THE WILD DOGS
in Life and Legend

This book is dedicated to

ROGER CARAS

Through his many books and national network radio and television news reports, he has demonstrated our brotherhood with the animals, and our need to protect them and their environment. Their environment is also our own. Since as early as 1700, great naturalists have spoken out against the witless destruction of that environment but none, I think, with a more intelligent and effective voice than Roger Caras. In addition, he has been able to put his own mind into that of the animals about which he has written so as to make their stories thoroughly believable. Few writers in any period have been able to do so as successfully.

THE WILD DOGS
in Life and Legend

by MAXWELL RIDDLE

Illustrated

First Edition — First Printing

HOWELL BOOK HOUSE INC.
230 Park Avenue
New York, N.Y. 10017

Library of Congress Cataloging in Publication Data

Riddle, Maxwell.
  The wild dogs in life and legend.

  Bibliography: p. 294
  1. Canidae.   2. Canidae—Legends and stories.
I. Title.
QL737.C22R53   599'.74442   79-18689
ISBN 0-87605-809-8

Printed in U.S.A.

Contents

About the Author 7

Foreword 9

Acknowledgements 11

1. Why You Should Know about Wild Dogs 13

2. What Is a Canid? 21

3. The Wolf in Legend and History 30

4. Wolf Children 37

5. The Legend of Wolves as Man Killers 44

6. The Literature on the Great Wolf Predators 48

7. The Biology of the Wolf 54

8. The Lore of the Coyote 73

9. The Biology of the Coyote 80

10. The Lore of the Red Fox 93

11. The Biology of the Red Fox 104

12. Biology of the Gray Fox 116

13. The Lore of the Arctic Fox 121

14. The Biology of the Arctic Fox 127

15. The Kit Fox and the Swift Fox 137

16. The Corsac Fox 141

17. The Lore of the Bat-eared Fox 144

18. The Biology of the African Large-eared Foxes 151

19. The Lore of the Jackals   158
20. The Golden Jackal   169
21. The Black-backed Jackal   175
22. The Side-striped Jackal   179
23. The Abyssinian Jackal   181
24. The South American Canids   183
25. The Lore of the Argentine Foxes   188
26. The Biology of the South American False Foxes   199
27. The Lore of the Raccoon Dog   219
28. The Biology of the Raccoon Dog   225
29. The Lore of the Dingo   229
30. The Dingo or Warrigal   239
31. The Lore of the Dhole   245
32. The Biology of the Dhole or Asiatic Red Dog   248
33. African Wild Dog   252
34. Exploding Misconceptions about African Wild Dogs   259
35. Neither Wolves nor Dogs: Falkland Islands Wolf,
        Aardwolf, Prairie Dog   272
36. Some Thoughts on Canid Reproduction   281
37. Alaskan Malamutes and Wolves   289
Bibliography and Supplementary Reading List   294

About the Author

MAXWELL RIDDLE is a dog journalist and judge of world renown.

His writing credits include reporter-columnist for *The Cleveland Press* for 25 years, a weekly column on dogs and other animals syndicated for many years in *The New York Post* and other newspapers, contributor of more than half the articles in *The International Encyclopedia of Dogs*, Associate Editor of *Dog World* magazine—and author of twelve books on dogs.

Past President of the Dog Writers' Association of America, he has won *all* of the Association's journalism awards. He received the "Fido" award for "Dog Writer of the Year."

Dog judging assignments, covering all breeds, have taken him to seven world areas: America, Canada, Europe, Australia, Asia, Africa and South America.

His extensive travels have enabled him to visit the major zoos of the world and the great game preserves and parks, and to make field study trips. These direct contacts enriched his interest in and knowledge of wild dogs. For example, on his first trip to South Africa in 1955, he watched Borzois course jackals on the veld where he was warned to shoot wild dogs on sight. They were then unprotected and he was advised that they were the most vicious, destructive and totally useless animals on earth. Not believing what he was told, he became interested in the animal then known as the Cape Hunting Dog. That interest led to two zoos giving the Cleveland Zoo a male and female of the species in Riddle's name.

As the animal expert for *The Cleveland Press*, Riddle was called upon many times to explode reports of wolves, sometimes from examining carcasses, sometimes from scanning foot prints. Twice he

was able to identify foot prints as those of domestic dogs. He learned
about desert foxes and Coyotes while living in Arizona.

In preparation for this book, the author consulted leading wild
dog authorities in America and abroad. He also deeply researched
the literature on the subject as his bibliography at the end of this
book amply attests.

The publishers are honored to present this worthy work and
believe it serves well the purpose of usefully informing general
readers about the wild dogs, in dispelling commonly held misap-
prehensions about them and in making a strong case for their
preservation. Some of them face extinction.

Foreword

IT IS A MAJOR PREMISE of this book that the wild canids of the world are facing extinction, and that they need our active support to save them. The sections on their biology, their lives, are not meant to be the exhaustive text books of science. But they are intended to give the reader a working knowledge of them, and to create an active sympathy for them.

This book links the biology of the canids to the legends and folklore which have been built up around them. Primitive people recognized their brotherhood with all of nature, and quite specifically with the canids. And so this book is also a plea for a realization that the canids are in a very real sense our brothers still.

Folklore, myths, and legends represent many things. These include fear of the unknown; man's efforts to answer such questions as: Who am I? Where did it all begin? Where will it end? Why is there both good and evil in the world? Were there, at one time, "the good old days?" In trying to answer these questions, primitive men linked their animal brothers to the problem. Thus, many ancient folk tales begin: "Long ago, when the animals could talk . . ."

In their efforts to solve the problems of Good and Evil, men of all eras have believed that a trick has been played upon them. A Trickster has robbed them of happiness, and has burdened them with disease, starvation, and ceaseless toil. For the Greeks, the Trickster was Prometheus; for the Scandinavians, Loki. The trickster is amoral, knowing neither Good nor Evil, but responsible for both. He is, in some cultures, both the creator and the destroyer.

Very often the Trickster is an animal. Adam and Eve were

tricked by the snake, which could talk—a snake which suffered from its own trick. In the lore I have collected in this book, the Trickster is often a canid. Among the North American Indians, it is the coyote. The fox assumes the role in Europe and in South America. It is the jackal in Africa and part of Asia; and the raccoon dog in Japan.

Many thoughtful people believe that our own Judeo-Christian culture is defective in its treatment of animals. Our position has been based on Genesis, or on a tragic misinterpretation of it. God said to them:

"Be fruitful and multiply, and fill the earth and subdue it; and have dominion over the fish of the sea and over the birds of the air and over every living thing that moves upon the earth."

Theologians have taken this passage to mean that, with respect to man, the animals have no rights at all. And so we have responded by working the most terrible cruelties upon the animals, whether wild or domesticated, and we have wiped out entire species, and continue to do so.

If at first in the Garden of Eden we were vegetarians, Cain's killing of Abel represented God's sanction that we should become meat eaters. "And the Lord had regard for Abel and his offering (of meat) but for Cain and his offering (fruit of the ground) he had no regard."

Adam and Eve were attempting to gain the knowledge of God; to answer the questions which we have given above. After their expulsion from the Garden of Eden, one can well imagine that they sometimes thought back to the "good old days." And that belief in such a time is still rooted deeply in our psyche. The great Spanish philosopher, José Ortega y Gasset, wrote that the "good old days" were in Neolithic times when man and dog could shake their cares and go hunting. He also wrote that both man and the domestic dog are degenerate animals.

Well then, let us recognize the wild canids as noble animals in all of their pristine glory, and thus worthy of our unflagging efforts to save them from extinction.

Maxwell Riddle

Acknowledgements

I AM DEEPLY GRATEFUL to many people and many organizations for their help and encouragement in the preparation of this book. Among those I would like to specifically thank are the following:

Canadian Department of Industry, Trade, and Commerce.

Canadian Wildlife Service.

Roger Caras who supplied many "leads" for information as well as offering his extensive photographic collection for use.

Herm David, who generously loaned rare and irreplaceable books from his cynological library, including those by St. George Mivart, Edward Topsell, Eugene Gayot, and Col. Charles Hamilton Smith.

Dr. Marion Ferguson of the Department of Biological Sciences, Kent State University, who took the time to read and comment on the chapter on canid reproduction, and who supplied information on texts which might be obtained, as did Dr. W. Jean Dodds, D.V.M.

Junko Kimura of Tokyo, Japan, whose researches and translations made it possible to correct English language texts which had confused the badger and the raccoon dog; and who retold for this book one of the legends told to her in her childhood. Miss Kimura also obtained the pictures of the raccoon dog used in the book.

Dr. Randall Lockwood, Department of Psychology, State University of New York at Stony Brook for his careful reading of the entire text, and his suggestions, and his corrections of errors. His recommendations have immeasurably improved the text.

G. R. Parker of the Canadian Wildlife Service, who donated the superb picture of an Arctic fox.

Dr. Leonard Goss and his staff at Cleveland Metro Parks Zoo, for their help and suggestions.

Dr. Stephen Seager of the Institute of Comparative Medicine, Baylor University, whose work with artificial insemination may save many of the endangered species.

Paul Toppelstein, *Cleveland Press photographer,* who copied many of the rare drawings and prints which appear in this book.

Mrs. Dean Harris who made the drawings for the book.

Jo Ann Sturm of the Oklahoma Zoological Society for granting use of the beautiful color picture of the Oklahoma Zoo's maned wolf.

Mrs. Louise Rucks of the Oklahoma Zoological Society who made helpful suggestions.

The entire staff of the Division of Science and Technology, Cleveland Public Library, who helped in researching information.

The Reed Memorial Library, Ravenna, Ohio.

Kent State University Library

J. G. W. Head of the Royal Agricultural Society of Victoria, Australia, for his help in locating material on the dingo legends of the Aborigines.

Philip Hershkovitz of the Chicago Zoological Society, Brookfield Zoo, and the Chicago Natural History Museum for permission to use his study of the small-eared zorro.

Texas Parks and Wildlife Magazine.

The wildlife divisions of a dozen states and provinces, with special thanks to the Texas Parks and Wildlife Division.

And to all those canid students whose writings have helped to make this book possible. Most, or all, are mentioned in the text or the bibliography. Others were specialists who contributed to encyclopedias, and whose work is especially appreciated. Among them are Dr. H. Wendt of Baden Baden; Dr. Detlev Mueller-Using, University of Gottingen; Dr. Michael Wolfe of Utah State University; and Dr. Erich Klinghammer of the Laboratory of Ethology, Purdue University.

And many others.

Maxwell Riddle

1 Why You Should Know about Wild Dogs

THE WILD DOGS of the world face extinction. They have been universally hunted and destroyed by man. In many cases, this has been caused by a desire for their skins and fur. Many of them, rightly or wrongly, have been considered to be livestock destroyers. And some have supplied man with furs, food, charms against disease and for medicine.

In addition, just as our exploding world population is destroying the habitat and living conditions of the few remaining primitive human tribes, so are we destroying the habitat and food supplies of the wild dogs.

The purpose of this book is to give the reader some knowledge of these wild dogs in understandable, non-technical terms, and to capture for the reader some of those features which make these animals unusually interesting. The author hopes his work will stimulate a desire to preserve them. For once an animal species has become extinct, it can never be reborn, and man is the loser.

It is necessary here to give some simple definitions of words so that the reader may have a precise understanding of them.

Carl von Linne, familiarly known as Linnaeus, was a Swedish botanist and doctor of medicine who was born in 1707 and died in 1778. He was the first to work out the principles of defining genera and species and to develop a uniform use of specific names.

He used Greek or Greek-Latin words. In his day all educated people learned Latin or Greek, or both. And thus Linnaeus's terms would be understood by scientists over all the world. Linnaeus's system, called *Taxonomy,* therefore went into world-wide use. For our purposes, taxonomy can be defined as the orderly classification of animals according to their presumed natural relationships.

Earlier we used the term *genera* which simply means "of a genus." And a genus is a group of similar species of organisms. Since Linnaeus's day, some animals have been moved from one genera to another. The reasons for this have been the influence of Darwin and Mendel, and the discovery by archaeologists of long extinct animals from which the modern ones evolved. Thus, we have a "fossil picture" which was not possible in Linnaeus's day. Yet his system has survived.

A simple dictionary definition of an *Order* is a category of taxonomic classification ranking above a family and below a class. Let us make a simple example at this point.

We have the *Order Carnivora.* Carnivora, of course, stands for the flesh eating animals. There are then two sub-orders. One is called the *Fissipedia.* It is made up of the land dwelling meat eaters which have separated toes. The second sub-order—the *Pinnipedia*—are the sea dwelling flesh eaters which have fins. Examples would be the true seals, sea lions and walruses.

The subject of this book is the wild dogs of the world. Or, to express it in taxonomic terms, Carnivora Canidae, which is to say the flesh eating members of the great dog family. There are 15 genera, although some zoologists would give certain animals a separate genera classification. While one genera might be represented by a single species, others might include a dozen or more living members.

Some authorities simply list the 15 genera separately. Some have divided them into two groups, while perhaps giving one "major group" status. For the purposes of this book and the reader's better understanding, the author has divided them into three groups.

The taxonomic name for the first group is Canis. A second word identifies the animal specifically. The domestic dog is Canis familiaris. Canis is always capitalized, and when the meaning is obvious, is reduced to C. The second word is not usually capitalized.

In this book we are not especially interested in C. familiaris, except to make comparisons between him and some of his wild

A canid prowls an ancient forest.

Lydekker's attractive drawing of Siberian
wild dogs, a species of Asiatic wild dog.

relatives. However, it will be helpful to remember that there are 400 or more dog breeds, of which about 200 are recognized by one or another of the world's stud books. Similarly there are possibly two dozen varieties of wolves. All are very much alike with only slight differences. They have not been genetically altered by man as dogs have been. Their variations are probably due to range, climate and separation from others of their brothers.

Jackals are normally described as *C. aureus,* even though this is only one species; actually there are four. The others are *C. mesomelus, C. ajustus,* and *C. simensis.* Slight local variants also exist but are not classified as different species.

By leaving out the domestic dog, we now have 15 or 16 genera depending upon whether we allow separate genera for two of the South American foxes. This, we are doing here. The Canis group includes:

Canis lupus, the wolf
Canis latrans, the coyote
Canis vulpes, the true foxes
Canis aureus, the jackal

We have split off three members of the "major group" as it is sometimes called, to form a second sub-family. This is made up of the beautiful South American Maned Wolf *(Chrysocyon brachyurus);* the Raccoon Dog *(Nyctereutes procyanoides)* of Japan, and parts of China and the Soviet Far East; and the Indian Dhole, or red dog *(Cuon alpinus).*

Much debate exists about Cuon. There are three or four members of the tribe. At times, one or more have been given separate genera classification. These animals have been called wolf or fox, depending upon their habitat. Today, most scientists make them minor varieties of Cuon dukhunensis. But of this, more later.

The other members of the canidae are:

Otocyon, the Bat-eared Fox of East Africa
Dusicyon, known as Azara's Fox, Patagonian Fox, etc.
Lycalopex, another South America fox
Fennecus Zerda, the smallest known fox
Urocyon, the Gray Fox
Speothos venaticus, the South American Bushdog
Atelocynus, the Small-eared Dog of South America

Maned Wolf, Oklahoma Zoological Park.
Photo by Herbert Bell

Miacis, No. 1 in the Family Tree.
Drawing conceived by Dean Harris

Cynodictis, first of the dog-like running animals.
By Dean Harris

Cerdocyon Thous, the Crab-eating Dog or Fox of South America
Cerdocyon magallanicus, the Cordillera Fox of extreme South America

In closing this chapter, we should repeat that debate still continues on the classification of some of these canids. Succeeding chapters will describe many of the varieties which have at one time or another been given separate genera, a status now denied them.

2 What Is a Canid?

SUPPOSE you were asked to describe your dog in reasonably precise biological terms. What would you say about it? You would probably begin by saying that it is a four legged mammal. But what is a mammal? The simplest definition would be: an animal which suckles its young, that is, one which nourishes its young by means of mammary glands (breasts).

But you should go much further than this. Mammals are born alive, and are quite well developed. Most are placental, that is, the fertilized egg is nourished internally by an outgrowth of the allantoic bladder, so that it can be nourished directly by the mother's blood.

This is in contrast to the *monotremes* of Australia, the duck-billed platypus and the echidna, which lay eggs, and to the marsupials. Young marsupials are born only in a partially developed stage and crawl to the marsupial pouch in which they "incubate" while nursing on mammary glands within the pouch.

Mammals also have body hair instead of feathers or scales. They are homeothermic, that is, they have an internal control system which permits them to govern their body temperature. They are thus able to maintain a relatively constant body temperature despite the outside temperature.

Mammals also have two sets of teeth. The first set is called the deciduous, or milk, teeth. The writer has often been asked why this should be so. What is the purpose, they ask, of the two sets?

One answer appears to be that the great powerful jaws of, say the dog, require a second set. The puppy is born with a foreshortened jaw. The jaw lengthens out as the puppy grows. At

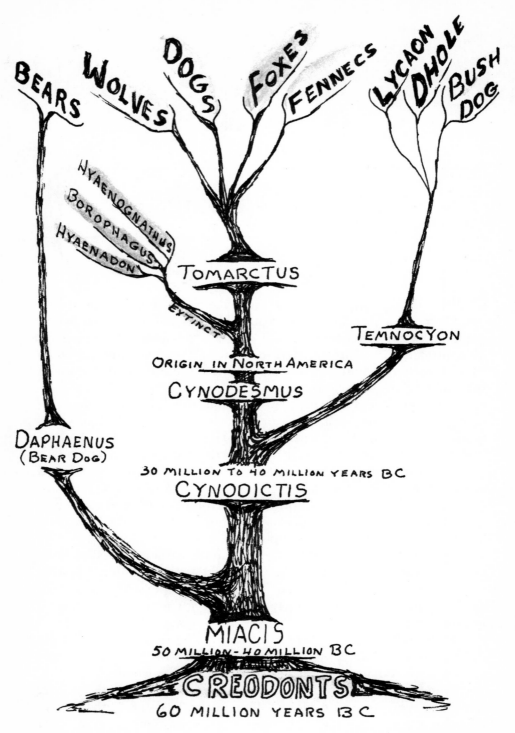

The Canid Family Tree showing some dead branches, and the split-off of the bears. *Drawing conceived by Dean Harris*

Cynodesmus, No. 3 in the canid family tree. *Drawing by Dean Harris*

Tomarctus, ancestor of many of the canids. *Drawing by Dean Harris*

A Dingo guards its mate. *Lydekker*

Dog saving ewe from wolf attack. *Illustrated London News*

weaning time, the sharp needle-like teeth probably stimulate the mother to wean her puppies.

The puppy may now live on the same food as its mother. Its permanent teeth are long delayed in making an appearance. They will not grow, except for the roots, after complete eruption. In the meantime, the puppy needs teeth. The mature teeth push out the milk teeth.

The canids are carnivorous animals, and so their teeth are specialized for flesh eating. It has been said that carnivorous mammals are fiercely rapacious forms, whose entire alimentary tracts are designed for highest efficiency.

For example, most or all of the canids, have teeth for tearing flesh, expandible gullets for swallowing huge chunks, and stomachs which may increase five or six times normal empty size to accommodate very large protein meals. Primary protein digestion takes place in the stomach; cereals, carbohydrates, and fibrous material are digested in the intestines. Canid intestines are therefore relatively short. All canids have a caecum, or appendix.

Uterine contractions during human labor apparently prepare the baby's genitourinary tract to function at birth. But in canids, and some other mammals, the tract is not mature at birth. All canid mothers lick the area to stimulate evacuation. They swallow the secretions and thus keep the nest clean. The period may last until the eyes are open and the pups are staggering about on their feet.

Here we can make some meaningful comparisons. The stomach of a medium-sized dog can hold one and a half gallons—that of man only 20 to 48 ounces. Further, a dog's stomach is about 60 per cent of its digestive tract.

The capacity of the dog's intestine is 1.7 quarts; that of man, three quarts; that of the horse, 25 gallons. Or, to put it a different way, the ratio of intestinal length to body length is 1 to 12 in the horse; 1 to 14 in the pig; and 1 to 6 in the dog.

The canid brain is relatively large, and the wolf's particularly so. Size of the brain does not necessarily correlate with intelligence. Size is perhaps less important than the shape of the head. The canids are said to have "nose brains." This is because air breathed in through the nostrils must pass over olfacory cells which are linked closely to the forward areas of the brain. These cells are protected and kept clean by a thin layer of mucous.

A man may have as many as 600,000 of these cells. Probably most canids have closer to a million. But an even more important factor is that there is greater air flow over these cells in the canid than in man. For the odor to be detected, odor molecules are caught by the mucous. Somehow they stimulate nerve messages to the olfactory centers of the brain.

Everyone is familiar with the domestic dog's habit of "marking" lamp posts, trees, and automobile tires with urine. Most wild dogs also use urine markings. It is said that a dog can detect one part of urine in 100,000 parts of water.

From a ridge the writer once watched wolves moving about in a valley. High power binoculars had to be used, and care had to be taken to prevent the wolves from seeing him or scenting him. Wolves would approach a marked area with care. It seemed to the observer that the wolves could then identify the marker of a previous animal, and from this probably understood whether the animal was healthy or ill, whether it had recently fed, where it had come from and was going, and certainly its sex.

Canids have their own type and range of "odor spectrum." They are interested in the odors of urine, sex, the musk of deer, meat, acids other than those in urine (for instance, sweat) and probably soil odors.

For example, sweat odors may be in the prints of prey which the canids are trailing. Musk odors will be strong in the prints left by deer. Soil disturbances may also carry a distinctive odor to the canid. An example of an acid which interests the canid is hydrochloric acid. This is produced in the stomach when food is being digested. So far as is known, all canids will carry food in their stomachs, and regurgitate it for their young. Similarly, the "fight or flight" reaction might cause the canid to vomit its food. Later it might be able to return and eat the food again. It would hardly do this if the acid smell was not attractive to it.

As a group, the canids have excellent eyesight. Probably the domestic dog has the poorest. It appears that all of the canids are color blind. Among other things, they are red-blind at night. As with human beings, night vision centers on the bluish-green of the spectrum.

Canids vary widely in their visual capacities. It will therefore be helpful if readers will remember the meaning of the following terms.

Diurnal, Animals chiefly active only during the day.

Crepuscular, Animals chiefly active in the dusk of twilight or dawn.

Arythmic, Animals active at any time, day or night.

Nocturnal, Animals active only at night.

So far as the writer knows, no canid is diurnal. Dogs, wolves and jackals are arythmic, and can see and be active nearly as well at night as during the day. The true foxes seem to be crepuscular, although as every fox hunter knows, they operate well at night also. The true foxes have upright, slit pupils; dogs, wolves, and jackals, rounded ones. There are also some truly nocturnal foxes which, like the fennec, must hide from the bright sun.

Most canids are well adopted for running and coursing. They have relatively long legs with four or five toes. They walk on their toes, and are called digitigrade animals. Bears walk on their heels and are called plantigrade animals. Canid toe nails are heavy, tough and have rather blunted ends. They are not retractable, as are those of the felidae. Nor are they intermediate, like those of the cheetah.

Canids have rather narrow, deep chests which may be a strong factor in their running ability. As a group, they are not noted for their speed. It has been claimed that the coyote can reach a speed of 40 miles per hour. But this may be doubted. Most of the canids have settled for moderate speed, a tireless gait and great stamina.

All wild canids have erect ears. They vary in size, but are triangular with more or less rounded tips. Puppies are born with drop ears, and this is called a larval condition. In breeding the domestic dog, man has been able to hold this larval condition. And he has been able to develop dogs with short legs, abnormally long bodies and barrel chests.

It is now accepted that the canids originated in North America from long extinct ancestors. The "plastic germ plasm," which has enabled man to breed such diverse dogs as the Chihuahua and the St. Bernard, was present in the first canids.

Their great adaptability permitted them to live successfully in a variety of habitats. Thus they spread to South America. In doing so they crossed the tropic barrier of Central America, an accomplishment few other animals have managed to do. They reached the Arctic and the Arctic islands and got as far south as Patagonia.

One creature, the Falkland wolf, even managed to reach the uninhabited Falkland Islands. More fox than wolf, this animal showed no fear of man and was quickly exterminated.

Other canids moved across the land bridge in the Bering Sea, populating all of Asia and Africa. Thus, the true canids have populated all of the world, except for New Zealand and some of the Pacific atolls.

Female canids have from three to seven paired teats. Males have a penis bone. Mating usually takes place in the winter or spring. Normally, the females come into heat only once a year. While female domestic dogs have been known to have litters of 17 or more puppies, the wild canids average three to five.

Wolves and African Hunting Dogs often live in large social packs. In the latter, females sometimes dominate the pack. Many of the foxes are monogamous and mate for life. In some canid families, both parents help to raise the pups. And many males are notably gentle with their pups.

Several of the foxes are able to climb trees, despite having claws which are not especially adapted for climbing. Although many domestic dogs fear water and some must be taught to swim, all wild canids are excellent swimmers. The South American Bush Dog is a superb diver. And one canid, the Raccoon Dog, hibernates in very cold weather.

"American Wolf" as drawn by famed English biologist St. George Mivart about 1871.

3 The Wolf in Legend and in History

"Better to Starve Free Than to Be a Fat Slave."

THUS SPOKE the wolf in Aesop's fable of the dog and the wolf. The dog met a hungry wolf and suggested that the wolf could get plenty to eat if it would join the dog in working for its master. At first, the wolf agreed. Then, seeing that the hair on the dog's neck had been worn thin by its collar, it refused. It preferred freedom even to life itself.

Aesop was himself a slave. He wrote about 2500 years ago, probably at Samos. No writer before or since has so perfectly described a major difference between the wolf and the dog. It is a difference no one should ever forget.

Man probably invaded the habitat of the wolf at least 60,000 years ago. Since then, he has shot, poisoned and trapped wolves. Wolf bounties have existed since organized governments came into being. And man has also destroyed the wolf's habitat. The wolf adjusted where it could. When it could not, it died. But it died nobly, and in freedom.

In our own North America, we began to cut down the forests and our ever increasing population moved westward. The wolf moved to the prairies and to the plains where other wolves lived on the buffalo herds. These we also destroyed. The wolves learned to respect guns and to avoid traps and poisoned baits, but they were pursued by professional bounty hunters. Today, through the efforts of the Red Wolf Recovery Team successful efforts are being made to save the pure, unhybridized American red wolf from extinction in its home in parts of Texas, Louisiana, and northern Mexico.

There have been areas where the wolf was trapped by its environment. The British Isles are surrounded by the North Sea and the Atlantic Ocean. So the British wolves had to stand and fight—and die. Records indicate that the last wolves in England were killed during the reign of King Henry VII about 1500. In the wilder areas of Scotland, they survived another 240 years. And in Ireland, the last were killed at about the time of the American Revolution. Intensive study in an effort to save them is being made of wolves remaining in Poland, Finland, Spain, Greece and Italy.

It is worthy of note that young nobles of both Europe and the British Isles were taught the art of venery (hunting) during their teens. So were the sons of the gentry. Wolf hunting was one of the sports taught, and in Ireland the Irish Wolfhound was developed especially for this sport. In Russia it was the Steppe Greyhound and his descendant the Borzoi, or Russian Wolfhound.

Despite Aesop's penetrating comment about wolves, which was meant to be understood as a human commentary, it is doubtful if he understood anything else about wolves. Instead, he simply followed the beliefs of the people of his times, whether accurate or not. Yet in studying the folklore about wolves, we must return to Aesop for other fables which used wolves. A fable is a short narrative, usually using animal subjects to convey a moral. It was developed by Aesop and, aside from the people of his time and a fox classic in France, it has been maintained chiefly by story tellers in India.

Every child is taught Aesop's fable of the shepherd boy who found fun in falsely shouting for help, claiming wolves were attacking his sheep. When wolves finally did attack, the would-be rescuers had been duped so many times they failed to respond. In another, a nurse tells the child, "If you don't be quiet I'll throw you to the wolves." Most of us are familiar with the wolf in sheep's clothing. And there are others: the wolf and the lamb, and the wolf and the crane.

Some Freudian psychologists have claimed a sexual content in the Brothers Grimm famous story, *Little Red Riding Hood*. The red is supposed to represent virginal blood, and the hood the hymen.

Even if so, the story is a classic children's tale which makes the wolf a villain.

It may seem utterly ridiculous to imply sexual connotations to the story of Little Red Riding Hood. Yet there is an ancient French saying still in use in many parts of France: "She has seen the wolf." It means that the woman has lost her virginity. In our own culture sexually predatory men are often called wolves. And there is the cynical saying that a gentleman is only a worn out wolf.

Roger Caras links sex and wolves in his modern classic wolf story, *The Custer Wolf.* As two young wolves, both unfamiliar with sex, begin courtship, Caras says, "These gentle agonies summoned up the wolf within the wolf."

In ancient Greece, it was a common belief that "If a wolf eyes you first, you will be struck dumb." This reminds us of our own saying, "Has the cat got your tongue?" Another belief, reported by the Roman author Aelian and others, is that squill would stupefy a wolf. Foxes were said to strew squill leaves near their dens to protect themselves from wolves. Anatolius recommended to shepherds that a squill bulb be tied on the neck of the bellwether of the flock to ward off sheep.

Oppian, about 200 A.D., gave an excellent account of wolves. They lived in the high mountains in summer, but descended to the plains in winter, driven by hunger into entering the towns. Yet Oppian reported that even the dead body of a sheep trembled and shook when a wolf approached. Plutarch reported that the flesh of a sheep, bitten by a wolf, tasted sweeter. He also said that a wolf's breath would soften the biggest and hardest bone.

German Shepherd breeders the world over bar white dogs. One of the reasons given is that a white dog might scare the sheep at night into stampeding. But the Greek, Columella, recommended white shepherd dogs because they could be more easily distinguished from wolves.

Aristotle was one of the greatest scholars in all history, so it is hard to forgive him for his claim that wolves have only one cervical vertebra. Actually, wolves and dogs have seven. Aelian said that the wolf had so short a neck it could not turn its head either left or right, and so had to turn its whole body. He went even further: men with short necks are as treacherous as the wolves, and so not to be trusted.

Though the wolf has always represented terror and, in some

cases, treachery, it has also symbolized strength and courage. Thus, men for many centuries have added wolf as a part of their names. As early as the 7th century of our era, the great epic masterpiece of Scandinavia, *Beowulf,* was written. The name was Beo, or Beaw, plus wulf.

Beowulf was a king's son from the land called Gautar by the Scandinavians. With 12 companions, he sailed to Denmark to help the Danish king, Hrothgar, whose hall or castle named Heorot had become uninhabitable. Arendel, a monster in human form, would force his way into the hall and murder one or more people nightly. Beowulf tore Grendel's arm off, so that he later died of loss of blood. He also killed Grendel's mother, who came to avenge the death of her son. Later Beowulf slew a dragon which was ravishing his own country.

However mythical the story may be, there seems to have been an actual hero, Beowulf, and even an earlier Danish hero of that name. As a symbol of courage and strength, the name still survives, as for instance in the Beowulf Kennels of Alaskan Malamutes of Beth J. Harris in Fair Oaks, California.

If one delves into Anglo-Saxon history, one finds dozens of examples of kings, monks, poets and bishops who incorporated wolf into their names. King Aethelwulf was the father of King Alfred the Great (848?-899.) Before and during Alfred's time, the Danes occupied Mercia and Wessex. One king of Mercia was named Eadwulf. Another Eadwulf, Archbishop of York, lived in the year 1000. And Wulfred was Archbishop of Canterbury in 940. It is easy to suppose that our present name Wilfred comes from this source.

In a later time, a Christian king ordered all the Jews to give up family names which might be called Christian. It is not surprising that many of them should have chosen wolf. For them, it symbolized the strength and courage they needed to survive. Others chose fox, since it stood for sagacity in an age when both wolves and foxes were being portrayed in stories.

The dog has been our domesticated companion and slave for at least 15,000 years. So it is strange, is it not, that we should speak of one of its habits, as well as one of our own, in wolfish terms. No dog owner has failed to note that the hungry dog bolts its food. And yet we say it "wolfs" its food. We say that we are as hungry as wolves.

The belief in werewolves has been common among all peoples

on all continents where there have been wolves. The name literally means man-wolf, or sometimes fiendish man-wolf. In areas where there have been no wolves, there have been man-tigers. In China, it was man-fox.

Either the man is changed into a wolf through witchcraft, or himself has the ability to make the change. Werewolves are supposed to have a taste for human flesh. In ancient Arcadia, there was a custom that in each generation, one man would have to change into a wolf. He was taken to a lake, stripped and forced to swim across. He then became a wolf and lived with wolves for nine years. At the end of that time, and provided he had not eaten human flesh, he could swim back, reclaim his clothes and become a man again, albeit nine years older.

The writer Agriopas recorded in the Olympionicae that the Arcadians had a custom of slaying a child and offering it as a sacrifice to the Lycaean Zeus. A man named Daemoetas of Parhasia tasted the entrails of the child and immediately was turned into a wolf. According to Agriopas, Daemortas regained his human form after 10 years, and later, about 480 B.C., won the Olympic wrestling championship. We will return to the Lycaean Zeus in the chapter on the African Hunting Dog.

In ancient Brittany people believed that the werewolf returned to human form at daybreak. He had to hide the skin because, if it was found and destroyed, the man would die. If the man hid the skin in a cold place, he would shiver all day. If he was wounded while being a wolf, the wound would be with him in his human form, and people would then recognize him as the werewolf.

This chapter began with a quotation from Aesop and some of his fables. They are fables which fit our text and for most of us they will be never to be forgotten stories of our childhood. So it is fitting that the chapter end with a wolf fable. But in doing so, we include a very brief outline of the history of fables.

Throughout all of recorded history, and probably long before, men used fables to record their wisdom and to instill it into their children. Probably no better method has ever been devised. A story involving animals would be easily remembered by children, as would the moral that went along with it.

Aesop had been a Greek slave. Perhaps he became a freed man.

Phaedrus, his literary descendant, was a Roman slave who became a freed man. Phaedrus was a poet. He lived during the reigns of four Roman emperors, but it is believed that he wrote his fables during the time of Tiberius, perhaps during the life of Christ. He used Aesop's fables, but added others, and did not hesitate to alter some of Aesop's, or to add to them. Babrius, another Roman who lived 150 years or more later, also copied Aesop.

There followed the so-called *Romulus Fox Tales.* The author is unknown. The fables are not limited to fox tales, and they are based on Phaedrus. The great beast epic, *Reynard, The Fox,* was spectacularly popular during the latter part of the 12th Century, and during the 13th. We quote from it later. It caused scholars to search for original texts, and from them to produce new editions.

Chief among these were Marie De France and Rabbi Berechiah ben Natronai ha-Nakdan, who may also have been known as Benedictus Le Puncteur. Berechiah couched his texts in Old Testament language, often quoted proverbs and other material from the Old Testament, and then added some comments of his own. The exact time of his writing is not known, but it was probably in the late 12th century. Using the title *Fables of a Jewish Aesop,* Moses Hadas translated Berechiah. His book was posthumously published by Columbia University Press in 1967.

To end this chapter we reprint the famous *Wolf and the Lamb* fable. Phaedrus wrote it in Latin poetry. The English poet, Christopher Smart (1722–1771) translated it into a charming English poem.

> By thirst incited; to the brook
> The Wolf and Lamb themselves betook
> The Wolf high up the current drank
> The Lamb far lower down the bank.
> Then, bent his rav'nous maw to cram
> The Wolf took umbrage at the Lamb.
> "How dare you trouble all the flood
> And mingle my good drink with mud?"
> "Sir," says the lambkin, sore afraid
> "How should I act, as you upbraid?
> "The thing you mention cannot be
> "The stream descends from you to me."

Abashed by facts, says he, "I know
" 'Tis now exact six months ago
"You strove my honest fame to blot"—
"Six months ago, sir, I was not."
"Then 'twas the old ram thy sire," he cried.
And so he tore him, till he died.
    "To those this fable I address
Who are determined to oppress
And trump up any false pretence,
But they will injure innocence."

Berechiah wrote in prose. His own comment added to this fable seems strangely modern and apropos.

"He that is stronger than his neighbor swallows him down. So do the judges and the bailiffs who pervert the justice of men and ransack their purses for silver and strip them of their fine garments in their very presence."

4 Wolf Children

WERE ROMULUS AND REMUS really suckled by a wolf? The question inevitably leads to another: Are there, or have there ever been, children who have been nursed by wolves? Or, for that matter, by any other wild animals? Let us begin by setting up a background upon which judgments can be made.

First, in all the centuries past, people have left their babies to be devoured by wild animals, to die of exposure or, with the hope that they would be rescued and adopted by others. Parents are still doing the latter in our own times. Families with too many children and without means of birth control, would abandon their later arrivals. But there were other reasons, too.

In his immortal tragedy, *Oedipus Tyrannus,* Sophocles has Laius, the king of Thebes, visit an oracle. Laius is told that he will be killed by his son, who will then marry his mother. So he exposes the son whom his wife Jocasta bears on Mt. Cithaeron, driving a spike through his feet. But the baby is saved and the prophecy is fulfilled.

In an effort to save Moses from death, he was put into a waterproof basket and was sent floating down the Nile. According to legend, Romulus and Remus were the twin sons of Mars and the Vestal Rhea Silvia. To save their lives from being taken by an imposter king, they too were placed in a "trough" and set floating down the Tiber. It is perhaps significant that Mars was usually accompanied by a sacred beast—a wolf.

According to the story, the trough ran aground under a fig tree which later became the site of Rome. There a female wolf found the twins. She and a woodpecker nursed them until Acca Larentia, the wife of a shepherd, found them and raised them. Historians who have puzzled over the story have pointed out that its main elements are Grecian, or even Cretan.

But Romulus and Remus were real people, apparently the sons of an overthrown king. When grown, they organized an army. Remus was slain. But Romulus restored the real king, became a leader and founded Rome on the site of the fig tree. He is credited with founding the military and civic institutions of the Roman Republic.

The question remains unanswered. Were they actually nursed by a wolf? In the ages since, there have been perhaps a hundred reports of children who have somehow survived in the wild. It has seemed to the people of the area that they could not have survived unless nursed and raised by some wild animal. So there have been the leopard child, the baboon child, and the wolf children. The authenticity of all these cases has been challenged, though in most cases no one has been able to disprove that some of these children did exist.

Several points must be understood. First, there are few valid accounts of wolves killing people, or even attacking them. As we shall see later, there is no valid proof of such an attack in all Grecian and Roman literature, except as supposed cases of rabies were held responsible. D. H. Pimlott, the noted Canadian authority on wolves, feels that the wolf has not regarded man as a prey animal. This, at least, has been the case since man developed weapons.

Second, wolves have long been noted for their gentleness with their own pups. They appear to tolerate much painful ear pulling and biting. And they also tolerate the pups of the entire pack. In areas such as an Indian jungle or European mountains, where wolves are not relentlessly shot, trapped and poisoned, there would be less fear of the man smell. And with their superior sense of smell the wolves would recognize baby smell even better than we do ourselves.

Finally, reports of animals adopting the babies of other species occur regularly and are thoroughly authenticated. For example, the writer once verified the following story. A spayed female Fox Terrier stole the kittens from a family's cat, carried them off one by one and developed milk by which she fed them. Dogs have tried to adopt lambs. Chickens have adopted ducklings and cats have adopted chicks. It follows then that the mother instinct is strong, and in some cases astonishingly so.

If a wolf did suckle Romulus and Remus if only for a couple of days, then the story would be true. But from evidence compiled on other wild children, and particularly those raised among wolves, this could not have happened for more than a few days. Human babies are highly adaptive. They absorb the culture of their parents, families and friends.

Wolves do many things by instinct, as all creatures do. But they must also go through a learning process taught them by their parents and other adult members of the pack. This learning process can rightfully be called a culture. Evidence exists that captured wild children have adapted to an animal culture. Judged in human terms, they have been wild animals in human bodies. Or, as some have said, they were all hopelessly retarded. Romulus, on the other hand, was a brilliant general and administrator. So any period which he spent with a wolf had to be very short.

Since one of the reasons for writing this book is the hope that it will help to save endangered wild species—and all the canids are endangered—another point should be made. We think of the sex drive as being one of our strongest instincts. Actually, it is at least partially learned. That is why so many zoos have had no luck in raising certain species in captivity.

Until quite recently gorillas could not be bred in captivity. Baby gorillas were captured by killing their parents. So they grew up knowing nothing of the culture of gorillas and nothing of courtship and mating. When babies did come the mothers, knowing nothing about nursing, abandoned or killed them.

Of all the stories of wolf children the best documented—and perhaps for that reason, the most bitterly challenged—is that of the wolf children of Midnapore. On October 17, 1920, the Reverend J. A. L. Singh, an Anglican clergyman who with his wife ran an orphanage at Midnapore, India, captured two children.

Reverend Singh went on regular mission journeys through the jungles in an area inhabited by aboriginal Indian tribes. On one trip he slept in the cow shed of a family belonging to the Kora tribe at or near a village called Godamuri. The village consisted of only a few homes, and investigators a dozen years later could not locate it. The villagers were terrified by what they called a ghost man.

The ghost-man was said to be living with wolves in an abandoned two-story-high white ant hill. Since the villagers would not go near the place, Reverend Singh hired men from another tribe to dig out the ant hill. He had observed the ant hill from a tree platform. This is what he said he saw:

On October 9, 1920, two grown wolves emerged from the ant hill. They were followed by two cubs.

"Close after the cubs came the ghost—a hideous looking being—hand and foot and body like a human being, but the head was a big ball of something covering the shoulders and upper portion of the bust, leaving only a sharp contour of the face visible, and it was human. Close at its heels came another awful being exactly like the first but smaller in size. Their eyes were bright and piercing, unlike human eyes. I at once came to the conclusion that these were human beings."

As they came out, each placed its elbows on the edge of the hole and looked about. Then they jumped out, running on all fours. Later, when the digging began, two male wolves came out and ran for their lives. But the female wolf tried to attack the diggers. The two cubs and the two children were found hugging each other in terror in a monkey ball. One or the other, including the wolf children, would make rushing sallies, growling and snapping their teeth, then retreating to form the ball again.

The diggers shot the mother wolf and captured the cubs and the children. The children arrived at the orphanage on Nov. 4. They had been robust and healthy. Now they were emaciated and in pitiful condition. Thereafter, the Reverend Singh kept a careful diary of their progress or lack of it.

The diary has been challenged as not containing enough evidence to satisfy an objective scientist as to its authenticity. But another scientist, after studying the report of one of them, wrote that, while the diary does not satisfy scientific criteria or prove the rearing of children by wolves, neither does it prove they were *not* reared by wolves. "They certainly may have been reared by wolves, since science has not proved that they were not."

Writing in 1940, Professor Arnold Gesell, M.D. and Director of Clinic of Child Development, The School of Medicine at Yale University, took an opposite view:

"This manuscript is unique," he wrote. "It portrays with simple, unassuming precision a series of remarkable events, such as no novelist's imagination could have invented. The events have a poignant significance for anyone also interested in the nature and growth of the human mind." And later: "There can be no doubt whatever that Amala and Kamala early in life were adopted by a nursing wolf."

Dr. Gesell might have added that few more tragic stories have ever been written than the Reverend Singh's manuscript and diary of the two children. The older girl, perhaps seven or eight, was named Kamala, and the younger, about two, Amala. Amala died Sept. 21, 1921 and Kamala Nov. 14, 1929.

The two children also shocked theologians, most of whom refuse to admit that an animal might have a soul. Could these children, living as wolves, and unable to develop normal human minds, have had souls? Perhaps this problem accounts in part for the rage and disbelief of so many.

Another scientist suggested that there is an embryology of the mind, just as there is of the body. Thus: "The highly abnormal environment created by contact of the infants with wolves, instead of human beings, affected deeply both their mental and physical development, each reacting on the other. They acquired a series of conditioned reflexes from imitation of the wolves, and at the same time the human aspects of their minds were completely in abeyance because of the absence of human models which could influence their mental and physical activities."

Bishop, The Right Reverend H. Pakenham-Walsh made from the diary a chronology of the lives and development of the two children. Using it, as well as Reverend Singh's own text, here is a brief account of the lives of the two children.

At first, they could not be clothed, but tore off everything. Eventually loin cloths were stitched on them. At first, they sucked milk from a cloth or lapped like dogs. They ate as wolves would do, not seeming to know what to do with their hands. They slept "overlapped" as puppies do, on the ground, refusing blankets or undercloths or rugs.

Aside from trying constantly to escape, they hunched in corners, refused to look at people or other children, and gazed off into space. Light hurt their eyes. They tended to be active only at night, arousing and becoming restless at about dusk. At night, their eyes glowed when light was shined into them, just as dogs' eyes do. (This is a phenomenon observed in certain people and indicates that the children may have been sisters.)

They had huge calluses on elbows and feet, and their toes turned upward. Neither could kneel or stand. Kamala went to eat with the dog, and became so ferocious when anyone tried to stop her that she could not be prevented from doing it. As they grew stronger in captivity, they began to crawl and then to go on all fours. Both could travel with remarkable speed in this way.

The calluses became huge suppurating sores which Mrs. Singh finally cured. She daily massaged the children with liniments and oils in an effort to straighten their legs. On Dec. 21, Kamala began to play with a boy named Benjamin. But disliking something Benjamin did, she bit him so severely he never again approached her.

Kamala could smell meat at great distances. Once she was caught devouring the entrails of a chicken. Neither child seemed to mind cold and neither perspired, even on hot days. After the death of Amala, Kamala formed a liking for goats' kids. She followed chickens, became friendly with a hyena pup and mourned when it died.

At first, neither child would touch salted meat, though later Kamala came to like it. On Feb. 27, 1922, Kamala stood on her knees alone for the first time, and on Mar. 2, she walked upright on her knees. On Mar. 6, she found a dead chicken which she carried into the bushes and devoured.

By Aug. 5, Kamala could stand on her knees to eat with her hands, provided she had support to keep from falling. But on Aug. 19, she was still placing food pans on the floor and eating wolf fashion without using her hands. By Nov. 27, she could say "bhoo, bhoo" when thirsty or hungry. Until that time, she had made no other sound except to howl at night.

On Aug. 13, 1923, she was seen to be sleeping for the first time with legs outstretched. On Dec. 29, she was shown raw meat, which was thrown into the bushes as far away as possible. She rushed for it on all fours, seeming to find it by instinct. Though at first she had fought baths and feared the day, now she liked baths and feared the night.

In September of that year, she began to accept clothes. On Oct. 6, 1925, she first used the bathroom to urinate, and on Feb. 10, 1927 she first attempted to wash herself after evacuation. Earlier, on Jan. 23, 1926, she took her first steps while standing on her feet. She sometimes walked then, but when she wanted to go faster she reverted to all fours.

In 1928, her health began to deteriorate. She began to fear the night, and became quickly irritated. She also reverted to going on all fours. She became really ill Sept. 26, 1929. But by Nov. 4, she could recognize and even name the attending doctor. She died, Nov. 14.

"In my opinion," wrote the doctor who attended both girls, "if the unfortunate wolf girls could have been kept alive and induced to take proper mixed diet with properly adjusted vitamins, improvement would have been more marked and they could have returned to an ordinary human condition from the stage of animal."

Two tears had been seen to drop from Kamala's eyes when Amala died. Our own tears must fall for a girl, bereft first of her human parents, then of the wolves, and finally of Amala, only to be left with human beings who could not understand her, nor she they.

A number of great authorities on wild wolves doubt the story of Amala and Kamala. However, the English investigative reporter and novelist, Charles McLean, made a most thorough search to discover the truth. He found lost records, interviewed Rev. Singh's widow, and Louise Mani Dar who, as a child, had been at the orphanage at the time of the wolf children.

He located the village of Midnapore. Its name had been changed, thus eluding other researchers. He interviewed Las Marandi, a Santal tribesman from Denganalia, who had taken part in the capture of the children. He found 23 pictures, most of Kamala. One shows the two naked children curled together like puppies, and sleeping on straw. His results appear in the book *The Wolf Children,* the first American edition of which appeared in 1977.

5 The Legend of Wolves as Man Killers

IN 1937 the University of Pennsylvania Press published the results of Richard Preston Eckels' researches into Greek lore on wolves. As a result of his studies, Eckels was able to say: "In Greek literature, we do not read often of men attacked by wolves, or even of their activities as scavengers . . . To summarize, it may be said that one looks in vain for valid evidence that wolves singly, or in packs, attack men out of hunger, or even out of malice."

How then how did the wolf, even in Grecian times, get its reputation as a killer? Eckels came to this conclusion: "The wolf is the vehicle of an unconscious abstraction which we may call the "Baleful Beast." We have seen earlier that, at least as a symbol of sexual aggression, the wolf had indeed been the "Baleful Beast." But as a killer of men, its reputation has been totally unwarranted.

Douglas Pimlott, the great student of wolves in a protected but large free range in the Canadian forests, has been able to find only two cases which could be authenticated. When he had run down the truth in one of these, he discovered that a farmer had been bitten by a wolf when he tried to break up a fight between the wolf and his dog. Thousands of people have been bitten when they tried to break up fights between dogs—and often the bites have come from their own dogs. In the other case the wolf was attacking while in the furious stage of rabies.

But even Pimlott, after years of study and intimate contact with wild wolves, records that he once had a feeling of unease while walking through wolf territory. He knew that wolves were carefully observing him, that one may have been walking stealthily parallel to his course. His unease was, of course, unwarranted.

The writer, too, knows this feeling. On a mid-December evening, at the northernmost tip of the North American continent, I decided to escape the continent by walking out on the Arctic Ocean ice. It was smooth at that point and snow was scarce. After walking for a time, the dark night seemed somehow to be filled with blinking eerie lights.

Suddenly the feeling came: How crazy can you get? You might fall into the breathing hole of a seal and be drowned. Somewhere out there a polar bear might be lurking. I knew there were no free roaming wolves that far north and that the probability of a wolf attack on a man was practically zero. Yet I could not control a mild anxiety which, combined with my other fears, caused me to return quickly to land.

Pimlott has said that he believes wolves do not regard men as prey animals; that hunting is not an instinct with them, but a learned process; and that man does not fit into the wolf's hunting pattern. Ernest Thompson Seton wrote: "These modern wolves have been educated, educated so that the fear of man, the terror of the man-smell is over all, both the great and the growing. Never will a modern wolf face, or fight, a man." But, as we have seen, this seems to have been true as far back as Grecian times. And if we follow Pimlott's clear thinking, these two predators, man and wolf, may have always left each other alone.

In Africa, it is said that leopards do not normally attack man. And as reported earlier, there has been at least one case in which a leopard supposedly adopted and nursed a human child. But the Africans also say that if a leopard once gets the taste of man blood and flesh, it then becomes an implacable killer of men. Then whole villages arm to kill the killer leopard, and skilled leopard hunters are brought in from other tribes, and white hunters as well. Bernard Grzimek has recorded the case of a man seized in his hunt by a leopard while in intercourse with his bride on his wedding night.

Seton, somewhere, has probably correctly ascribed the same motivation to European wolves which have become man killers. The taste of human blood and flesh could only be accidentally experienced by a normal wolf. But a psychological barrier would have been broken. Thereafter the wolf, probably already unbalanced, would become the enemy of man. It has happened only rarely in human history, and then chiefly in Europe.

Seton and Pimlott, as well as others, have researched the stories of these killers. Seton, as great a story teller as he was a naturalist, anatomist and artist, has not hesitated to embellish his accounts which he freely admits. His stories of Courtaud, the King Wolf of France, and La bête, The Beast of Gevaudan, make thrilling reading. And the stories are based on fact.

Courtaud lived and flourished about 1430. It was a time when France was being ravished by an invading army from Britain. Disease and hunger were widespread. France was infested by wolves, and they were hungry too. At that time Paris was a city totally on an island in the Seine River. Cattle had to be driven for long distances to the city. Wolves lined the roads, killing cattle. Moreover, there was a rocky area near one shore which was full of caves. Wolves in large numbers lived, bred and raised their pups in these caves. Today that area on the north bank of the Seine is known as Le Louvre, a palace filled with great art. But the name comes from Le Louvrier, the place where the wolves breed.

Courtaud was more than a man killer. Apparently he infected other wolves with his lust for human flesh and organized them into a massive army. Their killings of cattle and men struck terror throughout a major portion of France, and kept the Parisians near starvation. Courtaud and his army were finally lured into a Parisian square whose exits were blocked. There they were slaughtered by soldiers.

The Beast of Gevaudan lived between 1764 and 1767. His story was researched by Abbé Francois Fabre and later by Seton and Pimlott. As usual Seton did not hesitate to embellish his story with fiction.

Here are the facts. There were really two wolves, a male known as The Beast and a smaller female. She was killed long before he was. She was a large wolf by European standards with a dead weight of 109 pounds. But The Beast was a giant, with a dead weight of 130 pounds. European wolves simply did not grow to such a size. The Beast is credited with attacking at least 100 people and killing 64.

Because of his great size and unusual skull shape, it has been suggested that The Beast might have been a first generation cross between a giant dog and a wolf. The writer, though having no suggestion as to how The Beast could have reached such a size, doubts this supposition. For one fact, few dogs in that period ever reached such a weight. The giant dogs of today are a modern development. It has been suggested that hybrid vigor might have been responsible. Fox and Lockwood were able to produce wolf-Alaskan Malamute hybrids which were more than 20 pounds heavier than either parent.

Finally, Grzimek and others have reported on wolf-dog crosses. The first generation offspring have been pathetically timid creatures. And The Beast was anything but that. This writer and others have repeatedly asked Eskimos if they crossed wolves with their sled dogs. Always the answer was "no." The cross-breds were timid and too nervous to be trained successfully. However, Fox, Zimen, and others have reported that while some of the hybrids were timid, others were not. But then The Beast himself has been a rarity in human—and wolf—history, and his origins can never be known.

Great action picture of a northern wolf in full stride. *Photo by Tom W. Hall*

6 The Literature on the Great Wolf Predators

"The Assyrian Came Down Like the Wolf on the Fold."

THE ABOVE QUOTATION is one of the most famous first lines in poetic history. It comes from Lord Byron's poem, *The Destruction of Sennacherib,* which tells of the destruction of the Assyrian army and ends with: "And the might of the Gentile, unsmote by the sword / Hath melted like snow in the glance of the Lord." "Like the wolf on the fold" perfectly characterizes the predatory instincts of the wolf.

Man's war against the wolf probably did not begin until early man learned how to domesticate the plants and animals of his environment. Until then man and wolf were simply fellow predators. There was sufficient prey for both; their hunting methods were different; and they were not in competition. So it was likely that they either accepted or ignored each other.

The situation changed with the domestication of sheep and cattle. These animals were gradually removed from the wild. Another way of saying it is that man took important food sources from the wolf which could hardly be expected to understand or tolerate it. As men collected animals into herds, the wolves changed hunting tactics. Sheep and cattle were relatively stupid animals and became more so as man got interested in them solely as sources of food, clothing and leather.

We may say then that man's war against the wolf began some 15,000 years ago. Man has hated the wolf ever since. But the wolf has never returned that animosity. He has remained a predator, preying upon man's herds but not upon man himself. Or he has retreated farther and farther into the wilds, away from man. The wolf's survival against the incessant warfare against him has been due to his extraordinary intelligence, coupled with equally extraordinary senses of smell, sight and adaptability.

Yet the extinction of the wolf, as with most or all other wild canids, seems inevitable unless man himself stops the war. Man's hunger for land and the exploding population have destroyed the wolf's habitat as well as the wild creatures which afford food. The wolf, as Aesop said it, would prefer to starve free than to live as a fat slave. But if the wolf is stubborn in this respect, so is man on his part. Man would have to erase what has become a virtual imprint in his heredity—the Baleful Beast must be destroyed.

It is true that the wolf has never made his entire diet of man's domestic animals. Once he lived off the great buffalo herds on the western plains. Deer and antelope were on his food list. As the herds dwindled, he moved northward where great herds of caribou and musk ox lived. In times of hunger he proved a cunning hunter of mice and lemmings. In many ways he kept the balance of nature by controlling animal pests which could be, and sometimes are, the scourge of man. But it is as killer of domestic animals that man pictures the wolf.

Most authorities agree that few predators ever kill for any reason except hunger. A well fed lion may walk virtually ignored through a herd of zebras. But the wild creatures seem instantly to recognize the hungry predator, and they prepare to flee or fight. Generally speaking, the wolf kills only to eat.

There have been exceptions. Whether such wolves have killed out of hostility, an uncontrollable killing lust as an act of revenge against men, or simply from pleasure, can never be known. We simply cannot know the mind of the wolf. It is certain, however, that killer wolves have had a marvelously developed intelligence, a knowledge and cunning far beyond that of ordinary wolves.

As a result, men have been forced to admire them while hating them. And from this mixture of opposites has come the legends and the great stories of famous wolves. Many people have recorded the histories of these wolves. Of these, two are selected here because in many ways they stand out above all others. They are by Ernest Thompson Seton and Roger Caras.

We have referred to both writers before. Seton (born Ernest Seton Thompson) was a giant in many fields. First of all he was a great naturalist and woodsman. He was also a fine and careful artist whose anatomical studies of animals are without equal. During his long and restless life he wandered the American and Canadian West, observing and sketching and sometimes painting. Many of his anatomical studies are still used to illustrate text books.

Seton was a founder of the Woodcraft Indians, later to become the Woodcraft League. It was the first outdoor organization for boys ever to be organized. With Dan Beard, he was a founder of the Boy Scouts of America, became its first chief scout, and wrote its first handbook.

His literary output was enormous, and he was a magnificent story teller. Once the famed John Burroughs blasted Seton, but other naturalists came to his defense. And, ironically, he was later awarded the John Burroughs Medal and the Elliott Gold Medal of the National Academy of Sciences. They are the highest awards a naturalist can receive. Among other things the awards came for his eight-volume *Lives of Game Animals*. The studies in these volumes have never been equalled. Nor can they ever be, for the animal world in which Seton lived and wrote has almost totally disappeared. Seton was born in 1860 and died in 1946.

Seton's first marriage ended in divorce. A daughter born of that marriage is Anya Seton, one of the most respected and accomplished novelists of our time. His second wife, Julia, worked with him steadily. She and three secretaries helped in the final preparation of *Lives of Game Animals*. Julia Seton also collected his unpublished notes and journals, which were published by Doubleday in 1967 under the title *By a Thousand Fires*.

In this book appears one of Seton's masterpieces—The Development of the Animal Story—in which he traces the history of animal stories from the time of Aesops fables. Seton explains how a writer can try to put himself into the animal mind; how putting near human feelings within the animal may make that animal come alive for people. And how by embellishing the bare facts, the writer may reach a truth beyond the facts.

Seton did embellish the facts in his great stories of Courtaud and The Beast of Gevaudan, the man-killing wolves mentioned in the last chapter. And he did so also in the story of Little Marie and the Wolves, which he believed to be true of a little girl who was kidnapped by a wolf. But Seton had also been a "wolver"—a hunter-trapper and killer of the super-predator wolves which are the subject of this chapter. He told the stories of these wolves factually though his admiration for them is obvious.

Thus, two of his greatest stories are personal experiences. One is the famous *Lobo, The King Wolf of The Currumpaw.* The other is *The Wolf That Won,* the story of Badlands Billy, the big black wolf of Sentinel Butte. Lobo was a giant wolf, at least for New Mexico. Seton explains that the forefoot of the average wolf is four and a half inches long; that of a large wolf, four and three quarters. But Lobo's foot measured five and a half inches from claw to heel.

Lobo led a small pack, not larger than five in his latter days when Seton was trying to kill him. His mate was a small white wolf. Lobo is simply the Spanish name for wolf, and Blanca means white. These were the names which the Mexicans had given the two wolves. Blanca was killed. Seton, who had thus far failed in all efforts to trap or poison Lobo, now used Blanca's body as a lure. Lobo was trapped in this way, and Seton had the big wolf brought in alive.

Seton had trapped the wolf by ascribing to it an ability to feel love for its mate, so it is surely not anthropomorphic to believe that the big wolf did feel love in something like human terms. Seton had to admire Lobo so it is perhaps sentiment when he writes this about the trapped and imprisoned wolf: "His eyes were bright and clear again, but they did not rest on us. He lay calmly on his breast and gazed with those steadfast yellow eyes away past me down through the gateway of the canyon, over the open plains—his plains—nor moved a muscle when I touched him."

It may be sentiment. And yet one is struck by the Reverend Singh's account of the wolf children at his orphanage. The captured children would not look at people, but gazed steadily off into the distance. Lobo refused food and water, and was found dead a day or so later. His skin can be seen at the Seton Museum, Seton Village, New Mexico.

Badlands Billy was, as his name suggests, a wolf who lived in the Badlands of South Dakota. There the terrain made it difficult to follow a wolf, since the wolf could thread its way around and over rocks as horses could not do. Seton went out one day with a wolver named Penroof who had a pack of 15 hounds. Billy was pursued and apparently decided to make his stand on a rocky ledge. The dogs had to leap onto the ledge. As the astounded wolvers watched, Billy killed all 15 dogs. The watching men were so paralyzed with astonishment that they failed even to raise their rifles. Before they could recover, the big wolf bounded and disappeared.

Seton also went on several hunts near Medora, North Dakota, in an effort to kill two raiders. One was a white wolf named Wosca— the she devil—by the Indians. She was distinguished by a missing toe on each forefoot. A wolver named Bud Dalhousie had tried to kill her. When she fled, he found her den and dug out five pups. Four he killed. A fifth he kept alive, hoping with it to lure the mother into a trap. This proved unsuccessful. The red pup, named Shishoka, eventually became the property of Col. Buffalo Bill Cody. After a year in captivity, the red wolf escaped. He then joined his mother. Seton carefully researched the story and made it into *Wosca And Her Valiant Cub*. The story is told with little, if any, embellishment.

Roger Caras is a present day writer, a well known and respected TV and radio commentator on animal subjects, and the author of more than 30 books, including some on dogs. Caras carefully researched the facts about a white wolf which became nationally famous as The Custer Wolf. The name comes from the town and county of Custer, South Dakota. This wolf was a renegade, a lonely killer which killed from hunger and for pleasure. Or, as some said, in revenge against man.

The Custer Wolf's life probably spanned 10 years. He was trapped and shot in October, 1920, by a famed wolver named H. P. Williams. Williams had just come from Wyoming where he had killed another famous animal known as the Split Rock Wolf.

Caras says of the Custer Wolf that he was the author of a thousand useless deaths. Wolves do not normally kill for pleasure. Nor do most animals, responsible to and responding to their environment, waste its resources by useless killings. But the Custer Wolf did. It is officially recorded that, working alone, he killed 30 sheep in one night, partially eating only one. On another night, he killed 10 steers. He also delighted in chopping off the tails of cattle which he did not kill.

In an attempt to get at the truth of the wolf's life, and to try to understand it, Caras began his story with the meeting and mating of its parents. Wolves customarily mate for life and hunt together. Both parents help to raise the pups. Caras then tells of the fate of the parents and of the Custer Wolf's litter mates. In doing so, Caras brings to the reader a vivid story of the lives of wolves.

But Caras is also a strong voice urging Americans to give up their ceaseless war against the wild canids. And so in this story he has interwoven some tragic figures. Between 1915 and 1920—the last six years of the Custer Wolf's life—"traps, guns, and poison enough to wipe out every wolf that ever walked the face of the earth were stockpiled in the troubled areas. From 1915 through 1920, a 16 state war was waged that saw 128,513 assorted carcasses skinned and rotting in the sun."

But, of course, thousands of other animals, fatally poisoned, crawled away to live out their torture in hiding places where their bodies were never found. "Of the thousands of large predators destroyed in those six fateful years, however, only 2936 were wolves. In South Dakota, only 23 timber wolves are known to have been killed (plus) one bear, 58 bobcats and lynxes, and 794 coyotes . . . As a result of all this killing the rodent population exploded and in turn cost untold millions to bring under control."

The story of the Custer Wolf's last struggle to live is a great piece of writing, told almost without sentiment, but needing none. The Custer Wolf, caught by a forefoot, made so huge a lunge as Williams approached that he jerked the stake from the ground. He began to run, but the stake caught between two trees, turning him head over heels. Another mighty lunge broke the swivel.

Careful research indicates that the wolf ran a full three miles with the big trap chewing steadily into his foot before Williams could kill him. It was then discovered that the Custer Wolf, the scourge of ten counties, and the despair of hundreds who had tried to hunt him down, was only a very small wolf.

The Custer Wolf—Biography of an American Renegade was written by Roger Caras, and was published in 1966 by Little, Brown & Co. It was reprinted as a Bantam Pathfinder paperback in 1967.

7 The Biology of the Wolf

THE NUMBER OF SPECIES of wolves in the world has always been open to question. Depending upon which authority makes the study, there are six species of European wolf, and twenty in North America. Or, there are 24 species known as Canis lupus, plus the Texas Red Wolf, Canis rufus which is said to be a true sub-species and, which some would say, may have had three of its own sub-species. Some species are extinct. The Texas Red Wolf is close to extinction, and present efforts to save it may be in vain.

Trying to describe all these species and their minute differences can only serve to confuse the reader. For the purposes of this book, it suffices to say that there are the European wolf, Canis lupus lupus; Canis lupus, the Gray Wolf of North America which is also known as the Timber Wolf; Canis lupus pallipes, the Asian wolf which is said by some to be the ancestor of the domestic dog; Canis rufus; and Canis lupus tundarum, the Alaskan tundra wolf.

No point of origin for the canid family is known, only that its members have spread world wide. However, the wolves found the Central American and Central African jungles too difficult to pass. So the wolves of the world have adapted to life from the circumpolar or Arctic land masses—the Arctic tundras—to the mountains of Northern Mexico. In between they have prospered in the great forests and plains of North America. Others adapted to life in the Indian and Malaysian jungles. The largest wolves have been found along the Arctic land masses, and the smallest along the Mexican border and east to Florida. Wolves have shown remarkable versatility in making the required adaptations to whatever environment they have faced.

Stanley P. Young is said to have shot the largest wolf ever killed. It is claimed that it weighed 175 pounds and measured 38 inches tall at the shoulder. While Young's figures may be correct, one should point out that most reports of gigantic animals are open to question. For example, the heights and weights of domestic dogs vary with the liars who claim them. Though there are claims of dogs 38 inches tall, this writer has carefully measured a dozen such dogs and has found them to be 34 to 35 inches rather than 38. But when careful scientists make such claims, one must accept the fact that they are reasonably correct. Young also killed one weighing 116 pounds.

In the far north, male wolves average 95 to 100 pounds, with Young's kill at 116 pounds being maximum. Female wolves are always smaller than their mates in any given species; the northern females range between 65 and 100 pounds. In studies of Isle Royale wolves in Ontario, Mech, quoted by Rutter, and Pimlott give average sizes of 61 pounds and a maximum of 80 for males. Females average 54 pounds, with a maximum of 70. One female weighed only 39 pounds.

The Texas Red Wolf, Canis rufus, is the smallest wolf in the world. This species seems to have less variation in size than others do. The weights are given as 30 to 35 pounds, and the heights as between 19 and 22 inches at the shoulder. The Texas Red Wolf has a black phase which, once found in Florida, was sometimes called the Florida Black Wolf.

Male wolves seldom reach sexual maturity before the age of three; females at two. But Mech has reported successful breedings of both sexes at 9 to 10 months. The gestation period is about 63 days. Litters are generally small with three to five pups, but a litter of 14 was once reported. The pups are blind at birth, but the eyes are known to open at from 11 to 14 days. The pups are nursed until they are six to eight weeks old.

After mating, wolves usually dig dens. Both parents and even other pack members may help at this. Wolves have been known to use fox and beaver dens, or to make nests between the roots of great trees.

When weaning begins, the parents bring the pups out to see their surroundings. The pups gambol and play games much as dog puppies do. They may draw other pack members into their games. The genuine affection and tenderness which even older males show for the puppies are remarkable features of wolf-pack social life. When the pack goes off to hunt, an older wolf, often a female, is left to guard the puppies. She may allow the puppies to play in front of the den, but a single warning growl will send them scrambling into the den. If a wolf pair is living without pack members, both wolves may leave their puppies in the den while they hunt. In such cases, the puppies remain out of sight until their parents return. Other than man, wolves have no natural enemies. They may tussle with an occasional bear, but the argument is usually harmless for both. Thus, the puppy guarding instinct may be an ancient imprint in its pre-canid genetic code.

Wolves are great travelers. It has been estimated that they may travel as much as 35 miles a day. The Custer Wolf, for instance, had a hunting range covering at least ten large counties in South Dakota. Wolves seem to wander all of their lives, except during the mating season. At that time the den will be dug and the pack will remain in the area until the pups are sufficiently grown and trained to become nomads. The training will include conditioning for long hunts.

The parents and other pack members will bring food home for the puppies. This may be carried in the jaws, or it may be swallowed and then regurgitated when the den is reached. As the pups grow older, they are allowed to go on the hunts, but they appear not to be allowed to take part. In this way, the hunting technique is learned without the danger of having the pup killed by the kick of a cow, for instance. The pups are also learning woodcraft, the ability to find their way back to the den, and to know all parts of their hunting range.

As a general but not absolute rule one litter of pups is raised in a pack within a year. All members of a given pack may be related— father, mother, aunts and uncles. Young wolves may wander away to join other packs. Old and relatively useless wolves may be driven from the pack, as done with old lions in their prides in Africa. In this way, the pack will be kept efficient and within reasonable size limits.

In North America, at least, wolf packs number five to eight individuals, seldom more. The availability of food within the pack range may be a governing factor. Personal enmity may prevent a strange wolf from joining a pack or may cause a member to leave it. In southern and eastern Europe, where the population of both people and herd animals is great, larger wolf packs have been reported. It is in these areas that attacks upon people have been recorded. As a rule, the attacks have been against children who were sent out as shepherds. But even children have been able to chase off the wolves. Neither Scandinavia nor North America has ever recorded an authenticated death of a man by wolves.

Wolves are cursorial animals, that is, they must course or chase their prey. The big cats can stalk and pounce because they have the teeth and claws for such methods. But wolves, despite their mighty jaws and huge teeth, are not ideally equipped for such hunting. Also, wolf quarry is usually much larger than they are. So they rely on chasing the prey until it is exhausted. It is true, however, that in the absence of big game, wolves do stalk and pounce upon mice, lemmings, beaver, and other small animals. Big game is getting scarce even in the north.

It has therefore been estimated that each wolf must have about 10 square miles of hunting territory. A pack of five would then need 50 square miles. It is now well established that wolves mark their pack territories in a number of ways: males by raised leg urination; females by squatting; both sexes by fecal deposits (scats); and by scratching. As a rule, only mature animals do this, usually the dominant male and female. Most marks are on prominent spots, tree stumps, rocks, banks, etc. Scats are often left around rendezvous spots such as whelping dens. Also, wolves sometimes will bury a cache of meat, then leave their mark of ownership on the spot.

The habit wolves have of making up small nomadic bands is of great advantage to them. First, they are not so likely to exhaust their food supply, as would a large pack. Second, there is less likely to be disease epidemics as among large, closely grouped populations. As with other wild canids, wolves are heavily parasitized and are subject to viral, bacterial, fungal and other diseases.

During earlier centuries, wolves were supposed to be highly susceptible to rabies. Modern observers doubt it. All warm blooded animals can get rabies, and some certified cases have been reported in wolves. But if one couples an unusual susceptibility to rabies with man's traps, poisons and the destruction of the wolf's habitat and food supply, then it seems certain the wolf would have become extinct long ago.

Observers in other centuries may have mistaken running fits for rabies. It is well known that dogs heavily infested with worms may get running fits. During an Alaskan "rabies epidemic" during which many dogs were shot, a wise old trapper quickly stopped the epidemic. He fed the dogs horse hide with the hair left on. Huge quantities of worms were forced out with the stools, and the dogs quickly became normal.

Wolves have been known to be infested with at least six types of the adult forms of tape worms. Worms do not normally kill their hosts. But certain factors may be beyond their control. The infestation may become very large, and just at that time, the wolf may become exhausted, ill or weakened by wounds. Then the animal is in grave danger. Other factors may also drive the worms into killing infestations for causes that we do not know. It is possible and even probable that wolves, like dogs, may occasionally suffer from epilepsy or epileptiform convulsions which might be mistaken for rabies.

The life span of wolves in the wild has been put at ten years which is also the lifespan of the average dog. The seemingly high mortality rate among wolf pups, the small litters, and the late sexual maturity of the adults—all contribute to keeping wolf populations from exploding. Also, the female wolf comes into season only once a year.

Wolf howling is really wolf singing, though certain howls have certain meanings. Electronic analysis shows a range from deep base to high tenor, including tremolos, and harmonically are close to the human voice. Wolf howl parties have been organized in the Algonquin National Forest in Canada. Large numbers of people go into the forest at night just to listen to the wolves. Many tape the music. Some even imitate the howls and are delighted when they receive answering howls.

Wolves tend to move their pups to another den if disturbed. Or if they do not have a reserve den, they will still move the pups to what they consider to be a safer location, perhaps a fox or beaver den. Yet Murie reported crawling into a den with six pups and bringing out only one. He carried the pup off in his knapsack. The parent wolves barked and mildly threatened, but did not really interfere. These wolves did not move their pups. Farley Mowat also tells of crawling into a wolf den which contained pups and an older wolf. He was not harmed. We cite these cases, partly because of the strange gentleness of the wolves where people were involved, and to show that wolves do bark.

Wolves greet each other in much the same manner as domestic dogs do. There will be some circling, raising of tails, end to end smelling, raising of hackles, tail wagging and face licking. A submission gesture is to expose the throat, or to lie down, thus exposing throat and belly. The dominant wolf will show his dominance by placing its muzzle on the neck of the other wolf.

One rule commonly said about wolves and other wild canids is that the wolf will never attack when the other wolf gives the submission gesture. This is supposed to be a "law of the wild" which all wolves respect. Although this may be the rule in most cases, it is not a law of the wild. Wolves will kill dogs that make such gestures. And they may even kill other wolves despite the submission signal.

Murie reported a case in which a strange wolf sought to join a pack. When the pack wolves approached, the stranger lay down and exposed his throat and belly. But the pack wolves attacked him anyway. The stranger managed to scramble to its feet. It fled with the pack wolves chasing and biting at its thighs. When the pack wolves left the chase, the stranger rested, then tried to approach again. Again he was driven off.

Sir James Ware wrote a history of Ireland which relates how in 1658 the wolf hunter, Rory Carragh, a small boy and Carragh's Irish Wolfhounds killed the last two wolves in Ireland. In that day any writer, who wanted his works to last, wrote in Latin as did Sir James.

Carragh is said to have placed himself, dog and spear at one entrance to the sheepfold, and the boy, dog and spear at the other entrance. Carragh fully understood the habit of wolves of attacking from the front and rear at the same time. In attacking a single animal, one wolf would go for the throat while the other would try to cripple a hind leg. The two huge Irish wolves did as Carragh expected. The dogs engaged them, and the wolves were speared before they could kill the dogs.

Wolf packs seem to try to drive their prey in a circle. Pack members can then cut across the circle to meet the prey. However, many wolves simply rely on their superior endurance to wear down the quarry to exhaustion. It can then be attacked by the smaller animals in greater safety. In the far north it is said that wolves always single out the old, crippled or ill members of the herds of caribou and musk oxen. In this way, the inherent strength of the herd is maintained and greater food supplies are preserved for the healthy animals. Having singled out the animal to be killed, the wolves cut it out of the herd, much as skilled shepherd dogs cut sheep from the flocks of their owners. A wolf then attacks the throat and another the rear.

In 1977 Ron Nowak,. mammologist for the Fish and Wildlife Service, U.S. Department of the Interior, estimated that between 1000 and 1300 wolves still remain in the lower United States. He gave these figures: Minnesota 1000-1200, Michigan 50, Wisconsin 5, Montana 10, Wyoming 10, Idaho 10, Texas 30, and Louisiana 36. All are Canis lupus, that is, the Eastern Gray Wolf except those in Texas which are the Canis rufus, or Texas Red Wolf. He estimated 10,000 Canis lupus in Alaska.

The Canadian Wildlife Service lists three wolf species still existing in Canada. They are the Mackenzie Valley Wolf, Canis lupus occidentalis; the Eastern Wolf, Canis lupus lycaon; and the Hudson Bay Wolf, Canis lupus hudsonicus. The Mackenzie Valley Wolf inhabits the Mackenzie District, Northwest Territories. The Eastern Wolf is found in Northern Ontario and Quebec. The Hudson Bay Wolf lives on the mainland tundra. Some sub-species may exist in widely isolated areas, but if so, are very rare.

The Red Wolf of Texas

Earlier, we gave figures which show that there are only about 30 purebred Texas Red Wolves (Canis rufus, but previously called Canis niger or Canis rufus niger) in Texas. The 36 wolves listed for Louisiana are at least in part purebred Red wolves, but some are interbred with Coyotes. The Red Wolf has often been considered as a true separate species from the main stem of wolf heredity, but this is open to question. The argument has continued since at least 1851. It is the smallest member of the wolf family, only slightly larger than the Coyote.

One of the best articles on the wolves of Texas, the Gray Wolf and the Texas Red Wolf, appeared in the May, 1977 issue of *Texas Parks & Wildlife*. The author is the wildlife biologist, Joe T. Stevens, whose father was a "wolver." He points out that the Gray Wolf no

Texas Red Wolf puppy howls at the stars. *Photo by Perry Shankle Jr.*

Wolves photographed in the Lake Sasajewan Research Station, Algonquin Park, by Dr. D. H. Pimlott in 1961. *Ontario Department of Lands and Forests*

Wolf at rest. *Cleveland Press Photo Library*

longer exists in Texas, except for an occasional straggler from the pitifully small packs still living in the mountains of Northern Mexico.

The greatest authority on the Red Wolf is Dr. Howard McCarley, Professor of Biology at Austin College, Sherman, Texas. It was Dr. McCarley who, in 1962, alerted America's biologists and naturalists to the fact that the Red Wolf was facing extinction. Since extinction is forever, people began to rally to the cause of saving the wolf. Texans seem to have a hatred of Coyotes, as they once hated the Gray Wolves. The latter did not prey upon cattle, but did make forays against the farmers' hogs. Also, where the ranges of the Grays and Reds overlapped, cattlemen took out their anger against the Grays.

The Red Wolf, despite its small size, is longer legged in proportion to height than the Gray Wolf is. It has a more massive head and a broader muzzle than the Coyote. It also has a larger foot, so that its track is easily distinguished from that of a Coyote. The color is yellowish brown to reddish with cinnamon color on the muzzle and around the eyes.

Because of the alert sent out by Dr. McCarley, the U.S. Fish and Wildlife Service, the Texas Parks and Wildlife Department, and the Louisiana Wildlife and Fisheries Commission have cooperated to establish a Red Wolf recovery program. The Red Wolves, and those which have hybridized with Coyotes seem to be limited to three Texas counties: Liberty, Chambers, and Jefferson. This area amounts to 1,260,000 acres on the coastal prairie, with about 90,000 acres of forest. As indicated above, some have moved into Louisiana.

Highly trained personnel, operating out of Beaumont, Texas, capture the wolves, and subject them to intense study. A captive breeding program has been set up at the Point Defiance Zoo in Tacoma, Washington. Red Wolves deemed to be purebred are sent there. Some wolves are released as near their point of capture as possible. They wear radio telemetry devices which give the biologists important information as to their habits and movements.

The so-called black wolf of Florida is considered a color phase of Canis rufus. A breeding pair was sent to Bulls Island, a part of the Cape Romain National Wildlife Refuge off the South Carolina coast. They died of natural causes and were replaced by a second pair which was later removed.

In closing his article on Canadian wolves, Dr. Theberge wrote that he hoped another decade would find the Canadian wolves safe and prospering. Texans hope this will be the future of their native Red Wolf, Canis rufus.

Dr. John B. Theberge of the Faculty of Environmental Studies, University of Waterloo, Waterloo, Ontario, conducted a long study of wolf ecology in the north. The results, published in *Canada Nature* in 1973, under the title "Wolf Management in Canada Through a Decade of Change," gives great hope for the survival of the wolf, at least in Canada. Dr. Theberge points out that the present growing concern for wolf protection results from careful studies conducted in Ontario, Michigan, British Columbia and the Northwest Territories. Here are facts gained from these studies:

The wolf population in a given area will not increase indefinitely. Studies indicate that nowhere in North America have wolf populations exceeded one per ten square miles, even when there was a superabundance of food for them. The wolves on Isle Royale in Michigan, while limiting the big game numbers, still kept them within their normal food supply. But if big game animals have very dense populations, as for instance when men have interfered, the wolves could not limit the herds which then exceeded their food supply. Yet in the Algonquin Provincial Park in Ontario, wolves were a major mortality factor for big game animals. He concluded that the effect of wolves on prey populations varied according to other conditions.

Dr. Theberge points out that the effect of wolf predation is exactly the opposite from that created by hunters. And he cites proof from studies on Dall sheep, caribou, moose, and white-tailed deer. The hunters select the biggest and healthiest, those in the prime of their reproductive lives. Wolves kill the old, infirm, ill and the very young.

In the section on Coyotes, we point out how Kansas has set up a Coyote control program which corrects an individual problem. This is echoed by Dr. Theberge. "No longer should complaints of too many wolves be met with simplistic bounty programs and poisoning campaigns. A much more realistic and defensible approach to that of specific problems is that of specific solutions—removal of the individual wolf or pack causing a problem with livestock or with wild ungulates in a critical wintering area."

Eskimos at Point Barrow, Alaska, told the writer that prime wolf pelt was the finest of all furs. It carried prestige value for the person who dressed his parka with wolf fur. But, they said, it is the finest fur to have about the face—the warmest, and the one least likely to ice up from your breath.

It might happen then, if the demand for all furs increases and prices continue to rise, that the wolf will take on the status of a valued fur bearing animal. The effect, as far as Canada is concerned, might be that greater efforts would be made to control wolf killing. Or to put it another way, to manage wolf populations. It would not, however, banish the terrible cruelty of the leg hold traps. All over North America humane minded people have banded together to ban the use of this kind of traps, regardless of the species upon which they are used. So attempts to place the Canadian wolves on the fur bearing list would raise a tremendous outcry in the United States as well as in Canada.

The Arctic Wolves

Some 23 species have been identified as being true wolves, and there have been many sub-species and so many variations that only highly skilled wolf students with long experience in dissecting wolf bodies can tell the difference. We have pointed out that the Canadian Wildlife Service lists just three species of Arctic wolves. Stanley P. Young in *The Wolf In North American History* lists three species of Arctic wolf still existing in the far north. Besides the Mackenzie Valley Wolf already mentioned, he lists Canis lupus pambasileus and Canis lupus alces. The latter is an Alaskan Arctic Wolf. Neither of the above references refers to Canis lupus tundrarum, a name proposed by Miller in 1912. This wolf was described as being pure white, or a cream white, with darker hairs on the back and tail, thus showing faintly a wolf color pattern.

Young says that these Arctic wolves are the largest of all wolves. Ernest Thompson Seton killed one at Aylmer Lake which, being very gaunt, weighed 88 pounds after being bled. He estimated its weight when in good condition at 100 pounds. Seton called this wolf "the natural parasite of the muskox and the Barrenground caribou." As such, its natural hunting grounds would be the treeless barrens and tundra upon which the muskox and caribou lived. These Arctic wolves seldom enter forested areas, except as their quarry might.

Seton also observed that "sled dogs are a favourite prey with the wolves." Explorers from the earliest to reach North America have made similar observations. One of the earliest, commenting upon supposed wolf-dog crosses, said that the passion which wolves showed in killing dogs made this impossible. Wolves, he wrote, invariably kill dogs. Seton quotes Capt. George Lyon in the following passage:

"When the alarm was given (wolves were attacking his sled dogs) "and the Wolves were fired at, one of them was observed carrying a dead dog in his mouth, clear of the ground, at a canter, notwithstanding the animal was of his own weight."

Later, Capt. Lyon reported from Melville Island about an attack by white wolves:

"A fine dog was lost in the afternoon. The animal had strayed to the hummocks ahead of us without its master, and Mr. (Alex) Eldoer, who was near the spot, saw five wolves rush out, attack and devour it in an incredibly short space of time; before he could reach the place, the carcass was torn in pieces, and he found only the lower part of a leg bone."

This enmity between wolves and dogs is illustrated in a great book published in 1976 by St. Martin's Press. It is called *Tisha*. It is the story of Anne Hobbs Purdy, a young teacher who went to Chicken, Alaska to teach. Robert Specht has brought her story to life as few writers could.

In this true story, the sled dogs refused to go forward even when beaten. The driver, Fred, finally went forward. He came back with a piece of dog harness. All that was left of the dog was the skull, some broken bones and a little hair. Then they found another skull. And finally they came upon seven circling wolves. They were peering intently down a hole, and at first they didn't see Fred and Anne. When they did, this is how Anne described the wolves.

"Whatever it was that interested them, they didn't want to leave it, so they waited to see what we were going to do. The way they sized us up made my skin crawl. I'd always thought of wolves as smart dogs. This close they didn't resemble dogs at all. No dog had the huge head and powerful jaws these animals had, and no dog had

"Wolf Music," photographed by Tom W. Hall, Canadian outdoor photographer.

Roger Caras, internationally known animal writer and
TV commentator, gets initiated into the wolf pack.

their cold, shrewd gaze either. They were almost human. Or inhuman."

A sled had toppled into the hole. It contained a man who was dead, his wife who was pinned down by the sled, her young baby, a surviving dog, and one dog dead from a broken neck. The living were rescued. Perhaps one can say that the wolves were the real heroes of this episode, although unconsciously so. Had not their milling about the hole been noticed, the woman and baby would have died, and their bodies might never have been found.

The biology of these Arctic wolves does not differ sufficiently from that of other wolves to require much explanation. Some observers suggest that they may have smaller litters. When very hungry and the snow is deep, they have been able to kill Arctic foxes. Their main food is gained from the caribou and musk oxen in winter. In summer they have a variety of food, and even share the Arctic foxes' love of lemmings. Their chief enemy is winter starvation. In summer they probably do not range more than 10 square miles. In winter they may have to travel hundreds of miles in their search for food. Like other wolves, they are monogamous. It has been suggested that the pair bond may be weaker in winter when the long marches in search of food are made. But they still appear to mate for life.

The Future of the Wolf

At the present time, the Arctic wolves, or perhaps one should say the circumpolar wolves, are in no immediate danger of extinction. We know this to be true of Alaska and Canada. Reports from Siberia are scanty. Population pressures have squeezed the wolves in northern Europe and Russia. But there is little evidence as to Siberian pressures. In Alaska, the eventual effect of the Alaska pipeline with increased settlers, increased hunting, and dwindling herds of wolf prey animals cannot be estimated at this time.

According to a 1974–75 government report, in Canada the status of the wolf varies with each province and territory.

Newfoundland and Labrador form one area or province, but there are no wolves in Newfoundland. In Labrador, the wolf is a fur bearing animal and there are regulated trapping and hunting seasons for it. The population is listed as "adequate" and its general status as "satisfactory." Prince Edward Island, Nova Scotia and New Brunswick have no wolves.

Quebec lists the wolf as a fur bearing animal, and the population is considered to be adequate to abundant. Wolves are not protected, but a hunting license is required to take them. Latest available figures are for 1971–72 during which 732 wolves were killed.

Ontario ignores the status of the wolf, has no management program, but does use control measures where needed. At least 1156 wolves were taken during the 1971–72 season.

Manitoba, Yukon Territory, and Northwest Territories list the wolf as a non-game animal. Only 1227 wolves were killed during the above period. Wolves are neither protected nor managed.

Saskatchewan lists the wolf as a fur bearer and has a year round open season, but only about 200 are killed annually. Alberta has a regulated season, lists the wolf as a game animal, and reported 519 killed during 1971–72. In British Columbia, the wolf population is declining, is actually rare, and is an endangered species. Wolves are protected on Vancouver Island.

All the above figures are for trapping and do not reflect the unreported numbers killed by sports hunters.

At this point we should clarify the meanings of two words now used increasingly by ecologists. They are "endangered" and "threatened." "Threatened" is a term used for a species which is still reasonably strong, but which might suddenly suffer catastrophic losses sufficient to place it in the "endangered species" group. The Endangered Species Act of 1973 has placed the wolves of the lower 48 states in this category.

The major wolf population left in the 48 states is the Eastern Timber Wolf, Canis lupus lycaon. It has been squeezed into about five per cent of the range it once occupied. That area is basically Northern Minnesota. Earlier we have given government figures as to the wolf population in Minnesota, Wisconsin, Michigan, and other states. The reasons for the relentless war against the wolf may be summarized once again. They are:

Exploding human population.

Increasing demand for agricultural land

Destruction of the range land and forests, which has brought about the dwindling of the wolf's natural prey animals—deer, antelopes, moose, beaver and woodland caribou.

Destruction of farm livestock and dogs by wolves.

Dr. L. David Mech has devoted 18 years to the study of wolves. Probably no man in the world is so qualified to speak on the subject. For years he has been monitoring the wolves of Minnesota. He has written two books and dozens of papers on Canis lupus.

He is a singularly objective man. And so he is probably the one authority who best understands the need to preserve the wolf, and the feelings of farmers who lose cattle, sheep and dogs to wolves. Dr. Mech is a member of the Eastern Wolf Recovery Team which is made up of eminent biologists, all students of wolves, from Minnesota, Wisconsin, Michigan, the U.S. Forest Service, the National Park Service and the U.S. Fish and Wildlife Service.

As this is being written, the national Congress has before it recommendations made by this team. But as the subject is complex with political, sociological and human hatred of the wolf considerations. Since the wolf is presently on the endangered species list, it is illegal to kill one. And it is obvious that no Minnesota farmer who has a rifle will hesitate to break the law if he sees a wolf attacking his cattle.

A first recommendation is that the wolf be removed from the endangered species list and placed on the threatened list. This would mean that in areas where wolves particularly menace live stock, or where a wolf population explosion has begun, experienced government or state biologists could reduce the population. In this connection, see the section on Coyotes which deals with the methods being used by Kansas to handle individual Coyote cases.

Minnesotans complain of a decreasing deer population. One reason for this is the comparatively old age of the great wilderness area forests. The great trees offer no browsing for the deer. The Wolf Recovery Team has suggested that the forests either be logged or burned off and young trees be planted. Probably such a plan would include Minnesota's national and state parks. The plan would instantly raise a wolfish howl from conservationists and might contribute to flooding until the trees had reached considerable height.

The Team has divided Minnesota into five zones. Four of these contain altogether about 10,000 square miles. A fifth zone which contains about 21,000 square miles, has no wolves. In three of the zones, the Team suggests complete protection. In the remaining one, they ask that they be allowed to "manage" the wolf population. Dr. Mech is said to fear a population explosion in that area, although his own experience with the wolves on Isle Royal would seem to indicate a reasonably stable wolf population, according to its food supply. In Minnesota, the difference would be the pressure upon farm lands to the south, and the suppy of food which farm livestock would offer. But, if managed, it is estimated that the wolves would not exceed the one wolf per ten square miles which seems to be normal for the species.

In 1974 much publicity was given to the transfer of two mated pairs of wolves to northern Michigan. It was hoped that they would help to increase the struggling group in that state. But the experiment failed since all four wolves were shot within nine months of the transfer. This happened despite the fact that the wolves were on the endangered species list, and it was illegal to kill them. Michigan and Wisconsin, even in their northern areas, are growing more heavily populated. The danger to all the wolves is shown by the experiment. It is too easy for the hunter to say that he thought this was a Coyote or a dog gone wild.

The Recovery Team also has suggested a massive educational effort. This would be designed to allay human fears of wolves, to alert them to the danger that "extinct means forever," and to interest them in saving Canis lupus. In the Algonquin Provincial Park in Ontario, regular parties are organized so that people can go out into the wilderness and listen to, and even tape, the music of the wolves. This might certainly be done in Minnesota, Wisconsin, and Michigan. It might also be possible to set up tree house observation posts, such as those in Kenya, where people could go just to see and photograph wolves. The writer has known the fascination of lying along a ridge and watching wolves move along a valley.

Should people own pet wolves? Should they get wolf pups and try to domesticate them? The answer is "absolutely no." The wolf is a wild animal and should be allowed to remain in the wild. If raised in captivity, it can never be returned to the wild, and thus nature has been robbed of one more citizen.

8 The Lore of the Coyote

"The animal of this country called coyotl is very sagacious in waylaying. When he wishes to attack, he first casts his breath over the victim to infect and stupefy it. Indeed it is diabolical." Friar Bernardino de Sahagun, 1561

HISTORIANS rate man's discovery of fire, or at least his mastery of it, as one of the greatest leaps forward in human history. It is proper then that we begin this chapter on the legends of the Coyote with the discovery of fire. Edgerton R. Young was a missionary to the Indians and Eskimos of the far north. He was also a prolific writer and researcher, and he collected many of the legends of the Algonquins. His daughter, called Minnehaha by the Algonquins, was this writer's aunt. When we were children, my mother used to read Young's stories of the far north, and particularly from his *Algonquin Indian Tales* to my sisters and me at bedtime.

Here is the story of how the Coyote brought fire to man. It was told in an isolated wigwam on a bitter winter day to Minnehaha and her brother Sagastao. They had reached the wigwam with their father by dog sled. The aged Indian who told the story was Kinnesasis. It is reprinted here almost in its entirety as Edgerton Young took it down.

"It was long ago, when I was a young lad, that I heard the story from the old story-tellers of our people. I had traveled with my father for many days far toward the setting sun. We reached the land of the great mountains, and there, with our people of those regions, we spent many moons. It was while we were among them that I heard from the ancient story-teller the legend of how the fire was stolen from the center of the earth where it was kept hidden away from the human family.

"That there was such a thing as fire was well known. It had been seen bursting out of the tops of distant mountains, and there had been times in great thunder storms, when the lightning had set fire to dead trees—and indeed in this latter way the Indians had become acquainted with its value to the human race. But they had not taken care to keep it burning, and no one had been appointed specially to look after it.

"The reason why fire had not been from the first given to men was because when the race was created the fire was not much needed. The earth was then much warmer than it is now. There was no snow or ice ever seen except on the tops of the very highest mountains. Great animals now all dead, and others that could only live in the hottest countries, lived all over these great lands. Then there was abundance of fruit and nuts and roots that were all very good for food. Then some great disaster happened to the world and soon it began to grow colder and many animals, and even families, perished. Snow and ice appeared where they were never seen before. There was great suffering from the cold. The hunters began to kill the animals for food. They were now not satisfied with the fruit and roots, they wanted something better.

"So the fire was much needed. But where it was or how to get it, was the question. Fortunately an old dreamer dreamed a dream about it.

"As the council assembled to hear his dream he told them that the fire was preserved in the heart of the earth by a magician called Sistinakoo, and that it was kept very carefully surrounded by four walls, one within the other, in each of which was a single door. At the first door a great snake kept guard. At the second door a mountain lion or panther was the guardian. A grizzly bear guarded the third door, and at the fourth and last door Sistinakoo himself kept watchful care over the precious fire that smoldered on a stone altar just inside this last wall.

"When the council heard all this they were almost discouraged. They thought it would be impossible for anyone to get by all of these guards and steal the fire.

"They first asked the fox to try, but he only reached the first door when the great snake nearly made a meal of him. Thoroughly frightened, he rushed back to the top of the earth and told of his narrow escape.

"For a time nothing more was done to try and get the fire. The people continued to suffer, for the earth kept getting colder and colder and ice and snow were now to be found in lands that had previously been comfortably warm. So the council was called again, and the question again raised as to what could be done.

"It so happened that there came to the council a very old man who remembered a tradition, handed down from his forefathers, which said that part of the earth beneath us was hollow, and that some of the animals, even the great buffaloes, had dwelt in those underground regions before they came to dwell on the surface of the earth. He said that the Coyote, the prairie wolf, was the last one to leave, and that he was sure that he still remembered the route to the very spot where Sistinakoo, the head chief of the regions, guarded the fire so jealously.

" 'Why should they so guard the fire, and be so careful about letting people have it, when we know how good it is?' asked Minnehaha.

"Because," replied Kinnesasis, "there was a tradition that at some time or other the fire should get mastery over men, and the whole world be burned by it, and they thought that they would carefully guard it from getting scattered about by careless people who might set the world on fire.

"So when the Indian council heard this story they sent for the king of the Coyotes and told him of their wish that he should return to that underworld and bring up the fire for their use.

"To their surprise and great delight the Coyote said he would go, and he immediately began his preparations for the journey. So greatly had the cold increased that he found the dark mouth of the entrance under the mountains almost surrounded by snow and ice.

"After traveling for some time in the darkness he reached the outer wall, where he waited, a little distance from the door, until the snake was taking his usual sleep. Then he quickly stepped past him. Knowing the habits of the other animals, he waited until they were asleep and then he noiselessly passed them all. Even Sistinakoo himself was sound asleep. So the Coyote crept silently up to the fire and lighted the large brand or torch that was securely fastened to his tail. The instant it began to blaze up, as the Coyote rushed out through the first door, Sistinakoo shouted, 'Who is there? Someone has been here and has stolen the fire!'

"He at once began to make a great row and loudly called to the different keepers to close the doors in the walls. But the Coyote was too quick for them all, and ere the sleepers were wide enough awake to do anything he had passed through all the doors and was far on his way to the top of the ground. The fire was gladly received by the people, but after some time, when some big prairies and forests had been burned up by it, the men got fearful that the world might be destroyed, and so they intrusted it to the care of the old magician and his two daughters, with orders to be very careful to whom they gave any. It was from them Nanahboozhoo (Hiawatha, among the Onondagas, teacher of agriculture, navigation, and able to conquer all the forces that war against men.—M. R.) stole it, to scatter it once more freely among the people as we now have it."

In his monumental work, *The North American Indians,* Edward S. Curtis recounts a similar legend of the Jicarillas. In this case, it is the fireflies who guard the fire, and they live far underground, and can be reached only from a perpendicular hole. The Coyote gets "Little Tree" to send its roots down to the "Land of the Fireflies."

Coyote has cedar bark tied to his tail. After playing with the firefly children until their suspicions are allayed, he lights the bark and rushes to the hole. "Little Tree" helps him by quickly drawing up its roots. Coyote gets his tail singed, however, and that is why it has black on the end. According to the Yumas, Coyote brought the fire from the sun, and in doing so got his tail scorched.

Many of the Indian tribes considered Coyote to have been the creator, having been a son of Darkness. The Navahos said he stole the children of the water monsters, thus causing the flood. The Coyote sealed himself in a hollow tube, eventually landed on the top of a mountain. He is then said to have used turkey feathers to create vegetation. He traveled the world naming things. And his many mishaps and his ridiculous acts and sayings were said to be meant to teach men the folly of all things not normal.

The Monos said that the wolf and the Coyote rode out the flood in a boat, and then created the land. And Coyote was said to have created the stars by flinging bits of jewels into the sky.

These stories have a greater importance than most of us are likely to give to them. There is a definition of a myth which says that it is greater than truth itself. These stories and all other myths are attempts by human beings to learn who they are, and to know their place in the universe. It is surprising, for instance, to learn that all primitive people have stories of the great flood. And it is even more surprising to learn that they knew, what scientists now tell us, that at one time the earth was very warm.

Primitive societies have always had a closer relationship to the animals than we, who relentlessly destroy entire races of animals, have. Most of those societies believed that animals could talk, or at least that men could in some way communicate with them. They also ascribed certain human characteristics to the animals. That is why so many legends begin with something like this: "Long ago, when the animals could talk. . . ."

Dogs were said to be able to talk, and moreover, to have been great tattle tales. And since they were normally more loyal to their masters than to their mistresses, they were apt to report on the infidelities of the latter. In her book *God Had a Dog*, Maria Leach tells a Plains Indian legend of how the Coyote—again a cultural hero—robbed the dog of its ability to talk.

A Coyote found a group of women weeping. He asked the cause and was told that the men beat them. It was because, they said, that while out gathering wood or berries, they might give a kiss or an embrace to an old sweetheart. The dogs would report this to their masters who would then beat their wives. The Coyote put a stop to this by altering the muzzle of the dog so that it can no longer talk.

Fertility rites have always played a vital part in the lives of primitive peoples. The male sex organ, the phallus, was a religious symbol of the fertilizing power of nature. The Celts built gigantic stone phalluses and had spring dances about them. Christian missionaries simply substituted the maypole, and most modern people seem to have forgotten the original meaning of the dances.

The precariousness of their existence, coupled with a life span of about 33 years, caused fertility rites to become a vital part of primitive life. Many Indian tribes considered the Coyote to have been the creator of mankind. Carolyn Niethammer in *Daughters of the Earth, The Lives and Legends of American Indian Women* tells of an ancient legend that Coyotes copulated with the women in a spring rite. Later, men wearing Coyote skins, replaced their "little brothers." Just as Christian priests had stopped the Celtic Beltane rite, so white missionaries moving north hundreds of years later, failed to see any symbolism, only sin, in the Coyote rite. They stopped it.

Lest we misinterpret as did the Catholic Fathers, we might consider one of our own rites, and ask ourselves if we are so different from those Indians of long ago. How would visitors from outer space view an American football game? They would see two teams of warriors acting out a mock battle before 80,000 hysterically screaming people. The "totem" of one side is a tiger, so a man dressed in a simulated tiger skin prances about in front of the team's supporters. The "totem" on the other side is a bear, and so another man dances about in a bear skin.

Each side's shamans or witch doctors lead its supporters in organized cries for victory, and in victory chants. Bands parade, drums sound continuously. Experts tell the outer space visitors that, even though football fields are alike, the greater hysteria produced by the home side will help to provide the victory.

In another ancient legend, the Coyote is also portrayed as the actual creator of the modern races of men. The story can be found in *Mythology of the New World, A Treatise on the Symbolism of the Red Race of America* by Daniel G. Brinton. The third edition of Brinton's book was published in 1896, but he repeats the story from the earlier work *Indians of California* by Stephen Powers.

"The Aschochimi of California told of the drowning of the world so that no man escaped; but when the waters retired the coyote went forth and planted the feathers of various birds, which grew into the various races of men."

One of the most amusing Coyote stories was told by Edward S. Curtis. The story is a legend of the Chinookans. During a war on the river, the Coyote captures two slaves, both "small persons." He takes them to his house and puts one on either side of the doorway. But one swells up and finally bursts, destroying Coyote's house. He consults his "medicine"—his own feces—which tells him that when winter comes, he will see a small black spot in the snow on a hillside. He should set a trap there.

He does, captures his slave by the hand, and takes him home. Again it swells up, bursts, and destroys Coyote's home. This time the Coyote's medicine warns him not to try again, for if he kills the slave, winter will never go away.

"So Coyote had only one slave, and that was Flea. After the fight in which he was captured, Flea was in the bottom of the canoe in which the fighters were returning home. And he was so small that another slave sat down on him without seeing him, which made Flea flat."

The Caygotte, or Coyote of Mexico, as drawn by Col. Hamilton Smith 1839–40.

9 The Biology of the Coyote

THE SCIENTIFIC NAME for the Coyote is Canis latrans, meaning the "barking dog." For those who admire the Coyote, Hope Ryden gave it a better name—God's Dog. It has been called by other names—the prairie wolf, the steppen wolf, the brush wolf, and by terms less complimentary. The word Coyote comes from the Aztec word, Coyotl. Depending upon where you are, or even who you are, you will pronounce its name coy-o-tee, coy-ote, ky-ote (as in sky) or ky-o-tee.

Lt. Col. Charles Hamilton Smith wrote about the Coyote in 1839. He pointed out one of a number of strange resemblances of the Basque and Aztec languages and a little known and less remembered history of man's inhumanity to man.

"The Basque name, Caygotte, (pronounced Ky-go-tee, M. R.) bestowed by the Spaniards upon a Mexican canine, offers a curious coincidence with the indigenous name, Coyotl. In Bearn and the south of France, Cagot is a term of contempt applied to a race of human beings for ages persecuted and expelled social life. It is there interpreted for Ca-goth, Gothic for dog or Arian, but it seems to signify dog of the woods, or wood hound, which is synonymous with Coyotl. Is it therefore another instance where these two remote dialects resemble each other."

Hamilton Smith also mentions that a Capt. Belcher had seen on the banks of the Sacramento River in California an animal which he said was called a Cuyota, and which he called a "jackal-fox." Hamilton Smith had no doubt it was a Caygotte or Coyotl.

Some authorities have called it a small wolf, or little brother to the wolf. But such terms do not seem to be accurate. For example, the wolf is physically contrasted with the dog by its far mightier teeth, its greater leg bones, and its huge spreading feet. The Coyote contrasts with both dog and wolf by its very light leg bones and very small feet. Its jaws are narrower, and its teeth are relatively smaller. Even its ears are relatively smaller than those of the wolf. By general agreement, it is the most intelligent of all the canids. One proof of this has been its ability to survive despite the incessant war of extermination waged against it by man, and occasionally even by wolves.

The average height of Coyotes is 24 inches at the withers, or shoulders. Males average 24 to 25 pounds and females 22 pounds. Some meaningful comparisons for dog owners are these: Pugs are considered toy dogs, but some have weighed in excess of 25 pounds. English Springer Spaniels are supposed to be 20 inches at the withers and, if well proportioned, 49 to 55 pounds in weight.

Coyote color is usually light buff to gray. The muzzle, ears and the front of the legs are tinted with rust or a tawny color. There is a lighter, almost white color on the upper lips and under the chin. The gray body hair has black tipped guard hair, as do Norwegian Elkhounds and Keeshonds. The tail is very bushy, and is usually tipped with black.

The Coyote's range seems to affect both its color and its size. Those living on the prairies conform to the above description. Those living in mountainous country are usually darker in color, there being more black in the guard hairs. Seen from above, and in certain light, they may appear nearly black. Also, the higher the altitude and the farther north their range, the heavier they become.

C. Raymond Hall and Keith R. Kelson, in *Mammals of North America,* list 19 sub-species. The Coyote's range is from the Atlantic to the Pacific, and from the northern tip of North America to Costa Rica and Honduras. These sub-species usually inhabit fairly specific ranges of their own.

For example, there are Canis latrans latrans, the plains Coyote; Canis latrans incollatus, the northern Coyote; and Canis latrans thamnos, the northeastern Coyote. Some sub-species have been named after the people who first described them. For example, Canis latrans Dickeyi (pronounced Dickey-eye) and Canis latrans

Mearnsi (Mearns-eye). However, so little attention is paid to sub-species that when the writer asked the Colorado Division of Wildlife to name the species living in Colorado, the answer came back "I don't know what you mean."

It is generally agreed that the immense range of the Coyote has been caused by human pressure, or to be more specific, by white man's pressure. The Indians have always admired and respected the Coyote, and have lived peacefully with them. But the white man, with his passion for agricultural land and his sheep, forced the Coyote to expand his range into Central America and north to Point Barrow, Alaska. Its normal habitat seems to have been the great plains, which abounded in rodents, jack rabbits and similar food.

Coyotes, however, seem never to have entered tropical forests and swamps. For example, they do not exist in Louisiana and in certain areas of Mississippi. The tropical rain forests in Central America proved an impenetrable barrier for them, as in fact they did for wolves and most of the other North American mammals.

Although Ernest Thompson Seton and Stanley F. Young have reported that wolves will kill Coyotes, this is considered to be a comparatively rare occurrence. Wolves do not show the implacable hatred of Coyotes that they have for domestic dogs which they invariably kill when they can. When they do kill Coyotes it is apparently brought about by extreme hunger. Thus wolves and Coyotes inhabit the same ranges on a peaceful basis. That is, they do in those areas in which the wolves still exist. There is also the fact that both animals are wild. The wolf appears to hate the dog because the latter has cast its lot with man. Finally, the food habits of the wolf and Coyote differ when game abounds. The wolf selects larger game than the Coyote does.

There have been many major studies of Coyote diets. In such studies the stomach contents of thousands of Coyotes have been analyzed. They show that the Coyote lives chiefly on small animals—mice, rabbits, prairie dogs, carrion, grasses and fruits. In season, they also consume vast numbers of grasshoppers, and they seem to have a strong addiction for watermelons and grapes. Their grasshopper kill alone is a major advantage to farmers. They may be able to kill aged and weak deer. But they are always in danger of being trampled to death by moose and elk. It is obvious that by killing off weak and sick deer, when they can, Coyotes are contributing to the general health of the herds. And in addition, they are removing unfit food eaters from these herds.

Ranchers claim, of course, that Coyotes are major sheep killers. But one study showed that the loss from lambs in Utah where coyotes are present in large numbers, differed only slightly from losses in Ohio where there were no known Coyotes. (Perhaps half a dozen Coyotes a year are now being reported in Ohio). Since Coyotes do eat carrion, ranches often see Coyote tracks about a dead sheep and so infer that the Coyote killed that sheep. The ranchers make no effort to determine the actual cause of death of the sheep.

That Coyotes sometimes do attack sheep seems to be due to a man-made factor. Entire ranges were poisoned in an effort to eradicate both wolves and Coyotes. The poison, of course, made no distinction in animal species. Thus, it killed mice, rabbits, prairie dogs, skunks, badgers, vultures, and even eagles. In general, the Coyotes were too smart to take the poisoned baits. But being robbed of all other sources of food, except fruits and what frogs or crustaceans they might catch in streams, they might then be forced to attack sheep. In such cases, they would invariably select the sick or weak animals since these would pose less danger to themselves.

In the spring of 1977, United Press International reported from Sierra Blanca, Texas, that ranchers and farmers suffered annual damage of from $250,000 to $750,000 from the depradations of Coyotes. A small army of 130 professional Coyote killers, called predator control agents, spend $2,000,000 annually and kill about 20,000 Coyotes. These agents are supported by federal state and local funds. As was the case with the bounty hunters, these professionals will leave sufficient breeding stock to insure them jobs during the coming years.

"Every day," reports UPI, "the men drive hundreds of miles in the West Texas range area east of El Paso, looking for the next victim of their more than 10,000 coyote traps, laced with lethal cyanide powder. . . . The M-44 cyanide trap is the most effective, accounting for 6,000 Coyote kills in Texas last year (1976). Unfortunately, the traps also killed 1000 other animals, an agriculture report says, including 160 skunks, 350 foxes, 250 opossums, and 200 raccoons."

The report included this comment: "Environmentalists prefer

the cyanide trap to the agony of snares, bullets or steel leg traps, which still account for the largest number of coyote kills."

H. Wendt and E. Klinghammer reported a study made on an Indiana farm of a lone female Coyote. The study lasted about a year and a half, and since she was not seriously disturbed by man, she was easily watched. The farm had free ranging chickens and geese. Time after time the Coyote was seen to walk among the chickens without harming them. She was afraid of the geese which threatened to attack her when she approached. Her diet consisted of rabbits, mice, rats, and sometimes quail.

Coyotes are too small to travel well in deep snows. Thus, they may starve to death within a few hundred yards of deer. Those that survive often do so because of their astonishing ability to catch mice which travel under the snow. They are able to detect the passage of the mouse, then to pounce, burying their heads in the snow, but coming up with the mouse.

Hope Ryden reports in *God's Dog* that a biologist at the National Elk Refuge said he had seen only one elk killed by Coyotes in eight years. This was a new-born calf which was only half the size it should have been at birth. Ms. Ryden also watched Coyotes mingling with elk during winter, with neither seeming to pay attention to the other. Yet the Coyotes were watchful. When a bull elk would rouse itself and move, a Coyote would spring into the freshly made hoof print, and then spring out again. Many times, it would have captured a mouse in that one quick pounce.

Coyotes are less likely to form packs than wolves do. Instead a male and a female seem to pair for life. If more than the male and female are present, it is likely that these are pups. Two males may fight for a female, but it is she who makes the choice. And she may choose the loser in the fight.

It seems generally agreed that females do not breed until two years old, or nearly so. The female heat (oestrum) period is about two months in duration, but with only about four days being the actual mating period. If she is not bred during that time, she will not be for another year. (An occasional exception has been reported). Males also are not physically mature enough to mate at a year. They, too, might be two years old, or nearly so before making a successful mating. The breeding season is January and February.

The gestation period for Coyotes is about the same as that for the domestic dog, 60 to 65 days. Litters of five to seven pups are normal, but a litter of 13 has been reported. The pups are born blind, and are believed to open their eyes at from 10 to 14 days.

Coyotes live in the open and only make dens for the purpose of raising young. Both parents help in digging a den. But also, they may dig out the dens of other animals, make a den between the roots of great trees, or in shelters made by rocks. The pups are whelped in the den, but the parents normally remain outside. Coyotes often make several dens, and they will move their pups at the slightest suspicion of danger. It is perhaps this constant need to be alert to danger that has taught the parents to live outside the den.

The mother suckles her pups for six weeks or more. During that time, the male may do most of the hunting. He may carry home food for the mother, either in his jaws or in his stomach. In the latter case, he has freed his jaws for the possible catching of other food on the way back to the den. The food is regurgitated for the mother. Later, he will do the same for the pups.

Coyotes are among the higher animals in intelligence, and therefore they inherit less of the fixed genetic imprints which would, for example, govern the lives of insects. For this reason, they have a relatively long learning period. The pups play in much the manner of domestic dogs. But the parents have to teach them how to hunt. And in truth, the pups do not appear to be very successful until their permanent teeth come in. Even then, they are awkward and unsure of themselves for a long time. The parents must also teach the pups how to avoid danger, as well as what constitutes danger.

They are aided in this by what is known as neophobia—a type of fear. In the domestic dog, this is the period between about 14 weeks and six months. In human children, it may be during the second year of life and is shown by shyness with strangers, and fear of strange situations. In the Coyote, the period may last for nearly a year. It is during this period that the pups receive intensive training from their parents.

Ranchers sometimes claim that without rigid control, Coyotes would have a population explosion which would raise havoc with the flocks of sheep. But, in other areas where predators are not controlled, no such population explosion has ever occurred. Coyotes have too many enemies. These include the puma, jaguarundi, the

New World wild pig (peccary, javelin, or javeline), badger, and even the golden eagle. And they also suffer from external parasites, such as fleas, ticks and lice, and from a variety of internal parasites. In addition, they are subject to distemper, hepatitis, tularemia, and sometimes rabies. It is always possible for ranchers to stir up a Coyote kill session by claiming rabies has appeared among coyotes.

President Nixon signed a bill outlawing the use of poisons on the ranges. But one cynic commented that there was enough poison at the ranches to kill every living thing on the ranges. Enforcement has also been a problem. And as noted above, cyanide—a deadly poison—is being used in Texas and is being paid for by the federal government.

Hunting Coyotes as a sport has become popular in some of the western states. The cursorial hounds—Greyhounds, Borzois, Afghans, and Salukis—are chiefly used. Colorado requires such hunters to pay the same small game license fee as is charged for quail, rabbit and pheasant hunting. Permission of the land owner is also required.

The recent popularity of snowmobiles has also proven a particularly ugly new danger to the Coyote. Coyotes are too small to run well in heavy snow. So the snowmobilers run them down, sometimes killing them, and at others just leaving them with wounds from which they are likely to die. At the time of writing President Carter is considering legislation to prevent the use of snowmobiles in open country. But unless, and until such legislation is passed—and enforced—the snowmobile will continue to be a serious enemy of the Coyote. The Coyote's other winter enemy is starvation.

Once wolves were hunted in the open areas of the Minnesota and Canadian lakes area during winter from low flying airplanes. In Oklahoma, predator control officers now hunt Coyotes from helicopters. It was sufficient to embark upon such a program when the Oklahoma State University Experimental Sheep Farm claimed that Coyotes were killing prized registered sheep. The aerial killings were also justified by the claim that Coyotes were mating with wild dogs, and these posed a menace to children in populated areas. In 1976, Oklahoma's aerial hunting parties killed 2523 Coyotes.

During the first of the 1977 aerial hunts, Roger Caras, the noted author and ABC television animals editor, filmed part of the hunt. Caras also interviewed a rancher who said he had been ranching for 26 years, but had never had an animal killed by a Coyote. The 1976 aerial hunters used 889.3 hours of flying. It is also noteworthy that Oklahoma also began using the cyanide trap "under the less restrictive conditions imposed by the Environmental Protection Agency." Use of the trap then increased by 45% and Coyote kills by 69%.

Earlier, we reported that President Nixon had signed a bill outlawing the use of poisons on the range. But pest control operators are still using them, as noted in the case of the cyanide trap. But in addition, the deadly poison 1080 is still being used. Thus, says the Oklahoma report, "State Supervisor Peterson assisted state officials in the investigation of the accidental poisoning of three young children in Durant, Oklahoma. The incident resulted in the loss of a Pest Control Operator's license because of the shoddy manner in which a Compound 1080 derivative was being used and stored." What the report doesn't say is that all three children died.

One of the deadliest enemies of the Coyote is the predator whistle. The Coyote has a remarkable sense of hearing. And very early in life it learns to identify the distress call of the rabbit. This indicates to the Coyote that a meal may be near by, or at least a shared meal with some other predator. Men have learned to duplicate this distress signal so as to lure the Coyote within shooting distance.

Oklahoma Coyote kills for 1976 totalled 6844, of which 2295 were taken in leg hold traps, 172 by snares, 783 shot from the ground, 31 killed by dogs, 530 with cyanide M-44 traps, and 559 killed in dens. While the Federal Government no longer pays bounties, Oklahoma still does, apparently on a county basis. It paid $1,053 for 283 Coyotes killed. It is interesting to note that 501 opossums, 194 raccoons and 601 skunks also died during the program.

The Oklahoma damage figures for fiscal 1976 show more than the losses. They also indicate the widely varied diet of Coyotes. Since the value placed on livestock killed is that placed by the landowners themselves, they may be subject to downward revision. Also, it is possible that many of the losses ascribed to Coyotes were actually caused by wild dogs. Still, 13 dogs having a supposed market value of $470 were claimed to have been killed by Coyotes.

The report shows 797 cattle, market value $110,450; 1,283

sheep, market value $35,546; and then turkeys, chickens, hogs, goats, geese, ducks, etc. Most interesting is the claimed loss of 3,153 watermelons, market value, $4,389; and one half acre of peanuts, market value, $450.

A 1931 law which calls for the "destruction of all mountain lions, wolves, bobcats, prairie dogs, gophers, ground squirrels, jackrabbits, and other animals injurious to agriculture, horticulture, forestry, husbandry, game, and domestic animals" is still on the federal books. "Game" refers to animals which sportsmen wish to kill for themselves.

A report from Wyoming indicates that a million dollars annually is being spent on Coyote killing alone. But some states, notably Kansas, now have a system of controlled Coyote trapping. It is recognized that only an occasional outlaw, or atypical Coyote, preys on sheep. In Kansas, when such Coyotes appear, they are eliminated, and good citizen Coyotes are not disturbed. As a result, Kansas is now believed to be supporting the highest population of Coyotes in the nation. Their worth in controlling rodent and insect populations which would otherwise destroy millions of dollars worth of crops is well recognized.

The Audubon Magazine for September-October, 1953, carried an article by E..C. Shindorf, chairman of the board of directors of the Toponas Grassland Protective Association in Colorado. This group of ranchers had posted their lands to prohibit the killing of Coyotes and other predators.

"The reason for this attitude," he wrote, "is that for 10 years or so we have watched the steady increase of mice, gophers, moles, rabbits, and other rodents. Now we are at a point where these animals take up to one third of our hay crop and have cut the carrying capacity of our livestock on our range by as much as half . . .

"What with government hunters and government poison, the predators have a hard time. The coyote is nearly extinct in our part of the state. Foxes and bobcats have succumbed to the chain-killing poisons. There are fewer hawks and eagles every year and weasels are scarce . . ."

In the section on the lore of the Coyote, we told of the legends of so many Indian tribes which relate how the Coyote brought fire to mankind. Coyotes do have a strange habit which has, in fact, saved many a grass range from burning. It is their instant reaction to a small fire.

Everett McConahay of Cowley, Wyoming, demonstrated this for Hope Ryden by setting an envelope on fire and then tossing it on the ground. His pet Coyote immediately stamped on it, and then rolled on it, thus putting out the fire. Later, Dr. Michael Fox tried the same experiment with his captive Coyotes and got a similar result. The Coyotes reacted with lightning speed. Since most Coyotes were originally plains dwellers, this strange habit which has somehow become innate in them, whether wild or tame, must have had great survival benefit for them.

Coyote-dog crosses, and Coyote-wolf crosses are possible, and the offspring are fertile. Yet such occurrences among wild coyotes, either with dogs or wolves, must be very rare. In fact, controlled experiments have shown that Coyotes cannot be easily coaxed into mating with dogs in captivity. If a second generation of pen raised Coyotes must be coaxed into mating with dogs raised either with them or in neighboring pens, then wild matings must indeed be very rare.

This brings us to the puzzle of the New Hampshire canids. Some have said that they are the result of a wolf-Coyote cross; others, a Coyote-dog cross. That these mysterious New Hampshire canids could not have been the result of Coyote-dog crosses seems to have been proven by the work of Walter and Helenette Silvers. There is evidence that they are Coyote-wolf crosses with predominantly Coyote characteristics.

The careful work of Ronald Nowak, both in Southeastern Canada and New England indicates this is true. There may be a parallel in Texas. There, Dr. Howard McCarley has suggested that the Red Wolf of Texas may be the result of Wolf-Coyote crosses. In any case, the New Hampshire canid seems well established in Southeastern Canada, New England and New York, Pennsylvania and West Virginia.

Survival of the Coyote

As with the wolf, one must ask: Can the Coyote survive? No definite answers are possible. But it can be said that its chances of survival are greater than those of the wolf. The Coyote shows far greater adaptability than does the wolf. The relentless war against it

has eased just slightly, but it has eased in many areas of both the
United States and Canada. There is, however, a disturbing factor.
Coyote fur has suddenly become popular with the ladies. If the
current demand for the pelts continue, then the Coyote's chances of
survival are greatly lessened.

Recently, LeRoy Rutske, wildlife specialist for the Minnesota
Department of Natural Resources, mentioned that Coyotes are
completely unprotected in Minnesota. Then he added this: "We do
not know to what extent the current high price for Coyote fur may
be affecting the population."

Some idea of this may be gained from the figures supplied by
the Department of Trade, Industry, and Commerce of the Canadian government. During the 1974-75 season, some 44,366 Coyotes
were trapped, or otherwise killed for their fur. Their value was
placed at $1,416,512, or $31.93 per skin. During the 1975-76
season, 61,779 were killed for fur; their gross value was $3,150,383,
or $50.99 per skin.

On the other hand, S. P. Young and H. H. T. Jackson, in their
book *The Clever Coyote* (1951) wrote that trapping and poisoning
coyotes in order to reduce their numbers was like "digging a hole in
the ocean." In *Bulletin 1872, The Effects of Control on Coyote Populations,* Division of Agricultural Sciences, University of California,
Cooperative Extension Service, Guy E. Connolly and William M.
Longhurst report on a Coyote model simulated control. They
estimated that if 75 per cent of Coyotes could be killed each year, the
Coyote could be exterminated in slightly longer than 50 years. A 70
per cent annual kill would permit the Coyote population to maintain
itself.

"In this model," Connolly and Longhurst wrote, "coyote populations reduced by intensive control recovered to precontrol densities within three to five years after control was terminated. Under
current conditions, considering the restrictions placed upon control
methods, coyote densities probably cannot be significantly reduced
except in limited geographical areas."

They point out that sport hunting and fur trapping are non-
selective in their removal of Coyotes whereas Coyote killing to
alleviate livestock losses tends to be focused on localized conditions.

These authors and others have noted that severe control
methods can have an opposite effect in that the Coyotes left are able

Coyotes at San Diego Zoo. *San Diego Zoo photo.*

A Canadian coyote hunts for rodents moving under the snow.
Photo by Ed. Cesar, Canadian wildlife photographer.

to compensate by larger litters and fewer natural deaths. As populations increase, litters may be smaller and fewer animals may be able to breed. There may be a scarcity of food, fewer den sites and greater losses from parasites and disease.

Environmentalists and those interested in humane causes bitterly resent trapping and poisoning. (Poisoning has now been outlawed by Congress.) The reasons are that non-predator animals suffer heavily from trapping, and formerly from poisoning. Connolly and Longhurst think little sense is contained in those resentments. They argue that the non-target animals could have the same compensation abilities such as Coyotes possess.

"Also," they write, "the natural losses in the populations of these non-target species should be similar to those of coyotes so that population turnover is high and the effects of removing a few additional animals inadvertently would be insignificant and difficult to even detect. If this is true, predator control programs are not likely to eradicate or even seriously affect the non-target species. . . . None of this is to excuse the indiscriminate destruction of wildlife, but only to point out that the incidental catch of non-target animals in predator control programs is not, of itself, grounds for terminating predator control in areas of proven need."

However, it seems to the author that there is a very serious fallacy in the arguments of Connolly and Longhurst. That is this: Some of the non-target animals which will be killed in predator control programs may be endangered species themselves. The numbers killed in the indiscriminate trapping and poisoning projects may push the species beyond the point of no return. And this must be an overriding concern to those who want to see all wildlife species preserved and prospering.

10 The Lore of the Red Fox

In BEGINNING THIS SECTION, short introduction seems worthwhile. In this scientific age (which has sometimes been called "sterile") we tend to regard the people of the past as primitives, as children who did not fully evolve mentally. And yet by 400 B. C., the Greeks had developed a civilization unequalled in many respects in human history. At a later date Alexandria, where the Christian sermons using animals were written, was the seat of culture for all the world.

We need to remind ourselves that we, too, have our animal myths and legends. The "long ago when animals could talk" is with us still. When we were children, my mother used to read to us the stories by Joel Chandler Harris about Uncle Remus and B'rer Rabbit. And she read to us, and we ourselves read them over and over again, Albert Bigelow Paine's *Hollow Tree Snowed In* and *Hollow Tree Nights And Days*.

We have not escaped the fascination of those stories even in our adulthood and with our scientific training. The animals still talk to us. Few comic strips have enjoyed the world-wide popularity of Pogo and his friends. When a newspaper dropped Fred Basset, the public howled so loudly that the comic strip had to be restored—as it was with a front page announcement. Charlie Brown has animal friends who talk and philosophize.

The sermons of Physiologus seem to us to be shockingly naive, ignorant of natural history, and totally lacking in merit. Yet they were written at Alexandria. They were translated into many languages, preached by priests and popes alike, from Alexandria to

Reynard the Fox, as drawn by Edward Topsell for his *Historie of Beasts*, 1607.

THE CRVCIGERAN FOXE.

A second Red Fox picture taken from Topsell's *Historie of Beasts*.

Iceland, for a thousand years. They were impressive to minds which did not ask for science or logic, but only confirmation of doctrine. Thus, if the lion kitten was born dead and came to life after three days, it was only to illustrate the resurrection of Christ.

Millions of people the world over call the fox, Reynard. They may never have heard of the famous beast epic, *Reynard The Fox* but the title remains with us still. Reynard, Ysegrim the wolf, and all the other animals of the epic, were the Pogo and his friends from about 700 A.D. to the Renaissance. Anyone fortunate enough to find an English language edition will find the stories fascinating, and often very funny. (See the Bibliography under *The Epic of The Beast* for both *Physiologus* and *Reynard The Fox.*

The writer hopes that the legends and myths given here will be treated with the respect and understanding they deserve. Psychologically, we are closer to the people who worked out this folklore than we imagine. It is a part of our past, as it was of their present.

In preparing this section, we asked a dozen people to explain where, or how, we got the expression "sour grapes." Not one could tell us. It comes from a fable by Aesop, the slave of Cadmon of Samos, who lived between 620 and 560 B. C.

"A hungry fox spied some plump, juicy grapes high on a vine. He tried and tried to get the grapes but they were always just out of reach. At last he gave up. To hide his disappointment, he said: "I didn't want them anyway. They were obviously sour."

Aesop wrote many fables dealing with a fox. We like this one:

"A crow sat on a branch holding a nice chunk of cheese in her beak. A fox wanted the cheese and had a plan to get it. 'What a beautiful bird,' he said, loud enough for the crow to hear. 'Surely such a lovely bird has a lovely voice. How I long to hear it.' The foolish bird opened her mouth to sing. But all that came out was a caw and the cheese. The fox ate the cheese and said, 'I see you do have a voice, madam crow. What you seem to be lacking is brains.' 'Don't be fooled by flattery,' added Aesop."

Aesop did not always portray the fox as being so cunning.

"A dog and a cock, being great friends, agreed to travel together. At nightfall, they took shelter in a forest. The cock perched in a tree while the dog made a bed in the hollow between the tree's great roots. At dawn, the cock crowed several times. A fox heard the sound and wished to make a breakfast of the bird. He stood under the tree and said he desired to make the acquaintance of the owner of such a magnificent voice. But the suspicious cock said, 'Do me the favor of going around the tree to the hollow trunk below me. Wake my porter so that he may open the door and let you in.' When the fox went around the tree the dog sprang upon it and tore it to pieces."

The Physiologus was written about 150 A. D. at Alexandria. It was written in Greek which was still spoken at Alexandria at that time. One sermon deals with the fox, and we quote it in its entirety, as translated by James Carlill:

" 'The foxes have holes and the birds of the air have nests,' thus says the Scripture concerning the Lord: and in *The Song of Solomon,* Salome says: 'Bring us the little foxes, for they destroy the grapes' and David says in a psalm: 'They will become the portion of the foxes.' "

"Physiologus relates of the fox that he is a very crafty animal. When he is hungry, and can find no prey, he entices it thus: he seats himself in a warm place where there is chaff, or else casts himself on his back and holds his breath and swells up his body completely so that he appears dead. The birds believe that he is really dead, and they fly down to eat him up; but he springs up and catches them and eats them up.

"So also is the devil very crafty in his ways. He who would partake of his flesh dies. To this flesh belong adultery, covetousness, lust, murder. Thence also Herod is likened to this animal: 'Go,' says the Lord, 'and speak to that fox.' Well spake Physiologus of the Fox."

Few of us today study the "classics." So we know very little of the heritage from the past. We use words whose origins are lost to us. So not many of us know that Reynard the fox, Bruin the bear, and Chanticleer the rooster come to us from the Dark Ages. They are names which come from an epic whose origins began a thousand years ago, versions of which survive in French, German and the English translation by William Caxton, the first English printer, some time between 1401 and 1489. His translation was from the Dutch.

Reynard is cunning and wily, and his misdeeds cause him to be brought repeatedly before the court of the animals presided over by the lion. The lion summons all the animals to his court of justice. All come but Reynard. Bruin the bear is sent to bring him so that he can be hung for his misdeed.

But Reynard lures the bear to a huge log which has been partially split and contains honey. The bear gets its head and both feet in the log, and Reynard knocks out the wedges. Bruin loses the skin of his head and his ears. Dieprecht the cat is sent. But Reynard lures him into a trap.

Krimel the badger brings Reynard in disguised as a learned physician who can cure the king (an ant is in his ear). But the king must be wrapped in the skins of a bear and a wolf, and the hat of a cat, with a strip of stag's skin from the nose to the tail. He must also eat a boiled fowl and the haunch of a boar. This is done and Reynard gets revenge on his enemies. He then gives the king a hot bath, wrapped in the animal skins. This gets the ant so hot it leaves the lion's ear and the king is cured.

To give you some hint of the text we would like to quote two passages in which Isegrim (or Ysengrin) the wolf is Reynard's stupid enemy:

"Isegrim the Wolf, with his lineage and friends, came and stood before the King, and said: 'High and Mighty Prince, my Lord the King, I beseech you that, through your great might, justice, and mercy, ye will have pity on the great trespass and the unreasonable misdeeds that Reynard the Fox hath done to me and to my wife: that is, to wit, he is come into my house against the will of my wife, and there he hath bepissed my children where they lay, in such wise as they thereof are waxen blind. And, dear King, this know well many of the beasts that now be come to your Court. And further hath he trespassed to me in many other things. He is not living that could tell all that I now leave untold. But the shame and villainy that he hath done my wife, that I shall never hide ne suffer it unavenged, unless he shall make to me large amends.' "

The second story has been told in many forms about Bruin the bear and how he lost his tail. And there are similar North American Indian stories. Here, it again deals with the wolf, who again complains to the lion:

"My Lord, I pray you to take heed. This false thief betrayed my wife once foul and dishonestly. It was so that in a winter's day they went together through a great water, and he led my wife to expect that he would teach her (to) take fish with her tail, and that she should let it hang in the water a good while and there should be so much fish cleave on it that four of them should not be able to eat it. The fool, my wife, supposed he had said truth. And she went in the mire to the belly ere she came into the water, and when she was in the deepest of the water he bade her hold her tail till that the fish were come. She held her tail so long that it was frozen hard in the ice and (she) could not pluck it out. And when he saw that, he sprang up after on her body. Alas! there ravished he and forced my wife so knavishly that I am ashamed to tell it. She could not defend herself, the silly beast, she stood so deep in the mire. Hereof, he cannot say nay, for I found him in the deed, for, as I went above the bank, I saw him beneath my wife shouting and thrusting as men do when they do such work and play. Alas! what pain suffered I then at my heart. I had almost for sorrow lost my five wits, and cried as loud as I might: "Reynard, what do ye there?' and, when he saw me so nigh, then leapt he off and went his way. I went to her in a great heaviness, and went deep in that mire and that water ere I could break the ice, and much pain suffered she ere she could have out her tail, and yet left a bit of her tail behind her. And we were like both thereby to have lost our lives, for she yelped and cried so loud, for the smart that she had ere she came out, that the men of the village came out, with staves and bills, with flail and pitchforks, and the wives with their distaffs, and cried angrily: 'Slay! Slay! and smite down right!' I was never in my life so afraid, for we scarcely escaped. . . . . Se my Lord, this foul matter. This is murder, rape, and treason which ye ought to do justice thereon sharply."

Reynard, however, denied the charge. He claimed that she was so covetous that she kept her tail in the water too long. And when Isegrim came along, he was not raping her but only pushing and shoving to get her out. But when Isegrim began to curse him, he left.

American Indian Legends

In most of the American Indian legends, it is the Coyote who, after the great flood—the deluge—creates the land, the animals, and the people. But in his monumental, 20 volume set, *The North American Indian,* Edward S. Curtis records one creation myth in which the Fox is the creator and the Coyote is only his helper. Here we will quote brief passages from a rather long story.

"There was only water. There was a person, Qan (Silver Fox) who had a canoe in which he travelled about over the water. The canoe was filled with all kinds of seeds. He was alone. After many years another man flew down into the canoe. This was Jemul (Coyote). Qan asked him, 'Who are you?' He only pretended he did not know.

" 'Cousin, do you not know me? I am Jemul.' "

"Qan smiled and said: 'I know now. How did you come?' "

" 'I flew down as a spark,' " answered Jemul.

" 'Yes,' said Qan. 'I did the same way. But there is no land here.' "

But Jemul knows that Qan can do anything he pleases. So he begs Qan to do something, to create land. Qan has Jemul lie down, covers him with blankets, and during the next five days he creates the land, using a bit of dead cuticle from his scalp. He then scattered his seeds. When Jemul awakes, there are grasses, bushes, and trees and ripe fruit. Later he creates the deer, and finally people.

Curtis got this story from an Achomawi Indian, Henry Wool, whose Indian name was Lehutami. Another fox story told by the Indians portrays the fox as being somewhat stupid:

"One day Fox went to visit Owl because he was very hungry, with nothing to eat at home. Owl's food was nearly exhausted, but he had his wife pound some meat into a ball. The meat had no grease to hold it together, so Owl called for a sharp stick, with which he poked out his eyes. These he mixed with the meat to make it greasy. After the two had eaten, Owl rubbed his wings on his breast and rubbed his eyebrows. His eyes came back to him, so that he could see as before. Fox thought that was a very good trick to know.

"Some time later, Owl came to visit Fox, and it happened that Fox had plenty of meat, but no fat. He thought of what Owl had done, so called to his wife to bring a sharp stick, with which he poked out his eyes. They ate heartily, and, at the end of the meal, Fox rubbed his breast and eyebrows just as he had seen Owl do, but his eyes did not come back. He was blind."

In another story, the fox is also portrayed as being too smart for his own good. He travels with an opossum who digs up wild onions using his tail. Fox wants to know how he does this. Opossum tells him that he must put his tail into the ground, but only to an exact distance. Fox does this and gets wild onions. Then he thinks it is no

longer necessary to travel with Opossum. They separate, but Fox
suspects that Opossum was fooling him, and only wanted to get
more onions than he got. So he puts his tail farther into the ground
than the specified distance "just this once." But his tail is caught. He
goes round and round, but cannot get out. He finally starves to
death.

In another story, Fox pretends to be dying of hunger when a
man comes along carrying a heavy load of meat. He gives meat to
Fox who says he is too weak even to hunt. After the man goes on,
Fox circles him, pretends to be dying, and gets more meat. But the
fourth time he does this, the man sees particles of food on the jaws
of Fox. He runs away. Fox pursues, intending to eat the man as well
as his meat. But the man escapes.

The fox has been a prominent figure in Japanese fairy tales and
folklore. Much of what follows comes from two famous books which
have been re-published by the Charles E. Tuttle Co. of Rutland, Vt.
and Tokyo. The Inari Temple in Kyoto, which I have visited, was
dedicated to the fox-goddess, Inari no-jinja. Another temple dedicated to the patron saint of foxes was the Inari Sama. The Kyoto
temple was dedicated to a fox who is said to have blown the bellows
for a famous swordsmith, Kokaji, when he made his finest blades.

Kitsune Ken is a fox-forfeit game in which various positions of
the fingers represent the hunter, the fox and the gun. I once saw
this game played for my benefit during an evening at a famous
Japanese seaside resort home.

A Japanese fox fairy tale so typical of those of our own past is
The Foxes Wedding as re-told by A. B. Mitford in Tales of Old
Japan (1871) and reprinted by Tuttle in 1966 and later. In it, a white
fox falls in love with a beautiful vixen. Wedding arrangements are
made in typical human fashion, albeit Japanese. The vixen is carried
to the white fox's home during a shower with sunshine. (Such a
shower with sunshine is still called "the fox's bride going to her
husband)."

The happy couple marries. The pups are taken to the Inari
Sama Temple where prayers were offered that they be delivered
from dogs and other evils. "They're the very image of their old
grandfather," says the white fox's father proudly. All live happily
ever after.

According to legend, foxes were able to shave the heads of

travelers who went into the forest. In one such story, a man makes a bet that the foxes can't fool him. Along the way, he meets a beautiful girl who is going to her parents' home. However, the man believes her to be a fox in disguise. He convinces her parents that this is so. In trying to force her to show her fox's brush, he kills her.

The angry parents decide to kill the man. At that point a priest comes along. The priest convinces all that the man should be allowed to live provided he becomes a priest. This is agreed, whereupon the priest shaves the man's head. He thus loses his bet.

About 1900, Basil Hall Chamberlain who, according to Count Aisuke Kabayama, "taught Japanese and Japan to Japanese" began to collect materials for his book *Things Japanese.* The Tuttle Co. published it in 1971 as *Japanese Things,* and it has gone through nine editions. One of his chapters concerns demoniacal possessions.

In our Christian Bible, demons take possession of men and speak through them. Jesus once drove the demons out of the men and into pigs which then fled over a cliff and were drowned. In Japan, or at least in the Japan of 1900 and before, there were many cases in which foxes seemed to enter people, chiefly women, and then took possession of them. The foxes were said to enter between the flesh and the fingernail, or through the breast.

Hall quotes a Dr. Baelz of the Imperial University of Japan. We quote, in part, and then give an actual case which he relates.

"Possession by foxes (Kitsune-tsuki) is a form of nervous disorder or delusion, not uncommonly observed in Japan. Having entered a human being . . . the fox lives a life of its own, apart from the proper self of the person who is harbouring him. There results a sort of double identity or double consciousness. The person possessed hears and understands everything that the fox inside says or thinks; and the two often engage in a loud and violent dispute, the fox speaking in a voice altogether different from that which is natural to the individual. The only difference between the cases of possession mentioned in the Bible and those observed in Japan is that here it is almost exclusively women who are attacked—mostly women of the lower classes. Among the predisposing conditions may be mentioned a weak intellect, a superstitious turn of mind, and such debilitating diseases as, for instance, typhoid fever. Possession never occurs except in such subjects as have heard of it already, and believe in the reality of its existence.

"To mention but one among several cases, I was once called in to a girl with typhoid fever. She recovered; but during her convalescence, she heard women around her talk of another woman who had a fox, and who would doubtless do her best to pass it on to someone else, in order to be rid of it.

"At that moment, the girl experienced an extraordinary sensation. The fox had taken possession of her. All her efforts to get rid of him were vain. 'He is coming! he is coming!' she would cry, as a fit of the fox drew near . . . And then, in a strange, dry, cracked voice, the fox would speak, and mock his unfortunate hostess. Thus matters continued for three weeks till a priest of the Nichiren sect was sent for. The priest upbraided the fox sternly. The fox (always, of course, speaking through the girl's mouth) argued on the other side.

"At last he said: 'I am tired of her. I ask no better than to leave her. What will you give me for doing so?' The priest asked what he would take. The fox replied, naming certain cakes and other things, which, said he, must be placed before the altar of such and such a temple at 4 p.m., on such a day. The girl was conscious of the words her lips were made to frame, but was powerless to say anything in her own person. When the day and hour arrived, the offerings bargained for were taken by her relations to the place indicated, and the fox quitted the girl at that very hour."

Since in folklore, many animals are considered to be the little brothers of mankind, they sometimes turn into people. In such legends it is often a fox which turns into a beautiful woman. In his *Folk Legends of Japan,* Richard M. Dorson tells such a story. A beautiful woman asks a farmer to marry her. He does, and they have a child. The child becomes ill, and the parents tend the child so constantly that the rice fields remain unplanted.

One morning the farmer discovers that his fields are completely planted, but that the plants are upside down. He rushes to tell his still sleeping wife, and discovers a fox tail protruding from the covers. He realizes that his wife is a fox. She takes the child, goes to the fields, and repeats an incantation three times.

> "Be fruitful
> My child shall eat plenty
> The inspector shall pass over
> Bear fruit in the husk."

She gives the child to her husband. The rice plants immediately turn over. Then she waves at the sky, and day is turned into night. In the darkness, she disappears, rolled up in the leaves of arrowroot. That is why arrowroot leaves always show their under sides. The inspector came, but the rice plants had not come into ears, so he exempted the farmer from rice taxes. But no sooner had he left than the ears ripened into a plentiful harvest.

A Red Fox carries a rabbit which it has captured in the snow. *Photo by Wilford L. Miller*

11 The Biology of the Red Fox

*In the noble, and nearly forgotten
art of venerie: A skulk of foxes.*

THE RED FOX has the taxonomic name of Vulpes, and its various subspecies have additional titles to distinguish them. The great Red Fox of Europe, parts of Asia and a part of Africa is known as Vulpes vulpes. Other species inhabit Asia, parts of the Indian sub-continent and North America. In this section we are concerned chiefly with the European and North American species, the latter of which is usually called V. vulpes fulva. We will therefore content ourselves with giving short notes on the other major varieties.

The Tibetan Sand Fox is found in Tibet and Nepal. Since it lives at high altitudes where the weather is often severe, it has adapted by developing a particularly thick, long coat. (George Schaller, the legendary ethologist whose studies of African animals have made him world famous, photographed the tracks of a fox on a Pakistan glacier at 16,000 feet above sea level.) The Afghan Fox has also developed a long coat. The Bengal Fox, adapting to a warmer climate, is less valuable as a fur animal.

In eastern Europe, Russian Asia down to India and throughout Siberia there is the Hoary Fox, so named because of its frosty gray color over most of the body, except for the belly which is white. There is a desert form in Africa, between the jungles and the Sahara, called the Pale Fox. It is a light or golden buff color.

These are all true foxes, and they conform to a general description such as this: Small, medium sized, dog-like, with large erect ears, a narrow long jaw with somewhat slender teeth, elliptical eye pupils, which are yellow, an extraordinarily long, thick tail or brush, a thick undercoat protected by long, luxurious guard hairs. They vary greatly in size with the largest living in the northern latitudes, and the smallest living in the deserts but having the largest ears.

The European Red Fox and the North American Red Fox are the subjects of this section. The European variety has been raiding poultry yards for thousands of years. It has been hunted by horsemen with hounds, footmen with hounds, trapped for its fur, its dens destroyed by predator control officers, and it is the subject of countless legends and stories.

The origin of the North American Red Fox has been a subject of argument for three centuries. It is generally considered to be smaller, faster and wiser than its relative. At least along the Atlantic coast many consider it to be a cross between the European and native American foxes. In the section on the Gray Fox, we point out that George Washington hunted Grays because the Reds were unknown to the sportsmen of the day.

Yet in his *Travels in North America* (1770) Peter Kalm, a Swedish botanist, reported the Red Fox in New Jersey and Pennsylvania, although rare. He also wrote that the Philadelphia botanist, John Bartram, had told him that the Leni-Lenape Indians had sworn that the Red Fox was unknown to them until the Europeans came.

Many of the early writers gave the range of the Red Fox as extending to the "austral zone," that is, to the south, or roughly to the edge of North Carolina. But William Bartram, a far greater naturalist than his father, John, contradicted this in his famous *Travels of William Bartram,* published in Philadelphia in 1791. Bartram had wandered through Georgia, Florida, and the Carolinas from 1773 to 1778, studying and taking notes. We quote directly from him:

"The Foxes of Carolina and Florida are of the smaller red species; they bark in the night round about plantations, but do not bark twice in the same place; they move precipitately, and in a few minutes are heard on the opposite side of the plantation, or at a great distance; it is said that dogs are terrified at the noise, and cannot be persuaded to pursue them. They commit depredations on young pigs, lambs, poultry, etc."

In further dispute to John Bartram's Indians, in 1643 Roger Williams wrote *A Key to the Language of the Indians,* as he was returning to England. Williams had been kicked out of Massachusetts, both because of religious differences and because of championing the rights of the Indians. Williams then founded Rhode Island.

He wrote that the Indian name for the Gray Fox was "Pequawas" and for the Red Fox, "Mishquashim."

We explain later how it is possible to tell from their skulls the difference between the Gray and Red Fox. The bones of both breeds have been found in archaeological sites in New York, Rhode Island and Massachusetts. But while Gray Fox bones are plentiful in midwestern sites, those of the Red Fox are absent.

Those who rode to hounds had a passionate love of their sport. They had some great scholars who had the time and money to do the research. *The American Turf Register* for Sept. 1829 recorded the story of the importation of English Red Foxes. The editor, a famous sporting authority named Skinner, verified the story before he printed it.

In 1730, eight tobacco planters in Talbot County, Maryland decided to import some English foxes. They were dissatisfied with the sport as furnished by the Gray Foxes, and they longed for the type of sport they had enjoyed in England. In August of 1730, they commissioned the captain of the schooner Monaccasy to bring back some English Red Foxes. On his return from Liverpool, the captain delivered eight braces of Red Foxes. They were released. They thrived and reproduced. And they began to spread out into new territories. During the very cold winter of 1789–80, Chesapeake Bay froze over, and some of the foxes are said to have crossed into Pennsylvania and Virginia.

During that same winter, a Red Fox was killed in Perry County, Pennsylvania. It created a sensation. It was kept on display for about three days, and people drove from miles around to see it. Apparently no one had ever seen one before. However, a Jersey man had. He reported that it was an English fox. He added that an early governor of New York had imported some to Long Island. There they remained until one winter when the Sound froze over, after which some moved into New Jersey and Pennsylvania.

Joseph B. Thomas wrote one of the finest books on fox hunting

ever produced. It is called *Hounds and Hunting Through the Ages.*
Thomas records "that before 1812" a Dr. David S. Kerr chased a red
fox for a distance of 25 miles. The fox apparently brought the dogs
back to the place from which it was started. Thomas also found that
a Red Fox was killed in 1814 at Goochland on the James River, and
that it created a sensation among sportsmen. By 1829 the Red Fox
could be found in many parts of Virginia.

All authorities agree that foxes, except the Corsac and the
Arctic which are treated in separate sections, are home loving. They
tend to set up a small range and then to remain there. That is why
the men who do not hunt from horseback, and who do not kill the
foxes, get to learn the running habits of individual foxes. If we
assume that English Red Foxes were loosed in Maryland and Long
Island about 1730, then their migration into Virginia, Pennsylvania
and New Jersey took from 70 to 80 years.

It is therefore inconceivable that they could have spread from
the Atlantic to the Pacific, and northward to the Arctic Circle in
some 20 years. We have used 20 years, because in 1821, the
Hudson's Bay Company began to release figures on its annual fur
catches. The figures for 1821 would mean the catch for 1820.

Seton, who studied the records, reported that the lowest catch
year was 1826, with 2757. He totaled the reported catch for all
companies from 1821 to 1905, and found the average annual catch
to be 74,000.

It occurred to the author that one avenue which has not been
explored in the mystery of the Red Fox in America is that of Indian
legends and folklore. The Indians were very close to their "animal
brothers," and their folklore is rich in stories about them. Thus, if
the Red Fox existed in America before the Europeans came, then
there should be legends about them.

Indeed there are many stories which deal with foxes. In one, the
Kit-Fox is mentioned. In another section we have given the folklore
of the Arctic Fox. But other legends, except for two, simply speak of
"fox" without describing it as a Kit-Fox, Gray Fox or Red Fox.

One story tells how the fox got its coat "singed red." The other
deals specifically with a Silver Fox. And the Silver Fox is simply a
color phase or mutation in the Red Fox. These stories originate
among the Indians of the far west. The Silver Fox story was told to
Edward S. Curtis by the Achomawi of the Goose Lake Valley, near

the present town of Alturas in Northern California. The age of this story, pre-dating the coming of the Europeans, is indicated by the fact that it is a creation myth. These stories are told in the section on the Folklore of the Red Fox.

At the risk of adding more confusion to the mystery, we might advance the following theory. V. fulva fulva is at least a thousand year native American. Its habitat extended from northern California to southern Alaska, and across Canada to Labrador. It was comparatively rare in Minnesota and Manitoba, but probably plentiful in the Yukon and Northwest Territories. It was not found in the heavily forested North Atlantic States, but moved southward as the land was cleared and farms were set up.

It seems conceivable that, if Red Foxes could be brought from England to Maryland and New York, a smaller species of Red Fox might have been taken to Florida by Spanish settlers. That would account for Bartram's report. Meanwhile, the larger English Red Foxes would meet and mate with native Red Foxes moving to the south. This in turn would cause biologists to suggest that the foxes of the Atlantic Seaboard are only mongrel English Red Foxes, and so not entitled to the name V. fulva fulva.

It is also conceivable that the true habitat of the North American Red Fox was the Aleutian Islands, the coast of Siberia and Alaska. Since this fox is smaller than the English Red Fox, it would then be fully entitled to the subspecies name fulva. It is known that Russian trappers as early as 1769 were catching huge numbers of Red Foxes, including Silvers, and cross color phases in the Aleutians. Under this theory, fulva spread slowly across Canada, south to Northern California and, from Canada, south toward the North Atlantic and Middle Atlantic states.

The Red Fox is not truly red, rather it is the coppery golden color of some of the Golden Retrievers we see at dog shows. Rue has described the color as a deep burnt rust to golden. And in the Indian legend quoted in the Lore of the Red Fox, we learn how apt that description is. The color darkens along the spine and behind the head and lightens to near white on the chest and belly. The tail is dark and usually contain either black or black tipped hairs. The tail is always white tipped, whereas in the Gray Fox the tail is black tipped.

The throat, cheeks and inner sides of the ears are white, but the outer side of the ears are black. The legs are also black with the black sometimes extending nearly to the elbows. The nose and whiskers are black. The eyes are a bright yellow, and the pupils are elliptical. The elliptical pupil is possessed by all true foxes, and by no other member of the canid family.

Gray Foxes have often been called Black Foxes. But the true blacks are really melanistic mutant Reds, and range to the true Silvers. The Silver will at times appear black, but its silver hairs give it a beautiful frosted appearance. The Cross Fox is another mutant. The cross is formed by a darker than normal color along the spine, with a similar darkness across the shoulders. The so-called Samson Fox is one which has no outer guard coat, but only the thick undercoat. Its fur is useless in the fur market.

The European Red Fox is somewhat larger than is the North American variety. The average weight of the latter is about nine and a half pounds. There is great variance according to locality, and this variance has given rise to subspecies status for many of them. A Nova Scotia variety, rubricosa Bangs, is larger than the typical fulva, and has both deeper and darker color. It is the "reddest" of all. The Siberian and Scandinavian V. vulpes has coarser hair than most and is near yellow in color. So is Alascensis Merriam, an Alaskan subspecies which is also remarkable for its unusually long tail. A Minnesota form, regalis Merriam, is said to be the largest and palest of all the varieties found in North America. Weight variances in all of these varieties are so remarkable that foxes in the wild have weighed as much as 14 pounds. One raised on a fur farm weighed 16¾ pounds.

Total length of Red Foxes is 38 to 42 inches. The tail will be 14 to 16 inches, which normally equals the height at the shoulder. A variety found on Kodiak Island has an even longer and heavier tail than the 14–16 inches given above. This fox, harrimani Merriam, also has a sort of neck mane.

The Red Fox is actually a four toed animal, but like the domestic dog (and deer) it has a useless dew claw on each front leg. Dew claws are absent on the hind legs. The dew claw is a relic of the time when canids had five useful toes on each foot. Front feet measure 1¾ to 2 inches long and two inches wide; hind feet 1½ to 1¾ inches, long and wide respectively.

Like all dogs, foxes, wolves and coyotes, normal Red Foxes have

42 teeth. There are 12 incisors, four canines, 16 premolars, and 10 molars. The teeth are designed for seizing. If the Red Fox must chop up its meat, it then must turn its head to the side, and cut or shear it with its premolars. Its teeth are those of a carnivore and are poorly designed for grinding. And like dogs, wolves, and coyotes, the fox bolts its food. Its gullet is expansible for this purpose. The stomach also is expansible in order to accommodate large quantities of meat. An estimate of the stomach's capacity is 16 ounces of food. Since protein is digested in the stomach, this arrangement is perfect for the fox. It follows that the fox's digestive system is not well designed for cereals or for fibrous foods, which are digested in the relatively short intestine.

However, the fox often has been forced to take both fibrous foods and cereals. He prefers that these be predigested in the digestive tracts of its prey animals. But if forced to do so, it will raid gardens. The coyote has a passion for watermelons; the Red Foxes for strawberries, either wild or garden grown. They also enjoy grapes when they are able to reach them.

Foxes are great lovers of poultry, and they capture quail, pheasants, grouse and prairie chickens when they live within the habitats of these fowl. On the whole, they are a boon to gardeners, because they keep down pests such as mice. They have an equal fondness for rabbits.

We have already mentioned that the tail tip of the Red Fox is white while that of the Gray Fox is black. There are also skull differences. The temporal ridges of the Red Fox form a V while those of the Gray Fox form a U. The Red Fox has lobed upper incisors while the Gray does not.

The eyes of carnivores are always placed to the front. This affords them binocular vision. Rabbits, for example, have eyes to the side. They are not predator animals but prey species. So they must have some ability to look behind them. They do not need binocular vision. But the carnivores do to permit them better vision in seizing or pouncing upon prey. Wolves, coyotes, and foxes pounce upon such prey as mice. They lack the sharp retractable claws of the felines, and the greater angular or binocular vision of the cats. It is probable that they can see less well at night. Yet they do have the tapetum lucidum, or reflection blanket in the eye which permits them to pick up light rays which the human being cannot do.

The eyes of almost all creatures are designed for catching movement. Only the human being has been able to develop an eye which can clearly see objects which do not move. And every person who has thought about it knows that the still object is often difficult for man to identify. The distant inner tube lying on the highway, appears to be a dead animal until we approach closer; the tree stump appears to be a standing person until we near it.

It is not surprising, then, that the Red Fox can detect movement at a great distance, but does not realize that the still object is a man until other senses alert it. For the Red Fox, these senses are smell and hearing. The erect ears of the fox help it to hear at far greater distances than can a man, or for that matter, most dogs. The range of sounds is also greater so that the fox can hear higher pitches than can a man and, possibly, the dog.

The carnivores hunt "up wind." That is, they test the wind blowing into their faces. The fox is no exception. He may smell a rabbit at a hundred feet if it is up wind, but fail to detect it when it is down wind, and only ten feet away. When a fox curls up to sleep, it also points its nose up wind. And its sleep patterns are such that the scent of approaching danger, or of a feast, alerts or wakens it.

As we have pointed out earlier, the Red Fox is a home loving animal. It selects its range, and then tends to remain there so long as dens and food are available. In the lower midwest, where men gather together on hilltops to listen to hound music as the hounds chase a Red Fox, foxes are not killed. The foxes seem to know the hounds. And the listening men know the fox. The men have learned to know the evasive habits of each fox in the area. The Red Fox then takes its evasive action, runs its course and holes up when it is tired of the sport. It seems to delight in teasing the dogs into a chase.

English Foxhounds hunt with people on horseback. For this reason, they have been selected for an instinct to queue up, so that the horsemen are not left behind. But the American Foxhounds are individualists. They give tongue only when challenging for the lead, or when actually ahead. Thus, the sport for the listening men comes in knowing the voices of their own hounds, and in learning which hound is in the lead or challenging for it. In most cases, they are likely to know the course the fox will take, and so they recognize each fox. In riding to hounds, the fox is killed. But in the latter sport, it never is. It lives to run another day.

One can guess what happens with the fox. It is quietly hunting
for its supper. Far away, a hound strikes its "cold trail." A fox sweats
through its pads as well as by panting. The sweat leaves its scent for
the dogs. The fox, hearing the hound, has a somewhat similar
reaction to that of people who suddenly have fear. Its body prepares
for flight by clearing the blood of certain acids or impurities, and by
pumping sugars or adrenalin into the blood stream for quick
energy. The acids are excreted with the sweat. When the hounds
reach the spot where the fox first heard a hound's voice, the new
odor tells them they are now on a "hot trail." Their voices change,
betraying this to the fox and to the listening men. The real chase
then begins.

The Red Fox is monogamous. The male and the vixen will
remain together during their lives. The vixen comes into heat only
once a year. This is usually in late winter; in southern areas earlier,
in northern latitudes later. After mating, the pair will seek a den.
Often, the den selected is one abandoned by a woodchuck. Wood-
chucks dig down three or four feet, then level off for 15 or more,
and then dig an outlet which forms an escape route. The Red Fox is
seldom satisfied with this, and so may select a den with multiple
entrances and exits, or may add more. As many as 15 to 20 have
been noted. This means that, combined with the earth and rubble
which the foxes have removed, the den can be spotted from great
distances. Predator control officers have little trouble locating them.

The gestation period is 51 to 57 days, although seldom so long
as 57, and more often closer to 51. Pups average four to eight per
litter, though much larger litters of 10 or 11 have been reported and
verified, and even one of 17 was reported. A first litter may be small,
and succeeding ones much larger. Then as the vixen grows older,
litters may become smaller. A number of complex factors, aside
from age, are also involved.

The pups are born blind but their eyes open at nine to ten days.
The eyes are blue at birth, as with the dog. The vixen refuses to
allow the male to enter the den from just before whelping until the
pups have their eyes open and are about two weeks old. The male
does the hunting and leaves food for his lady.

At two weeks, the vixen leaves the den and begins to help in the
hunting. The male is now welcomed back to the den. Both parents
may, as a part of the weaning process, regurgitate food for the pups.

A red fox puppy. *Cleveland Press photo library*

Red Fox, Vulpes vulpes, San Diego Zoo. *San Diego Zoo photo*

Perhaps to draw attention away from the den, the parents visit it only to bring food to the pups, or the vixen returns to nurse them.

At about five weeks of age, the pups are strong enough on their legs to begin cautious looks at the outside world. At six, they are beginning to make short forays outside the den. They retreat precipitately at the slightest sound of danger, and literally tumble into the den. Since they are wild animals, the pups are far more alert than dog pups are at the same age. They·also seem to have an inexhaustible amount of energy, and play constantly when out of the den.

The mortality rate among young foxes is fairly high during the growth period, for they are prey animals for fishers, lynx, bobcats and wolverines. Even wolves may seize a fox puppy for its supper, or for its own pups. Adult foxes also have a strong fear of wolves, even though wolves do not regularly feast upon them. Eagles also prey on pups and occasionally on adults.

As the pups become steadier on their legs, they take short hunting trips with their parents. In this way, they learn the dangers they face and how to find meals of their own. What they get will depend partly upon where they live.

In marsh areas they may be able to catch baby muskrats. In most areas they are able to find mice, ground squirrels, and moles. In Alaska, the young foxes join their parents in feeding on lemmings, the Alaskan ground squirrel, the varying hare and other small animals. As autumn comes the foxes fatten up on nuts and berries. Red Foxes may also cache food as the Arctic Foxes do. They may also raid the nests of yellow jackets, and they feed on all sorts of insects. Grasshoppers seem to make a tasty dish for them.

The young foxes may have to move out to unfamiliar territory as winter approaches. This is often the time of greatest danger for them. They are in unfamiliar territory. There may be a food shortage. And they face many enemies alone. Among their enemies are trappers, hunters and farmers' dogs. They also have the problem of parasites. Internal ones include various types of worms. External ones are fleas, ticks, lice and other insects. Occasionally they are killed by infectious encephalomyelitis and rabies. The life span is about ten years.

Carl Sagan, the astronomer-philosopher has a bit of curious speculation in his book *The Dragons of Eden.* He suggests that we think of things as being "right" not so much because we are right handed, as because primitive tribes, having no toilet paper, used their left hands. Joe Taylor, a predator control officer has an equally curious bit of speculation which Leonard Rue reports in *The World of the Red Fox*. Taylor found that 90 per cent of the foxes he trapped were caught by their right foot, forcing him to conclude that they were right footed, and the ten per cent left footed.

The 1975 report by the Canadian Department of Industry, Trade and Commerce, is the latest available on the status of the Red Fox or as it terms it, the "Coloured Fox." It includes the Red, Cross and Silver phases. Its own latest figures are for the trapping season of 1971–72. It reports 55,403 pelts for all phases, and suggests that a "potential harvest" of 70,000 is possible without danger to the species as a whole.

It gives the general status as "excellent to abundant," and states that the population is abundant to sustained over most of its range.

During the 1971–72 season, Red and Cross Fox pelts sold for an average price of $16.19 and Silvers for $16.45. After the following season, Red and Cross pelts averaged $29.27 on the fur market, and Silvers $23.63.

Pure blooded Silver Foxes were first produced on a New Brunswick fox fur ranch in 1910 by Charles Dalton and R. T. Oulton. That year, they sent 25 pelts to the London Fur Market. They created a sensation. In the 1972–73 season, purebred Silver pelts averaged $66 each.

It has been suggested that printing pelt prices is an invitation to trappers' greed, and not to conservation. Yet they show that the prices of pelts have not been high enough to stimulate trappers to kill to the limit of the "safe level" given by Canadian wildlife authorities. Second, fur farms have shown that in specialty fields they can compete successfully against the trappers. But more important, if humanitarians can only convince the world's women not to buy natural furs, trapping will cease.

12 Biology of the Gray Fox

"The fox of Carolina is gray but smells not as the foxes in Great Britain and elsewhere. They have reddish hair about their ears and are generally very fat; yet I never saw anyone eat them. When hunted they make a sorry chace because they run up trees when pursued."—A NEW VOYAGE TO CAROLINA, by John Lawson, 1709.

GEORGE WASHINGTON was a lover of fox hunting and Foxhounds. He loved to get up at daylight and ride with his hounds in the exciting chase of trying to catch a fox. Knowing this, General Lafayette sent him some French hounds following his return to France after the American Revolution. Washington told about these hounds at some length in his diary, and among other things, said that they had "voices like the bells of Moscow." Since Washington had never been to Moscow, the comparison is simply a fanciful allusion meant to be very flattering.

The Red Fox is the darling of fox hunters. But there were no Red Foxes in Virginia during Washington's time. The foxes he hunted were the Gray Foxes which are the subject of this article. The Gray Fox belongs to the genus Urocyon cinereoargenteus; the Red Fox to the true fox genus, Vulpes. The Gray Fox and the Corsac fox have an ability to climb trees which is not shared by any other fox. When chased, they may climb a tree, and they have even been known to nest and whelp in trees.

The range of the Gray Fox is from the Canadian border through Central America, and even to the northern areas of South America. It inhabits dense cover areas, swampy grounds and even

Half grown gray fox yelps at photographer Allen M. Pearson.
U.S. Department of the Interior, Fish and Wildlife Service

rocky ledges. Since it climbs trees, it naturally prefers a heavily wooded area. This, added to its dislike of running from the hounds, does not endear it to those who chase the fox while on horseback. In such cases, the Gray Fox tends to move quickly to an underground den, to climb a tree or to scale rocky ledges which give the hounds great difficulty. Their procedure also leaves fewer tracks for the hounds to pick up and follow. Washington was thus denied the greatest thrills of riding to hounds which comes with chasing the Red Fox. In the west, the Gray Fox prefers to live in areas fairly densely covered with chaparral, mesquite and other desert vegetation.

The Gray Fox is about two feet long and weighs 6–8 pounds. Its muzzle is quite long, and it has fairly large, rounded ears which, however, have rather strong erectile powers. An adult has a very bushy tail about 15 inches in length. The Gray Fox has a black tail tip. It has three basic colors: the back is gray; the sides of the head and neck and legs are reddish brown; the underparts are cream to white.

Very early writers spoke of silver and black foxes. But since these are mutant strains of the Red Fox, it seems likely that they were referring to Gray Foxes, some of which would appear silver and others, in certain light, nearly black. One of the earliest accounts was made by Roger Williams. He had been forced to flee for his life from the Plymouth Colony, partly because of his espousal of equal civil rights for Indians.

Williams founded the colony of Rhode Island, and then took ship to England in an effort to gain a royal charter for the area. During the voyage he wrote a curious *Key into the Language of America.* He reported that the Narragansett Indians called the Gray Fox "pequawas."

Gray Foxes do not mate with Red Foxes. Other than obvious physical differences, there are apparently sufficient chromosomal differences to make such matings, if attempted, unproductive. The Gray Fox has very prominent temporal ridges which form a distinct "U." In the Red Fox, these ridges are less distinct and form a "V." The Gray Fox has larger foot, or toe pads, but the foot itself is actually smaller than that of the Red Fox.

There is a saying among squirrel watchers that red squirrels will drive out grays and blacks. The reverse has been said of foxes, in that the Gray will drive out the Red. But while the Gray does appear more aggressive than the Red, it does not rob the Red of its territory. Thus, hunt clubs on Long Island, New York, would start both Red and Gray foxes on their hunts.

The food of the Gray Fox is varied. It prefers woodrats, rabbits, squirrels and white footed mice. It also enjoys insects, berries and various fruits. It appears to be less of a predator of chicken yards than is the Red. Yet there have been instances when it seemed to kill for pleasure. In this, there are indications that it shares the habit with maverick wolves and coyotes. That is, only an occasional maverick fox will do this. Arctic foxes store food for winter. Gray Foxes may bury what they can't eat at once, urine mark it, and then return later to finish the feast.

Urocyon cinereoargenteus has a relative which lives on the Channel Islands off the coast of California. This subspecies is smaller, and has a relatively smaller tail. There are no good speculations as to how it arrived there. Arctic foxes migrated to islands on ice floes. But this was impossible for the Channel Islands Gray unless it arrived on the islands during the Ice Age.

Squirrel watchers, particularly those who live in cities, have noted that red squirrels are subject to mange. The parasites cause the squirrels to lose their hair. Skin sores occur from scratching, the mange spreads, and eventually the affected squirrels are killed by the parasites. Oddly, something similar happens with foxes. The Pennsylvania Department of Health examined the pelts of more than 60,000 Red Foxes and found that nearly 900 had some degree of mange. But of about 56,000 Gray Fox pelts studied, only two cases were found.

Ordinarily, parasites do not kill their hosts. If the hosts die, it is usually because they become so weak that they fall prey to some other illness. A weakened Red Fox might be unable to find sufficient food to survive. But city red squirrels with mange are often well fed by neighborhood people. Yet they die anyway. The writer has not been able to discover a connection of red coat to mange parasites, yet the evidence in these four species—red and gray squirrels, and Red and Gray Foxes—may indicate a close relationship.

Gray Foxes are normally nocturnal, as are so many canids, the dog excluded. When they do forage during the day, it is in heavily brushed country. When they move, their tails are carried in a line with the back. As mentioned earlier, they may make whelping nests in high trees, given sufficient room. But normally they den among rocks, under ledges and sometimes in fallen, large hollow logs. Breeding season is in late winter and the pups are born about two months later, or about 65 to 67 days. The pups are born blind. They grow rapidly, and by late June are old enough to be taught to hunt by their parents.

Man is their principal enemy, followed by dogs. They may also become the victims of the golden eagle. A danger to pups is the golden eagle and large hawks. Coyotes and cougars are enemies within their range.

Gray Fox, Urocyon cineroargentens. *San Diego Zoo photo*

13 The Lore of the Arctic Fox

IF ONE GOES OUT onto the frozen Arctic Ocean during the long months of darkness, an illusion will be created. There is no horizon. The sky meets the ice. Just beyond the reach of your clear vision pale forms seem to dance to eerie lights. You might shiver in fear that Polar bears are stalking you. Perhaps in the darkness just ahead there is a seal's breathing hole into which you might fall and drown. Or, if you are an Eskimo, those seemingly dancing forms might be the souls of your departed ancestors.

Now if you lived intimately with the wild and often terrible nature of the Polar regions; if your life depended upon the killing of the animals for food, clothing, and even for the oil which you used for cooking and for light, then you might feel that the animals are both your brothers and your enemies. You might try to propitiate them, to gain in advance their willingness to be killed and their forgiveness as well. And you would develop rituals and taboos concerning each of the animals upon which your life depended.

If you did not adhere strictly to these rituals and taboos, the spirits would be angry. They might cause your harpoon to miss; cause your wife to have a miscarriage; cause some monster out of the deep to destroy your kayak; keep the whales from coming close to shore. But the coming of Christianity would gradually change many of your concepts. And even by 1900 the old stories and legends would begin to disappear. The old traditions, the rituals and the taboos would gradually be forgotten. Later, modern radio would replace the art of the story teller.

Superb picture by G. R. Parker of the Canadian Wildlife Service shows an Arctic Fox in the great wastes of ice, snow, cold and mists which form its habitat.

Here we have collected some of these legends and taboos as they concern the Arctic Fox. In several of these, there is a striking resemblance to the myths of ancient Greece in which there is marriage between a god, or the sun, or moon, and a human being. In those of Greece, the person, usually a woman, was warned not to look at her mate, or she would lose him.

In 1908 Knud Rasmussen's *People of The North* was translated from Danish into English. Rasmussen had taken down many of the ancient stories. There are two, taken from different areas of the Arctic, which tell of the marriage of a man to a fox. We give them here, exactly as Rasmussen took them down.

"It is the old story about a bachelor again. His countrymen urged him to marry but he would not. One day he set a fox trap. When he looked at it he had caught a fox and he killed it. The next time he went to look at his trap there was something in it again; this time a she-fox.

"He took her home with him and kept her, like a dog, under the window. When he had a meal he gave the fox the bones, and then she lay there and gnawed them. That was how things were between him and the fox; and then one morning he went out seal hunting in his kayak. It was not very long before he used to find that the skins of the seals that he caught were dressed when he got home; yes, and at last they were even spread out to dry on the staging outside.

"By-and-by, he noticed that his lamp was also attended to, while he was away, and never went out. When he came home, he found the pot boiling over the lamp fire, without any person being in the room. As he could not understand the meaning of these things, he hid himself one day behind a rock to watch, and behold! a lovely woman with a great knot of hair and broad hips. It was the fox, who could change into a woman.

"When she went inside, the bachelor sprang in after her, Inside the house, he saw something dark disappear under the window. The pot was turned but there was not a person in sight. The next day he hid himself again, and again there came out of the house a woman with a lovely big knot of hair. When she went back in, he ran after her and caught hold of her before she got under the window. And then he made her his wife. She was so beautiful that she was like the white men's women. While he was living with her as his wife, one day there came a man on a visit.

" 'Shall not we two change wives?' asked the stranger one day, when they were out in their kayaks.

" 'Impossible! She gets so easily jealous.'

"And the stranger had to go away without getting his will. The bachelor had not wished to lend his wife because there was this peculiarity about her, that she smelt like a fox when she perspired. But one day the stranger came again on a visit, and again proposed the exchange of wives; and as the bachelor did not see any way out of the difficulty, at last he consented. So one day he went in his kayak, over to the wife of the stranger; but before he started, he begged him not on any account to make remarks, if by any chance his wife should happen to smell of fox. She was so hot-tempered!

"The stranger then lay down by her side, and it was not long before the woman began to perspire; and she, who was more beautiful than other women, began to smell of fox. The man tried hard to restrain himself from saying anything, but the smell grew stronger and stronger, and at last he burst out—

" 'But where on earth does this stink of a fox come from?' "Then he caught the scream of a fox. 'Ka, ka, ka, ka!' "The woman had sprung up from the couch and dashed out. The man rushed after her. But he only saw a fox spring up the cliff. Then he went home and told the man that his wife had run away.

" 'Did I not tell you that she was very hot-tempered, and that you must say nothing, if she should smell?' said the man, who was very angry.

"Then he looked for the fox, and called her to come back; but the fox never came. They say he is still wandering about the hills looking for her."

The second story has some essential differences. It also involves the exchange of wives, but it includes several other animals.

"There was once upon a time a man who thought he would like to take a wife who was not like everybody else's wife, and he caught a little fox and took her with him to his tent. One day he had been out seal-catching, and came home and found his little wife, who had changed into a woman. She had a very big knot of hair on her head; that was her tail. And she had taken off her shaggy skin. And when he saw her so, he thought her very beautiful. Then she began to want to see other people; and so they moved away and settled down elsewhere.

"There was one of the men there who had taken a little hare as wife. The two men thought they would like to exchange wives, and they did so. But the man who had borrowed the little fox-wife despised her when he had lain down beside her. She smelt so strongly of fox, and it was not pleasant. And when the fox saw it, she was angry, because she was so anxious to please men; and she put out the lamp with her tail, sprang out of the house, and fled far away into the hills. Up there she found a worm and stayed with him. But her husband, who was fond of her, went after her, and found her at last with the worm, who had clothed himself in human shape.

"But it so happened that he was the man's mortal enemy of yore; for it appeared that once, a long, long time before, he had burnt a worm, and that worm's soul was the very one that had changed itself into a man. The man could see, too, that its face was all burnt. The worm then challenged the man, and suggested that they should pull each other's arms, and so they wrestled, but the man found the worm very easy to vanquish, and then he went out and would have nothing more to do with his wife."

The Smith Sound Eskimos told Rassmussen this story, here somewhat abbreviated:

Avuvang—he was invulnerable. When men tried to kill him, he took with him the skin of a dog's neck. His enemies fell upon him "but behold!" no weapon could touch him. Avuvang went south to buy wood. He took a wife, a very beautiful woman. The other men desired her and decided to kill Avuvang. One stabbed him in the eye, and the others seized him and pushed him through a seal breathing hole under the ice. The wife escaped. But in an attempt to catch a seal, the men drove over slippery ice. The ice broke and many men were drowned.

Later on, the survivors noticed a fox in their path, and they set off after it too. But in pursuing it they drove at a furious pace up an ice elevation, fell down on the other side, and were killed. It was the soul of the invulnerable Avuvang, who had changed itself first into a seal, and then into a fox, and thus brought destruction on his enemies."

Among the other legends and taboos are these. Lice have been a scourge of Eskimos and their dogs until quite recently. This amusing legend indicates this.

"There was once a giant; he was so big that he called the Polar bear a fox. He was so big that his lice were foxes."

A woman who has had a miscarriage cannot eat the flesh of bears, foxes or rough seals. She cannot sew an undressed fox skin. If a freshly caught fox is in the house, and its nose has not been split, she must have nothing to do with fire.

The fox is cunning in the search for food and guards himself cleverly from its enemies. So, if a man has a piece of a fox's head, or a piece of old, dried dung sewn in his clothes, the cunning of the fox will pass into him.

Here is an ancient magic hunting chant used by Greenland Eskimos before going out on a seal hunt:

> "In what shape
> Shall I wait at the breathing hole?
> In the skin of a fox
> Will I wait at the breathing hole
> In the skin of a leaper (a mythical monster, M. R.)
> Will I wait at the breathing hole
> In the form of a wolf
> Will I wait at the breathing hole
> What do I want at the breathing hole?
> To catch seals."

Rasmussen once witnessed an incantation in which a magician-medicine man tried to cure a sick child. His diagnosis was that the illness had been caused when, in fun, her fox-skin breeches had been put on a puppy.

14 The Biology of
the Arctic Fox

GREAT WARS have been fought for control of the fur trade. Much of the exploration of America's far north was stimulated by European and Chinese demand for furs. Jacques Cartier reached the big Indian village on the St. Lawrence, called Hochelaga, meaning "Beaver Dam" on Oct. 2, 1535. There he founded Montreal. He found the Indians going naked in summer and clothed in rich furs during winter. Cartier could get all the furs he wanted in exchange for cheap baubles. He was impressed. And so were the French when he returned to France with a ship laden with furs.

The furs Cartier took home were red and black fox, Arctic white and blue fox, marten, mink, and beaver. Under the patronage of Aymar de Clermont, Samuel de Champlain was sent to Canada—the Iroquois name for "village." His patron had been given exclusive fur rights, and Champlain, whom we think of chiefly as an explorer and later governor of Canada, was one of its first fur traders.

The famed "couriers de bois" were men sent out to buy furs from the Indians. They became smugglers, dealers in whiskey, served as double agents and spies for both the English and French, fomented armed conflict and some, having "gone native," joined the Indians against both the English and the French.

Champlain first reached Canada when he was 36 years old in 1603. He founded Quebec, but was forced to surrender to the

Lydekker's drawing of Arctic Foxes showing one
in winter white and the other in summer black.

A captive Arctic Fox at San Diego Zoo. *San Diego Zoo photo*

English in 1629. When Quebec became French again in 1633, Champlain returned as its governor.

Two of the couriers de bois—Sieur de Grosseilliers and Pierre Redisson-joined the English. They helped to form an English company known as "The Governor and Company of Adventurers of England Trading into Hudson's Bay." This company was granted an unlimited monopoly in 1670 by King Charles II.

It became the greatest fur trading company in world history, and the longest lived, but not without a struggle. The two couriers de bois, Redisson and Grosseilliers, deserted back to the French and helped to organize a French company. Battles between the two brought on armed conflict, and became a factor in the 100 years of French and English war for Canada.

At that time, China was the world's greatest fur market. And the lure of Chinese fur money was a major factor in stimulating the search for a Northwest Passage. The English organized the Muscovite Company. It traded guns and other goods to the Tsars in return for furs. This helped to open up Siberia.

In 1810 an American, John Jacob Astor began to dream of a world fur empire. He founded the town of Astoria at the mouth of the Columbia River in the northwest tip of Oregon. It became his shipping port for China. The city of Astoria is now a major salmon canning area instead of a fur exporting city.

The couriers de bois had to yield to discipline. They disappeared and were replaced by "voyageurs" who travelled the rivers of Canada buying furs from Indian and white trappers and from the Eskimos. What it was like was described by Edgerton R. Young in *Three Boys in the Wild North Land*. "Brigades of boats" would come to York Factory on Hudson Bay. Ships from England would unload supplies for the trappers, and Hudson Bay Company personnel, and then load the furs for England and Europe.

The heavily loaded boats carried carefully sorted and packed bales of furs weighing 80 to 90 pounds each. One boat had capsized in some treacherous river rapids. The bales had been recovered, but they had to be opened and the furs dried out.

"There were no less than six varieties of foxes, the most valuable being the black and silver ones. Then there were cross foxes, blue foxes, as well as white and red ones. There were rich otters and splendid black beavers . . . and prime bear and wolf skins."

The greed and brutal methods of the couriers de bois had almost wiped out the beaver populations and also had reduced the mink and marten numbers. They would never fully recover. But far to the north of Montreal and Quebec lived the Arctic Fox. It lived and prospered roughly from the Arctic Circle north clear around the world.

They have been found in all of northern Canada and Alaska, in all of the Aleutian Islands, on Pribilof Island in the Bering Sea, on relatively isolated St. Lawrence Island, at the northern tip of Ellesmere which is north of the American continent, in Greenland, and even in far off Iceland. They seem virtually immune to even the lowest Arctic temperatures. And while they are land animals, they have often been seen riding ice floes far out to sea, and apparently healthy and unconcerned. It seems probable that they reached Greenland and Iceland by riding the ice floes.

It is possible that more Arctic Foxes have given their lives to clothe people than any other fur bearing animal in the world. The merciless trapping of nearly four centuries has not endangered the species, although it is rare or has disappeared from many of the Northern Pacific islands. Canadian populations are still so large that, other than establishing a trapping season, Canada has made no move to protect the species.

The scientific name for the Arctic Fox is Alopex lagopus. It comes from a combination of three Greek words—Alopex for fox; lagos for hare; and pous for foot. One might say, therefore, that the Arctic Fox is a "hare-footed fox." The sole of the foot is covered with a dense coat of bristles. There are two color phases, white and blue. So the early French trappers and couriers de bois called them Renard blanc and Renard bleu.

The Siberians call it Isatis; the Eskimos, Ka-tug-u-li-o-quk; the Chippewan Indians, Et-thip-py. In Greenland it is the Greenland dog. Others have called it the Polar fox, sooty fox, pied fox, and snow dog. English speaking people call it the Arctic Fox.

It is a true canid, and the smallest one in the Arctic. Yet it is not a true fox, whose genus is Vulpes. Attempts to cross it with the Red Fox have failed. While the writer knows of no chromosomal studies of the two species, it is evident that they differ too widely to make cross mating possible. They are therefore more widely separated than are the ass and the mare, or the zebra and the horse. They are about the size of a middle weight domestic cat, ranging from about 5.5 pounds to 20. They are close to the Polar hare in size. The largest apparently lived on the North Pacific islands. New born pups have been weighed at two and a quarter ounces.

As its name suggests, its heavily furred feet help to protect it from the Arctic cold. Also, its feet are large, being up to four and a half inches in length. This gives it exceptional running ability on snow. Its tail is 30 to 35 per cent of its total length. Ernest Thompson Seton gives measurements of 31 inches total length and tail ten and one quarter inches. The muzzle is shorter than that of the Red Fox and the ears are smaller. These, combined with the dense coat and bushy tail, plus heavily furred foot soles, give the Arctic Fox nearly perfect insulation. They seldom seek shelter except during particularly severe storms. They may then dig a hole in the snow and curl up, perhaps go into a breeding den or shelter in an esker—a narrow, sinuous mound of sand and boulders deposited in or under a glacier.

The various names, such as white, blue, pied and sooty, have been given to it because of the blue and white color phases mentioned earlier, and because the winter and summer coats differ greatly. In the white phase, the winter coat is a pure white, thus making the fox extremely difficult to see against the snow, even when moving. The undercoat is exceptionally dense and woolly, and the outer coat extremely heavy. But as the snow begins to melt in May, the fox develops a thinner coat which has been described as a two-tone brown. As the short Arctic summer begins, the back, tail and legs are a dark brown, while the belly is a buff or tawny color. These color changes account for the pied and sooty names.

The blue fox is a color phase which comes up in all populations much as blacks appear in gray squirrel families. However, a Canadian study shows that more blues appear along coast lines and in areas which remain relatively ice free. In winter the blues are a pale blue-gray; in summer they become a darker blue. Canadian government figures indicate that only about five per cent of Arctic foxes trapped in Canada are blue. Yet blues predominate in Greenland and Iceland, and on the latter island the blue shading remains about the same the year around.

In the Northern Pacific, blues predominate in the area bounded by the Bering Sea, including Pribilof Island, the Aleutians and the

Alaskan Peninsula. The farther north one goes, the fewer the blues until on Alaska's north coast they are virtually absent.

Taxonomists have claimed to recognize six species of which Lagopus Linnaeus is considered the typical type. It is European and Russian-Siberian. It is, or was, common in Lapland. Hallensis Merriam is also Asiatic, although it has been found in the Bering Sea islands. It is smaller than lagopus, and has a broader and shorter skull. The other members of the family are believed to be North American in origin.

Innuitus (after Eskimo) Merriam is normally white in winter. Its skull is somewhat pear shaped. Ungava Merriam is slightly larger than innuitus. Pribilofensis Merriam is the largest of the six, and its head is closer to that of the Red Fox in shape. P. Merriam may now be extinct. The rare Beringensis Merriam is also larger than the European form, and is predominantly blue.

The great Arctic explorer, Vilhjalmur Stefansson, a Canadian born of Icelandic parents and educated at the University of Iowa and Harvard, believed that the Arctic Fox spends 90 per cent of its time during winter on the ice. This would, of course, apply only to those foxes living along the sea coast. In summer they prefer the open plains, or very wild and rugged country, and especially dry, sandy areas such as the eskers mentioned earlier.

It may be deep snow that causes the Arctic Fox to travel out to sea. There it can survive on the auks or other birds which fly or swim about the ice floes during a part of the winter. As spring comes the foxes move to shore. There they frequent the nesting areas of birds and water fowl, feasting on them and their eggs.

Those foxes which are far from the coast line, and those which come off the winter ice, live chiefly on lemmings, other small rodents and upon Arctic hares. The lemming, sometimes called the snow mouse, is a vegetarian. It exists in the millions primarily, it seems, to feed the foxes. They are abundant in every part of the Arctic Fox's range, and at all seasons of the year. However, lemming populations rise and fall, and if they fall, so must the ranks of the Arctic Fox. Lemming population cycles seem to run a course every three to four years. From its peak, the lemming population may drop to a level 20 per cent or less. Then it will gradually return to a peak. But occasionally, there will be a 100 per cent increase.

Many foxes will starve during the low point in the winter

lemming population. The survivors will breed in the spring. Then the fox population will reach its own peak a year behind that of the lemmings. However, the foxes have learned to prevent part of the starvation process by hoarding. They will kill large numbers of lemmings during the summer which will be buried in the permanent frost—the permanently frozen ground of the north which is below the level the summer sun can warm. Men have found as many as 50 lemmings in one such burial. Perhaps those foxes which live on the ice have an easier time. They are known to follow the polar bears, and to scavenge on their leavings.

Assuming a hard winter, the foxes which have survived are in a weakened condition. They mate and try to raise their pups. But if food supplies remain scarce, the parents may abandon the pups. Sometimes, the starving pups kill the weaker members of the litter and eat them. The parents may then be able to feed the smaller family. Such actions are rare among other canids.

But Arctic Foxes have very large litters, in fact, the largest of any members of the canid family, and larger also than any other known mammal. S. W. Speller, writing for the Canadian Wildlife Service places the mean litter size at about 11. This is double the mean for the Red Fox. Speller also mentions a litter of 22 reported from the Soviet Union.

It seems probable that the atypical canid behavior of the Arctic Fox in abandoning its litter, or in allowing the pups to kill and eat other pups, is a necessary survival act which has become built into the animal's genetic inheritance. At other times, the male is a far more attentive parent than most other canids are. Let us follow the mating and rearing cycle:

Before the end of winter, the Arctic Foxes begin to pair. They mate and then during a gestation period of 51 to 57 days, they select a denning site. Since the snow leaves high ground before it does on lower ground, the pair seeks a den in an esker, or on the sandy bank of a river. It is estimated that some dens are up to 300 years old. Some may have as many as 100 entrances. Both foxes select a particular den, then busy themselves cleaning it out and sometimes building or digging a new entrance. Both may feed themselves. But as whelping time nears, the male will hunt for both. And he does this also during much of the nursing period. For a time, he is feeding his mate, the pups and himself. The pups are born blind and helpless, but are well covered with fur. Their eyes open at 11 to 14 days. They are able and willing to take food brought to them by the male at about four weeks and are weaned at six. At 14 to 15 weeks they begin to leave the den. At 10 months, they will mate and whelp at about a year of age.

Speller reports the food requirements in lemmings for a litter of 11. When they are just starting to eat solid food, they will need 30 lemmings per day. By the time the pups are ready to leave the den, that is, at about 15 weeks after birth, they will be requiring 100 a day. During the denning period, the pups and their parents will have consumed 3500 to 4000 lemmings. Of course after weaning the vixen will help in hunting. The two will hunt through the sunlit Arctic night from about 4 p.m. until 11 the next morning. They may make as many as 15 hunts a night. When lemmings are plentiful, the foxes may hunt over a territory of two and a half to five square miles. At other times their range may be greater.

The little foxes do not have a long training period, such as wolves and coyotes must give to their pups. By October, the young foxes are on their own. They must strike out for new territory. The family is broken up. There is evidence, however, that the parents have mated for life and remain together.

Great migrations of Arctic Foxes have been reported. The reasons are not known. But it is possible that the need to find new territories is one reason. In such migrations, it is the young foxes which take the trek, not their parents. They never return to the area of their birth. Many perish during the trek.

Some writers have called the Arctic Fox stupid. But, if we remember their relatively short youth, and the lack of training given by their parents, then some of the things they do appear to be truly clever. Here is an account by Julian W. Bilby, who spent 12 years with the Eskimos of ice bound Baffin Land. (Bilby uses Eskimo as both singular and plural, as did many early writers):

"or it may be that an Arctic Fox decides to spend the day seal hunting. He glides over the snow, an almost invisible shape, like nothing so much as a white wraith of the desolation around. His scent having guided him to a likely spot, and being unable to do his house-breaking by brute force (the Polar bear simply smashes in the seal pup's shelter M. R.) he adopts a peculiarly wicked plan of his own. Planting all four feet together, pivot-fashion, he spins himself around and around, his paws forcing a way through the snow until he corkscrews his unwelcome presence into the seal's retreat. The baby, again, falls helpless victim."

Since so many Arctic Foxes have been killed and skinned over the centuries, one wonders what has happened to the meat. White explorers have written that the meat has an excellent flavor, likening it to chicken, rabbit or young goat. But foxes which lived along the sea coast were said to have a rank flavor because of their fish and carrion diet. Since the Eskimos, when starving, would eat their dogs, presumably they would also eat fox meat, at least in emergencies.

Charles F. Hall, in his *Narration of The Second Arctic Expedition, 1864–1869*, made this report. Hall, with the Eskimos, Ou-e-la and Ar-too-a, were on a sledging trip when they turned aside to investigate a reindeer deposit. Noticing the tracks of a fox, on close examination, they found a hole in a snow bank which covered the cache, and on loosening the stones, discovered a fox within.

"He was dead and frozen hard as a rock. The hungry fellow had burrowed through the drift and forced his gaunt body in through a very small hole between the stones. But he had so gorged himself that it was impossible for him to get back through the hole he had entered. The meat was left untouched for the Innuits (Eskimos) cannot eat what a fox has meddled with."

Canadian studies say that the Arctic Fox is seldom heard to make a sound; that he does not bark as most canids do; and that he is heard chiefly during mating time, or when trying to set up his own hunting territory. Then his voice is said to be a sort of high pitched whine.

But early writers reported that the foxes seemed not to be afraid of them, that they barked at them and even followed them still barking. Oestrum in the vixen is about 40 days, with acceptance being only about four days of this period. In many of the Polar areas, this time is called the "barking time."

After World War I breeding farms were set up in both Canada and Alaska and the nearby islands. But Canadian breeding farms died out rather quickly. Blue Arctic Fox farms were set up on many of the islands in the Aleutians and around the Bering Sea. Often these islands were uninhabited. Fox farmers simply leased entire islands from the United States, or they moved in and claimed "squatters rights." There the cold, great humidity and spring rains were conducive to the growing of prime coats. There also was a plentiful supply of fish which could be captured, smoked and preserved for fox food. The fox roamed free.

The islands have very few trees and consequently not a great deal of shade. However, the climate is very damp, with much fog, rain and snow. Sunlight tends to bleach the blue fur. During the shedding season the blue hair tends to turn brown. Occasionally what is known as a "Samson fox" is born. These foxes have no outer guard hair coat. What is left is a dense, woolly coat which is useless for the fur trade. These and other inferior foxes are quickly culled before they have a chance to breed their kind.

The National Board of Fur Farm Organizations lists 38 fur farms in the lower 48 states. They are located in Colorado, Georgia, Illinois, Indiana, Iowa, Massachusetts, Michigan, Minnesota, Missouri, Montana, North Dakota, Ohio, Pennsylvania, South Dakota, Utah, Virginia and Wisconsin. The organization's record does not list the colors raised by individual farms. But it is believed that a majority raise silver foxes which belong to a different genus. Canada is believed to have no fox fur farms at this time except on Prince Edward Island where white foxes are raised.

Fashions in furs change, and new furs like the nutria from South America are now being raised on American fur farms. The pelts of white and blue Arctic Fox are used as trimmings, neck pieces and, to a lesser extent for jackets and coats. Alaskan blues are considered the best of the blues, and wild trapped Polar whites the best of that color.

The Canadian Department of Industry, Trade and Commerce reported a catch of 31,913 Arctic Foxes during the season of 1974–75.

15 The Kit Fox and the Swift Fox

THERE are said to be eight subspecies of Kit Foxes and then there is the Swift Fox. The problem is that the terms Kit Fox and Swift Fox have been used interchangeably for many years. Moreover, authorities do not agree as to whether subspecies distinction among the Kit Foxes is genuine. And a few feel that there is insufficient difference between the Kit and the Swift to merit separate classification. Carol Snow, research biologist at the Endangered Species Library of the Bureau of Land Management, Denver, has stated that more critical study is needed to resolve the arguments.

What is more important here is that the Swift Fox is already extinct in the Canadian provinces of Saskatchewan and Manitoba, and all of these foxes are dangerously close to extinction in the United States.

The Kit Fox is officially named Vulpes macrotis, and the Swift, Vulpes velox. They are claimed by some to be the fastest four footed animals in North America. This is, however, an illusion based on their remarkable running grace, and their closeness to the ground. They are considered by many to be the greatest of all scavengers and the finest sanitarians on the continent.

All of these foxes share general species characteristics. They have unusually large ears. They are quite small, varying in weight from three to six pounds. Their body length ranges from 15 to 20 inches; the extremely bushy tail, from nine to 12 inches. Back coloration ranges from gray with rust to nearly brown; gray brown

Desert Kit Fox, Vulpes macrotis. *San Diego Zoo photo*

with grizzle, or pale brownish yellow. This fades to near white on the belly and in the ears. The tail tip is black as is the anal scent gland. There is a black spot on each side of the muzzle.

It has been said that where long legged mice do not occur, neither do Kit Foxes. While the so-called grasshopper mouse is a staple food, the diet of the Kit Fox is varied and includes jack rabbits, cotton-tail rabbits, some ground nesting birds and their eggs, snakes and other reptiles, and insects. Some foxes store food, but the Kit Fox usually does not, since its bountiful year round food supply makes this unnecessary.

Pair bonding has been known to last for three years. Occasionally, lactating females may share both a den and a male, but this is not common. During the non-mating season—winter—males and females have separate dens. But after the pups are born, males bring food to the mother and her whelps. In the fall, both parents help to teach the pups to hunt. The dens are often so far underground that a study of mating and weaning habits is extremely difficult.

The whelping den is usually lined with grasses. As do most canids, the mother keeps the nest and tunnel scrupulously clean. Litters range from five to seven. Mortality rate among the pups is not high, although Kit Foxes appear to be seriously pestered by lice which can attack the pups in such large numbers as to make survival difficult.

It is believed that the mother nurses the pups for about 10 weeks, although weaning starts earlier as the male brings food to the den. In the fall, after they have learned to hunt, the pups start out to establish territories of their own. The parents, however, are not nomadic and remain in the den areas and in the territory which they themselves have staked out. This observation led originally to the belief that mating was for life. And as pointed out above, this is not true.

The fur of the Kit Fox is not as valuable as is that of the Arctic Fox, and the pelts are smaller. But at times, Kit Foxes have been heavily trapped. Authorities do not agree on either the cunning or the unwariness of the Kit Foxes. Their decimation in certain areas has thus been laid to their lack of cunning and their consequent capture in traps. However, the major sources of death for them are poisons put out for wolves and coyotes, night hunting by "sportsmen," and the use of dune buggies and snowmobiles in running them down. Encroachment and destruction of their territories by agriculture are also a factor.

V. macrotis is environmentally adapted to the desert areas of the Southwest whereas V. m. Velox, the Swift Fox fits into the great prairie regions of Northwest Texas, Kansas, Nebraska, North and South Dakota, and the eastern parts of Wyoming and Montana.

While both Kit and Swift Foxes are nocturnal, the former has been known to hunt as early as an hour before sunset and as late as an hour before sunrise.

It has been suggested that neither the Kit nor the Swift Fox defends its territory to any extent. For it has been observed that the same territory may be hunted by two different groups, though not at the same time. Harold M. Egoscue of the Smithsonian Institute and the National Zoological Park, Washington, has recorded five vocalizations of Kit Foxes found in Nevada—a bark, a purr, a growl, a croak and a snarl. Egoscue also designated one vocalization as a "lonesome call." Both adults and pups made it, and he decided it was made when the foxes, particularly the pups, got separated.

16 The Corsac Fox

THE CORSAC FOX deserves special consideration because biologists and taxonomists are in disagreement as to whether the Corsac belongs to the genus vulpes—that of the true foxes—or is a relative of the Arctic Fox, Alopex lagopus. If the latter, then it is intermediate between wolves and coyotes and the true foxes. It is about the same size as the Arctic Fox and therefore larger than most of the true foxes. Some have been measured at nearly 12 inches in height at the shoulder, and a maximum weight of 19 pounds has been recorded. But most are somewhat smaller, with 11 pounds being a good size.

The winter coat is grayish white, and it is so long and heavy that only the tips of its ears protrude above the neck and skull fur. During the summer the coat thins out and turns to a tawny or reddish color. Corsacs have been trapped for centuries, and royalty often hunted them with golden eagles. Also, because they become quite tame, gentle and playful, they were often kept as pets.

The Corsacs differ from other foxes in several other respects. They are very active during the day. This has made hunting them with tamed eagles possible and has helped to make them satisfactory pets. They also lack the sharp, and to most people, unpleasant odor of other foxes. This, too, has helped to make them desirable pets.

The habitat of the Corsac Fox ranges widely from Mongolia and North China across the steppes to the Volga River. Unlike most other foxes which are relatively "stay at homers," the Corsac is a nomad which wanders ceaselessly over its vast range except during the mating season and the months when the whelps are too young to travel.

Corsac Fox with pups. *Berlin Tiepark Zoo photo by Gerhard Budich*

In the wild, Corsacs mate in January to mid-March. The gestation period is 50 days, give or take a day. As with other foxes, Corsacs seldom dig a den. They prefer to move into one which has been vacated by some other animal. Corsacs pair bond for life, and the males help their vixens in preparing the den and later feeding the whelps.

The sex ratio is normally one male to one vixen, and litters range from two to ten though larger ones have been reported. Vixens become sexually mature just short of their third birthday. Young Corsacs stay in the den until about four weeks of age when they begin to peek out at the world. At six to seven weeks, they wobble out to explore, but tumble quickly into the den when startled. They are strong enough to begin short hunting forays at about four months.

The Arctic dwelling Corsacs find their major food source in pikas and voles. The former are about the size of cavies (guinea pigs) with short, rounded ears and a very short tail. Voles are related to the lemmings and the common American field mouse. In the summer and in warmer areas Corsacs hunt for frogs, lizards, injured or sick birds and insects. During periods of food shortages they may scavenge and also hunt for Arctic hares.

Corsac Fox as drawn by Meyers.

17 The Lore of
the Bat-eared Fox

As STATED in the previous chapter, little is known about the bat-eared foxes. But here is an entrancing story of an orphan. It was written by Kay Turner, and it appears in her charming book *Serengeti Home*. Myles and Kay Turner lived in a home at Seronera on the fabulous game area known as the Serengeti. Here, with permission from Dial Press—James Wade Books, we give you her story.

"One hot afternoon at Seronera I heard Myles' Land Rover draw up outside the house. Calling to me, he reached into his pocket and held out one of the smallest animals I had ever seen. It lay in the palm of his hand with eyes shut and an enchanting expression upon its tiny face."

" 'A present for you,' Myles said. 'Know what it is?' "

"A mongrel dog?"

"He shook his head."

"A Wild dog?"

" 'No,' Myles answered. 'Try again.' "

"Jackal? I was beginning to run out of ideas."

" 'Wrong again,' Myles laughed. 'It's a bat-eared fox.' "

"I wondered how he could possibly tell. The cub's ears, normally the most noticeable feature of its species, were so small as to be virtually nonexistent. Myles told me he had found it abandoned on Lanai airstrip, in the north of the Park. To enable the mother to retrieve it, he had left it for an hour while he went about his work.

But the small creature was still there on his return and, rather than risk having it killed by jackals or birds of prey, he decided to bring it home. Foxes are normally concealed by their parents until several weeks old; it was rare to find a cub so young in the open, and Myles wondered if in fact the baby was a runt, rejected by its mother.

"I was delighted to have it and immediately set about choosing a name. Finally we decided on Mchutu (pronounced Mmchootu) the Waikoma word for bat-eared fox. Our cub quickly came to know his name, for he was never called by any other.

"To begin with it was not easy looking after the little animal, who weighed less than 5 ounces. Within two days of his arrival I travelled by road to Kenya to visit the children at half term and Chutu came with me, cradled inside my shirt for warmth. Unhappy with the milk formula I was feeding him, he looked exhausted and weak by the time we reached Nairobi, nearly 300 miles away, and I drove directly to see Tony Harthoorn, a leading veterinarian experienced in wildlife work. In Tony's opinion the cub's only hope of survival would be to find a nursing cat or dog. As this was not possible, the fox and I spent another miserable night.

"The following day, while lunching with friends, Chutu lay still and lifeless against my skin. Each time I thought about him the tears rolled down my cheeks, which was embarrassing at a popular Nairobi hotel. In desperation I phoned the Wildlife Orphanage for advice. They said they could not help, their only experience at the time being with young jackals, but they suggested that I strengthen the milk formula and that I provide a hot water bottle at all times for extra warmth.

"This proved the turning point for Chutu. Within a few days he had gained in strength and was a frisky ball of mischief. I added baby cereal, egg, and insects to his diet, and his weight soon doubled. In six weeks he had gained 2 pounds; by the time he reached maturity, he weighed 8 pounds, the average weight of a male fox. We never discovered his sex, and even our Serengeti Research vet was perplexed; but judging by Chutu's subsequent behaviour when he lived wild, I believed him to be a male.

"From the start Chutu was an enchanting pet, rushing about like an animated toy, fluffy tail in the air. Whenever he greeted us, he would wriggle his body with pleasure and roll over to be tickled. His most marked characteristic was joyfulness, which gave him a particularly attractive personality. Exhausted from playing, Chutu loved to sleep in my lap, lying on his back with front legs limply bent over, back legs stretched straight out, and a blissful expression on his tiny face.

"During his first two weeks the little fox tried each morning to leap from the floor to my bed which seemed an impossible feat at the time, for he was no more than six inches long. His gymnastics would begin before dawn when I was only dreamily aware of the jump-thud sounds Chutu made as he leaped up and fell back again. Having been roused several times in the night by his piercing yells for food, I generally turned a deaf ear, trusting hopefully he would come to no harm. But one morning I heard the familiar jump followed by silence instead of the usual thud as he hit the rug. My eyes flew open in alarm. To my surprise I saw Chutu standing on the pillow with his head on one side, looking the picture of impish mischief as he gazed triumphantly down at me. From then on he lived on my bed.

"Although as a very small cub he hated being in the open, Chutu followed me on walks, calling constantly in a nervous birdlike chirrup. It seemed to be the only sound he could make, apart from furious snorts and growls when playing or feeding. He was a glutton, so that we all worked ourselves to a frazzle each day collecting grasshoppers and other insects to keep him going. On rainy nights I thankfully filled up as many jars as I could lay my hands on with flying ants. But these lasted for only a day or two, and he would again be seen hanging about at mealtimes, looking pathetic and hungry. One day to appease the little animal, Myles handed him a piece of steamed pudding. To our astonishment Chutu seized and devoured it instantly, his bright eyes looking up eagerly for more. Our feeding difficulties were at an end, for we soon discovered our ravenous small fox would accept anything that came his way, snarling and growling continuously like a kettle on the boil. Amongst other things his diet eventually included eggs, bacon, pork, chocolate cake, biscuits, sausages, chicken, and fresh toast, prefera-bly buttered with a touch of Marmite (yeast extract). Later, small snakes and mice were added to his menu, and these he loved most of all.

"Chutu sometimes displayed this same aggressive behaviour when playing, particularly with Myles's smelly tennis shoes. He loved to chew on them, grunting and growling, and usually ended the game by urinating on them, much to Myles' displeasure. But woe betide anyone who tried to interfere or take the shoes away! Another of Chutu's favorite games was to have a dressing gown or towel waved in front of him, at which he promptly charged. With ears flat, plumed tail waving, and an expression of ecstasy on his small face, he would leap straight off the ground and go down fighting savagely inside an entanglement of cloth.

"Apart from this frenzy whilst feeding or playing, Chutu showed us great affection and was a most lovable pet. Before reaching maturity, he could be picked up and cuddled, and would make soft mewing sounds of pleasure, burying his wet nose in my neck or hand.

"As the weeks went by our fox grew more and more beautiful, his main features being the huge ears and luxuriant black-streaked tail that swept the ground. His coat changed from rough and woolly to silky, with an unusual patch of short fur in the middle of his back. His ears swivelled constantly at every sound and he would react violently to any sudden noise, such as a sneeze, dashing beneath my bed from the depths of sleep above it. He also disliked rain, again cowering under the bed until the storm had passed. Once when he was caught outside in a downpour, he rushed to the fireplace of the unlit bathwater heater and emerged in a hurry with paws and fur slightly singed from the live coals that were covered by a layer of ash. It took a few hours to soothe the perturbed little cub, who had just taken to spending a lot of time outdoors.

"Chutu was now about six months old and we were beginning to feel dubious about the nocturnal habits of bat-eared foxes; we were also skeptical about their mainly insectivorous diet and ability to locate beetles and mice inches underground with their enormous ears. Our fox still slept soundly all night; the noise his ears located best was the clatter of our meals being brought in, when he would come skidding along the slippery floor, plumed tail aloft and round black eyes gleaming. By this time he was hunting for about two hours each morning, digging shallow holes in short bursts and pouncing ineffectively into the grass. During long periods of immobility after a digging frenzy, he would listen intently, nose to ground, immense ears cocked, and one delicately shaded paw folded backwards. Even in the house he sometimes began digging frantically;

under the door, the sofa, or the boot of someone sitting in a chair. At feeding times it was best not to interfere.

"Time passed and Chutu became increasingly restless at night. He would now keep us awake by scratching at the door and chewing on anything he could find, and Myles urged me to set him free. But with leopards prowling round our house at night I was nervous and doubtful about his ability to fend for himself. For a while I banished him to the spare room where he promptly ruined my best rug and was miserable at being left on his own. Finally, in some trepidation, I released him into the night. Chutu was eight months old.

"The next morning, to my relief, I saw our cub curled up asleep in the sand outside the bedroom. He had by then taken to sleeping in the open at all times and I missed not seeing his familiar figure on my bed.

"For a few days we had no problems. During the day Chutu slept outside, tucked into a corner of the house where I could see him; dusk he vanished in search of adventure. On his second night of freedom, Bobby Kennedy (son of the late Senator Robert Kennedy) saw Chutu outside 'the Taj' guest house where he was staying, and brought him back to our house, thinking the fox had escaped. Bobby was fourteen years old at the time, and he had grown fond of our little fox while on a visit to the Park.

"A week after Chutu's return to the wild he disappeared. Noticing he was not in his usual 'burrow' one morning, I set out across the plains to look for him.

" 'Have you lost your fox?' Bobby asked, when I passed the guest house where he was breakfasting. I nodded and at once he joined me. But our search proved fruitless. For eight more days I walked morning and evening, calling Chutu's name, until I decided he was dead. My loss of hope filled me with sadness.

"Exhausted from days of anxiety, I slept soundly that night for the first time since Chutu's disappearance, no longer listening for a scratching at the door nor getting up to investigate any obscure noises. All at once a sharp bark outside our window woke me instantly. I leaped from my bed, knowing it was Chutu, although I had never before heard him bark.

"Rushing out, I saw three bat-eared foxes racing round and round the house. Each time they circled one of them barked as it passed our window. I called Chutu's name, but the foxes raced on, until in the end I began to doubt our fox was amongst them. Suddenly one of the little animals broke away from his companions and shot through our bedroom door in a state of high excitement. It was Chutu.

"Beside myself with joy, I hurried to defrost some pork, his favorite food. The delicious smell of cooking pork made Chutu frantic, and he scrabbled at my legs, more ravenous than usual, while I murmured consolingly to forestall his impatience. To add to the turmoil, a disgruntled voice called from the bedroom: 'If I came in at one o'clock in the morning, you wouldn't make all this fuss!'

"Although he sounded indignant, I knew that Myles too was delighted at Chutu's safe return. But his exasperation increased when the ecstatic animal insisted on joining us in bed, after he had wolfed his meal. With Chutu's small wet nose tucked into my neck, we did our best to doze peacefully together. He was covered with fleas and his increasing restlessness made sleep impossible. After twenty minutes we could stand it no longer. I opened the door, regretting that Chutu's nocturnal habits had prevented us from enjoying his company any longer. He raced out, and stood for a moment on the top step with every sense alert. Finally he stepped into the night.

"At once his two companions bounded towards him out of the darkness, apparently amazed at his safe deliverance from the house. They raced after one another in a game of tag, their long tails sweeping out as they sped around the lawn, until eventually they disappeared from sight and did not return. I felt elated at Chutu's return, and relieved that he had learned to take care of himself and was accepted by the wild foxes.

"After that first visit Chutu returned many times to the house; sometimes he scratched at the door with his sharp claws, while at others he appeared suddenly in our midst during the early part of an evening. I never again heard him bark. He now hated to be picked up, and if people attempted to stroke him he was liable to bite them, being always in an excitable state. Eventually no one dared to pet him, with the exception of Myles and myself. Even Myles could not lift him, and when I did so Chutu sometimes turned and sank his teeth into my arm, but without drawing blood. Then he would gradually relax in my arms for a short time before struggling to be put down. In a world populated by predators, he had learned to be both defensive and aggressive and his immediate reaction to being touched was to resist.

" . . . on this occasion I decided Chutu was male. After eating his meal, he trotted a short distance across the lawn and waited expectantly. Suddenly two foxes raced up to him and one of them engaged Chutu in a seemingly fierce battle. At times the two bodies struggled at my feet, locked in combat, and I wondered whether to step in and separate them. But Chutu seemed to be enjoying the fight tremendously, racing away with tail arched and closing again with his opponent, while the third fox looked on with interest. In the end I decided the two combatants were old friends, enjoying a mock battle for the favors of their lady friend. They seemed to be having so much fun that I left them to it and went back to bed.

"The last time I saw Chutu was the night before I flew to England to settle the children at their new schools. Knowing I was to be away for several weeks, it was particularly gratifying to be visited by my erstwhile pet, after a fortnight's absence. At the time we were entertaining friends to dinner, and our cook noticed two bat-eared foxes trotting past the kitchen. He called Chutu's name and immediately one of the foxes swerved from its companion, and hurried behind Fundi into the dining room. By good fortune we were eating pork. Scooping Chutu into my lap, I suffered a threatening half bite as he readjusted to his other world. Everybody offered him scraps from their plates, which he gulped down eagerly before struggling to be released. He looked sleek and well and waved his tail ecstatically while he rushed about the room. When he finally left to rejoin his friend, I watched him go with a feeling of sadness, wondering if we should meet again.

"During my absence in England Myles wrote from time to time to say that Chutu had called. He came often at first, searching the house and wandering in and out of all the rooms, which he had not done before. Each time Myles showed him affection and fed him heartily; but after awhile Chutu's visits ceased altogether. I returned a month after his last visit to the house and tramped the plains calling his name to let him know I was home. But he never came back. I liked to think he had moved out of the area altogether and that he lived to a normal old age."

18 The Biology of the African Large-eared Foxes

AFRICA has four varieties of large-eared foxes, all of which are called bat-eared foxes. Three belong to the genus Vulpes, the fourth to Otocyon. There is also the very large-eared fennec. To avoid confusion, it seems wise to limit the use of bat-eared foxes to the three vulpids, and to use only the proper names for the other two. So little is known about the three vulpids that the facts are often conflicting. For example one fox is said to have a gestation period of seven to eight weeks; another nine to ten. One species is said to be solitary, though pair bonding, while another authority states the same fox is communal. Since these foxes are closely related, it seems to the writer that their gestation period would be roughly the same. With this reservation, we have listed the supposed gestation period for each.

All three are heavily hunted and trapped, both for their meat and fur, although the latter is prime for only a short time. They are therefore in danger of extinction, and for two added reasons. One is the exploding human population, the other the encroachment of human settlements and agriculture. At least two species have never been known to touch poultry, the third only rarely.

The three vulpids under discussion here are the Pale Fox (Vulpes pallidus; the Sand Fox (V. rueppelli); and the Cape Fox (V. chama). The latter, as its name suggests, is named after the Cape Province of the Republic of South Africa. The Sand Fox is sometimes called Ruppel's, or Rueppel's fennec. But it is not a fennec,

African foxes are noted for their big ears. This one is
Vulpes chama, the Cape Fox. *San Diego Zoo photo*

Bat-eared Fox, Otocyon megalotis. *San Diego Zoo photo*

which is a much smaller animal and will be described later.

The Pale Fox is found from northeastern Africa to Libya, south to Chad and westward through northern Nigeria, Mali and Mauretania. They live on the great grassy, treeless plains within the above range. They are communal, with six to a dozen or more denning together, or gathering at waterholes. Their weight is about four and a half to six and a half pounds. They are sandy in color with a sort of dirty white belly. The gestation period is about nine weeks, and a litter of three to five pups are born. It is believed that they are blind until 10 to 14 days old. As with most other wild canids, the parents teach them to hunt and avoid danger. Danger often comes from the sky where eagles watch for adults and pups. However, the Pale Fox is nocturnal and remains in the den, or in hiding places out of the sun during the day. The diet consists of insects with a special preference for locusts, dung beetles. It also eats small rodents such as gerbils, lizards, snakes, fruits and vegetable matter. Its habitat has helped to make it omnivorous in an environment in which living is not easy.

The Cape Fox is larger than the Pale Fox, weighing six and a half to nine pounds. It is not limited to the Cape Province but is found in Namibia, and north to Angola. It lives in desert areas. Its diet is about that of the Pale Fox, but it includes even grains. Some authorities credit it with a seven to eight weeks gestation period, but this seems unlikely to the writer. The head and legs are yellow; the back, sides, and tail are silver gray; the belly whitish. It lives alone or with a mate. It is difficult to keep in zoos. The life span in the wild is not known.

The Sand Fox is, on the average, slightly smaller than the Cape Fox. Its range is from Libya across northern Africa, Arabia, Iran and Afghanistan, and south along the Indian Ocean coast in Somalia. It prefers rocky terrain. It, too, is killed for both its flesh and its fur, and it is also difficult to keep in zoos. The gestation period is probably about 60 days. The back, upper sides and the nape of the neck are a light reddish brown. The flanks are silver gray and the belly white.

Bat-Eared Fox (Otocyon megalotes)

This fox is considered to be one of the most primitive of the canids, along with the raccoon dog, and a species living in South

America, the bush dog. Various authorities give it a dentition of 46 to 50 teeth, and it may be that the confusion results from a study of different specimens which do differ in this respect or perhaps image. At any rate, whether it is 46 to 50, this is more than any other canid possesses. Most of the canids, including the dog, have only 42.

O. megalotes has a maximum length of two feet, and is about 16 inches tall at the shoulder. Its tail is long and very bushy. The legs are slightly longer in proportion to body than is true with the other African foxes. The huge ears are funnel shaped. The face and ears are blackish brown and the tail and front sides of the legs are only slightly more brown. Most of the body is grayish brown. However, the color lightens in some areas, possibly due to sunlight. This is so even though the animal is nocturnal. It is also possible that this slight variation may be a species variation, even though Otocyon megalotes is generally considered to be one species. Similarly, some observers have said that the Bat-eared Fox lives in pairs, while others comment on their communal living. This may be due to behavioral differences in different areas.

The communal living seems to be closer to the truth for most Bat-eared Foxes, and particularly those living close to villages or towns. Domestic dogs have spread canine distemper to the Bat-eared Fox, at times decimating the population. This would not be so likely to occur if these foxes lived in pairs and set up territories of their own.

O. megalotes is found in Ethiopia, the Sudan, Somalia to the Cape of Good Hope. They are also found in Namibia, although they avoid the desert areas. Their omnivorous diet includes all kinds of insects, birds' eggs, birds, lizards, berries and fruits. The gestation period is 60 to 65 days, and litters consist of two to five pups. Communal groups follow migrating locust hordes. Thus, like the foxes mentioned earlier, they are important in keeping down insect pests. Or, one should say, they are of great general importance in the control of all insect and rodent pests.

Although the African natives hunt the Bat-eared Fox for its meat and fur, it is protected in South Africa and in the game parks. It is often seen in zoos where it adjusts well. The National Zoo in Washington, D.C. was the first to produce a successful mating in 1950. Other zoos have had similar successes since.

The Fennec

The Fennec (fennecus zerda) is the smallest living canid. Its average weight is slightly under three and a half pounds, and its length is from one to one and a half feet. Its ears are four inches long, or longer, so that they are about a fourth of the body length. So not only is it the smallest canid, it also has proportionately the longest ears. They are funnel shaped with rounded tips.

The hair is long and soft, and is slightly woolly, especially on the forechest. The color varies from cream to light brown. The foreface is brown with white bars above the eyes, and the muzzle and cheeks are a cream white, but with brown streaks from the point of the inner eye down to the juncture of the lips. The eyes are large and brown with round pupils. The bushy tail has a brownish-black tip. The exposed inner ear surface is brown but is fringed with cream white. The nose is black. The animal gives the impression of being a cuddly puppy, or an unbelievable, animated stuffed toy. This is heightened by its rather whimpering voice.

The Fennec is a true desert dweller, and its habitat is the desert areas of all North Africa, the Sinai Peninsula and Arabia. Some authorities have said that the Fennec can get its entire water requirements from the food it eats. However, the truth seems to be that they can go for many days without water. They then replenish their needs by gathering at water holes which they are able to find. It can be said that they have the most remarkable kidneys of any of the canids. Their diet is made up of locusts and other insects, small rodents, lizards and birds.

The thick coat is not typical of desert animals. However, it may serve to some extent as insulation both from the heat and from the cold of the desert nights. And this may have some bearing on their ability to go without water for such long periods. Fennecs are able to dig with such rapidity that they can be out of sight in less than a minute. The hairy soles of their feet help them to run with great speed over the sand. Perhaps, like the American Kit Fox of the desert, their small size makes it appear that they are running faster than they really are.

Fennecs dig tunnels which are often interlocking, and which lead into a chamber. They avoid the desert heat by staying under-

Fennecus Zerda is the smallest fox and
has the largest ears. *San Diego Zoo photo*

ground until evening. They are social and up to a dozen may share a series of tunnels and chambers. It is believed that they pair bond, and that both parents help to raise the young. The mating season comes in February or March. Gestation is reported to be 50 days plus, and litters of two to four are born.

Although members of the French Foreign Legion are said to have captured pups and made pets of them, Fennecs are very shy. They have been difficult to keep in zoos. In zoos, they have been shown to have a liking for fruits and berries—food that would be difficult for them to get in the desert on any regular basis. Since they are great diggers, it is possible that they have satisfied some of their water requirements by digging deeply to get at the moisture carrying roots of desert plants.

While they have been bred successfully in zoos, the parents normally do not take care of their offspring. This is often true with animals far higher in the scale of intelligence, for instance chimpanzees and other anthropoids. Baby care may therefore be less innate than behavior learned in a social group.

As with the other foxes of Africa, Fennecs are hunted mercilessly, and their aid in keeping down insect hordes is ignored. In some areas of their habitat they are becoming quite rare. They are on the world endangered species list.

A fennec which Col. Hamilton Smith called Laland's Zerda. It is believed Zerda is an ancient Persian term for fennec.

19 The Lore of the Jackals

WE HAVE SEEN that the fox was the trickster in medieval Europe, and that the Coyote takes its place in the legends of the North American Indians. In Africa and in India, it is the jackal which is the cleverest of the animals. Sometimes legends develop out of man's urge to explain things. Thus, we have told the Algonquin Indian story of how the coyote got the black tip to its tail. Other animal stories carry a moral. Both appear in the lore of the jackals. And always, it is the lion who is stupid.

Outa Karel was a famous black story teller of South Africa who died in 1911. He often told his stories to the white children—to the "baasjes." Sanni Metelerkamp listened to Outa Karel's stories, took them down, and they were published in 1914—by Macmillan of the United States.

Among them are tales of the jackals (sometimes spelled jakhals). They fascinated children then, and they should fascinate adults who remember their own childhood.

How The Jackal Got His Stripe

"The sun was a strange little child," said Outa. "He never had any pappa or mamma. No one knew where he came from. He was just found by the roadside.

"In the olden days when the men of the Ancient Race—the old, old people that lived so long ago—were trekking in search of game they heard a little voice calling, calling. It was not a springbokkie, it was not a tarentaal, it was not a little ostrich. They couldn't think what it was. But it kept on, it kept on.

"They hunted amongst the milk-bushes by the roadside, and at last under one of them they found a nice brown baby. He was lying quite still looking about him, not like a baby, baasjes, but like an old child, and sparks of light, as bright as the sparks from Outa's tinderbox, seemed to fly out of his eyes. When he saw the men, he began calling again.

" 'Carry me, carry me! Pick me up and carry me!'

" 'Arre! he can talk,' said the man. 'What a fine little child! Where have your people gone? and why did they leave you here?'

"But the little Sun wouldn't answer them. All he said was, 'Put me in your awa-skin. I'm tired; I can't walk.'

"One of the men went to take him up, but when he got near he said, 'Soé! but he's hot; the heat comes out of him. I won't take him."

" 'How can you be so silly?' said another man. 'I'll carry him.'

"But when he got near, he started back. 'Alla! what eyes! Fire comes out of them.' And he, too, turned away.

"Then a third man went. 'He is very small,' he said. 'I can easily put him in my awa-skin.' He stooped and took the little Sun under his arms.

" 'Ohé! Ohé!' he cried, dropping the baby on the red sand. 'What is this for toverij! It is like fire under his arms. He burns me when I take him up.'

"The others all came round to see. They didn't come too near, my baasjes, because they were frightened, but they wanted to see the strange brown baby that could talk, and that burned like a fire.

"All of a sudden he stretched himself; he turned his head and put up his little arms. Bright sparks flew from his eyes, and yellow light streamed from under his arms, and—hierr, skierr—the Men of the Early Race fell over each other as they ran through the milk-bushes back to the road. My! but they were frightened!

"But someone had been watching, my baasjes, watching from a bush near by. It was Jakhals, with his bright eyes and his sharp nose, and his stomach close to the ground. When the people had gone, he crept out to see what had made them run. Hardly a leaf stirred, not a sound was heard, so softly he crept along under the milk-bushes to where the little Sun lay.

" 'Ach, what a fine little child has been left behind by the men!'

he said. 'Now that is really a shame—that none of them would put him into his awa-skin.'

" 'Carry me, carry me! Put me in your awa-skin,' said the little Sun.

" 'I haven't got an awa-skin, baasje,' said Jakhals, 'But if you can hold on, I'll carry you on my back.'

" 'Where do you want to go? asked Jakhals.'

" 'There, where it far is,' said the baby sleepily.

"Jakhals trotted off with his nose to the ground and a sly look in his eye. He didn't care where the baby wanted to go; he was just going to carry him off to the krantz (cliff) where Tante (wife) and the young Jakhalses lived. If baasjes could have seen his face! All wereld! He was smiling, and when Oom Jakhals smiles, it is the wickedest sight in the world. He was very pleased to think what he was taking home; fat brown babies are as nice as fat sheep-tails, so he went along quite jolly.

"But only at first. Soon his back began to burn where the baby's arms went round it. The heat got worse and worse, until he couldn't hold it out any longer.

" 'Soé! Soé! Baasje burns me,' he cried. 'Sail down a little further, baasje, so that my neck can get cool!'

"The little Sun slipped further down and held fast again, and Jakhals trotted on.

"But soon he called out again, 'Soé! Soé! Now the middle of my back burns. Sail down still a little further.'

"The little Sun went further down and held fast again. And so it went on. Every time Jakhals called out that he was burning, the baby slipped a little further, and a little further, til at last he had hold of Jakhals by the tail, and then he wouldn't let go. Even when Jakhals called out, he held on, and Jakhal's tail burnt and burnt. My! it was quite black!

" 'Help! help!' he screamed! 'Ach, you devil's child! Get off! Let go! I'll punish you for this! I'll bite you! I'll gobble you up! My tail is burning! Help! Help! And he jumped, and bucked, and rushed about the veld, till at last the baby had to let go.

Then Jakhals voertsed (apparently a word of Outa's coining, M.R.) round, and ran at the little Sun to bite him and gobble him up. But when he got near, a funny thing happened, my baasjes. Yes, truly, just when he was going to bite, he stopped halfway, and shivered back as if someone had beaten him. At first he had growled with crossness, but now he began to whine from frightenness.

"And why was it, my baasjes? Because from under the baby's arms streamed brightness and hotness, and out of the baby's eyes came streaks of fire, so that Jakhals winked and blinked, and tried to make himself small in the sand. Every time he opened his eyes a little, just like slits, there was the baby sitting straight in front of him, staring at him so that he had to shut them again quick.

" 'Come and punish me,' said the baby.

" 'No, baasje, ach no!' said Jakhals in a small little voice, 'why should I punish you?'

" 'Come and bite me,' said the baby.

" 'No, baasje, no, I could never think of it.' Jakhals made himself still a little smaller in the sand.

" 'Come and gobble me up,' said the baby.

"Then Jakhals gave a yell and tried to crawl further back.

" 'Such a fine little child,' he said, trying to make his voice sweet, 'who would ever do such a wicked thing?'

" 'You would', said the little Sun. 'When you had carried me safely to your krantz, you would have gobbled me up. You are toch so clever, Jakhals, but sometimes you will meet your match. Now look at me well.'

"Jakhals didn't want to look, my baasjes, but it was just as if something made his eyes go open, and he lay there staring at the baby and the baby stared at him.

" 'You'll know me again when you see me,' said the baby, 'but never again will you be able to look me in the face. And now you can go.'

"Fierce light shot from his eyes, and he blew at Jakhals with all his might; his breath was like a burning flame, and Jakhals, half dead with frightenness, gave a great howl, and fled away over the vlakte.

"From that day, my baasjes, he has a black stripe right down his back to the tip of his tail. And he cannot bear the Sun, but hides away all day with shut eyes, and only at night when the Old Man with the bright armpits has gone to sleep, does he come out to hunt and look for food, and play tricks on other animals."

How Jakhals Fed Oom Leeuw

So often when the story tellers recite the legends which have been so carefully handed down to them, generation by generation, they say something like "Long ago, when the animals could talk." In one of Outa Karel's greatest stories, the one we are about to give briefly, he admits adding a few "modern" details for the benefit of the white school children to whom he is talking. Then he adds this rather surprising observation: "But the real story was made long, long ago, perhaps when baasje's (white boss's) people went about in skins like the Rooi Kafirs, and Outa's people were still monkeys in the bushveld."

The story of how the jackal fed the lion is quite long. In selecting from it, we hope to give something of Outa Karel's colorful story-telling, as well as his knowledge of the animals. This is how the story begins.

"One day, in the early morning, before any people were awake, Jakhals was prowling round and prowling round, looking for something to eat. Jakhals is not fond of hunting for himself. Oh, no! he likes to wait till the hunt is over, so that he can share the feast without having had any of the work.

"He had just dragged himself quietly to the top of a kopje (small hill)—so my baasjes, so—with his ears moving backwards and forwards . . . to hear the least sound. Then he looked here, he looked there, he looked all around and yes, truly! whom do you think he saw in the kloof (ravine) below? No other than Oom Leeuw (Uncle Lion) himself, clawing a nice big hamel (castrated ram) he had just killed—a Boer hamel, baasjes, with a beautiful fat tail. Oh yes, Oom Leeuw had picked out a good one."

The jackal then figures out a way to get the ram. He finds a piece of paper which he takes to the lion, saying it is a message from his wife. The lion can't read but, saying he has lost his spectacles, asks the jackal to read the message. The jackal pretends to read the message, saying that Oom Leeuw's wife and children are very hungry, and he must kill a fat ram and bring it home at once.

Oom Leeuw says his wife is not well, since the donkey she killed and ate a couple of days before did not agree with her. Jackal then agrees to take the dead ram to the lioness and her kittens. Where-upon, Oom Leeuw says that for his trouble, the jackal can have the offal. The jackal, however, carts off the meat and then beats the lioness and her kittens with the offal. The lion promises revenge.

He kills and eats a young Steenbok, and goes off to sleep during the heat of the day in the shade of a cliff. The next morning, he spots the jackal on top of a cliff, sitting by a fire with his wife and children. He tries to climb the cliff side, but always after getting part way up, he falls. He then tries to be friendly, and asks the jackal to go hunting with him.

"At any other time Jakhals would have skipped with delight, for it was very seldom he had the honor of such an invitation, but now he was blown up with conceit at having cheated Oom and Tante Leeuw so nicely.

" 'Thank you, Oom, but I am not in want of meat just now. I'm busy grilling some nice fat mutton chops for breakfast. Won't you come and have some too?'

" 'Certainly, with pleasure, but this krantz is so steep—how can I get up?'

The jackal says that he and his wife will pull him up. They get rather weak ropes, and when the lion is part way up, they saw each rope against the sharp cliff edge. The ropes break and 'kabloops' down fell Oom Leeuw to the hard ground below."

After repeated falls, the lion is exhausted, whereupon the jackal says he will toss down meat to him. He wraps a red hot coal in meat, tells the lion to open his mouth, then tosses in the meat.

"And then, my baasjes, there arose such a roaring and raving and groaning as had not been heard since the hills were made. The dassies (probably dassie rats, M.R.) crept along the rocky ledges far above and peeped timidly down; the circling eagles swooped nearer to find out the cause; the meerkats and ant-bears, the porcupines and spring-hares snuggled further into their holes, while the frightened springboks and elands fled swiftly over the plain to seek safety in some other veld.

"Only wicked Jakhals and his family rejoiced. With their bushy tails waving and their pointed ears standing up, they danced round the fire, holding hands and singing . . ."

The lion, of course, died.

The Jackal, the Hare, and the Cock

Earlier, we have shown that, at least in Africa, the jackal sometimes is shown to have outsmarted himself. The following story is from the Swahili, as translated by Capt. C. H. and Mrs. Stigand. It was published in 1904 by Houghton Mifflin. Again we quote it in part, trying to convey something of the original story.

"Once upon a time there was a hare who was cunning with great guile. That hare went to the jackal and said, 'I want to make friends with you, jackal. Our friendship will be that we walk about together and agree in every matter. Everything that I do you must do also, and everything that you do I must also do.'

"When the jackal heard those words of the hare he was very pleased, and he thought, 'This will be very good to have the hare for a brother for he is very clever.'

The partnership worked quite well until one day the hare said that the jackal should kill his mother, and the hare would kill his. It was agreed.

The hare hid his mother in a cave and smeared his knife with the red sap from the Mtumbati tree. He showed the knife to the jackal to prove that he had killed his mother. The jackal, not wishing to kill his mother, hid for a few days, then reported that he had indeed done so. But since he had no bloody spear or knife to prove it, the hare knew the jackal was lying. The two then went to the jackal's home and the latter slew his mother.

The hare then said that they must eat nothing but insects, and so they went to the forest to try to catch them. But while the jackal slept, the hare went to the cave and was fed by his mother. The poor jackal starved to death. This affair was so scandalous that the other animals called a conference to see what could be done.

A cock agreed to punish the hare, saying that he could outsmart him. It was decided he should try. So he invited the hare to dinner for the next day. When the hare arrived, the cock lay in the yard, his head under his wing. His family told the hare that the cock had had to send his head to the Sultan for a business discussion, but that the head would return soon.

While the hare was eating, the cock got up, went into the house and apologized for the delay. The hare then invited the cock to come to his home for dinner. He then instructed his family to cut off his head, saying that if the cock could send his head to the Sultan on business, so could he. Of course he died, and the cock was able to report the good news to the conference of the animals.

JACKAL LEGENDS FROM INDIA

No one knows when the Panchatantra was written, but it might have been as long ago as 2600 years. Some have said that Aesop got the idea for his animal fables from India; some have said that the reverse was true; some have said that the beast epics of medieval Europe came from India. Still others believe that the stories arose independently, since all peoples of an earlier time had a closer bond to the animals than modern man does.

Whatever the source, the Indian stories usually pointed up a moral. And it is the jackal who is the wisest of the animals. In most of the stories he is less a trickster than than a very wise benefactor who comes to the aid of the other animals.

In 1924, Stanley Rice, who had been in the Indian Civil Service under Britain's rule of India, translated stories from the Panchatantra. They were published under the title *Ancient Indian Fables and Stories* in 1924 by John Murray of London. Here we give some of the delightful stories which deal with the troubles of the animals and the sagacity of the jackal in solving them. As in true fairy tale fashion, many of them end with "and lived happily ever after."

The Crow and the Jackal

"In the forest of Pratama Sachi lived a crow who had built his nest in one of the highest trees. Under the same tree a huge snake had taken up his abode in a white-ant's mound. When the crow found that he had such a dangerous enemy for neighbour, he tried either to get rid of him or to destroy him; but as he could do neither and could not live at ease beside such a neighbour, he sought out a jackal and told him his troubles, asking his advice how best to bring about the destruction of the snake."

The jackal then tells a story which demonstrates how cunning can be used to destroy an enemy, and says he will think of a plan. Whereupon the crow takes him to the place where his dangerous neighbour lives.

"While this was going on, the king of the country happened to be hunting in that jungle and, being tired, lay down under the tree where the crow's nest was. He took off his golden collar and his other ornaments and was soon asleep. The jackal at once made a sign to the crow; the latter flew down and, taking up the collar, hid it in the snake's hole. Then they quietly withdrew.

"But one of the king's men had seen what happened and told his master as soon as he was awake. The king thereupon set his people to dig up the place where the collar was hidden. Out came the snake in a rage, ready to attack those who had disturbed him; but the people were on their guard, and soon crushed him with big stones; they continued their work and recovered the collar.

"The crow, having achieved his end, lived happily in the tree with his family. 'So it is,' remarked Damanaka (the story teller) 'that we can defeat by cunning those whom we cannot defeat by force, for as the saying puts it: Strength dwells in the brain, not in the body; he is the strongest who is the cleverest.' "

The Jackal and the Lion

"Once upon a time in the forest of Madunata there lived a lion named Pundarika, the terror and the scourge of all the animals that lived there. Fearing to be exterminated, they resolved to find a forest beyond the reach of their enemy, and were about to carry out their intention when an old jackal advised them to wait.

'Why,' said he, 'leave in such haste the place of your birth and the land of your fathers? Let us first see if we cannot come to terms with our enemy and live here in peace.'

"The animals agreed to take his advice, and at once deputed him to make terms with the lion, or at any rate to reduce the slaughter, and to find out on what conditions he would let them live in peace.

"Accordingly the jackal went to the lion.

" 'Why do you try so foolishly to destroy our race?' he said. 'At the pace you are going there will soon be nothing left in the forest, and you yourself will die of hunger. If you will have a clear understanding with us, we will undertake to provide for all your needs and to keep you supplied without any effort on your part.'

" 'What is that?' cried the lion fiercely, amazed at such language from a jackal.

" 'Yes,' answered the latter, 'if you will let us alone, we promise to bring you one animal a day to satisfy your hunger.'

"The lion agreed, and the animals faithfully kept their promise and sent him an animal every day to eat. Each kind sent one in turn, and at last it was the turn of the jackal. On the day when he was to be the victim he assembled the beasts and explained that the remedy was in fact only temporary, since they were all being devoured in turn, and he added that if they were not to be ruined, the only chance was to destroy their enemy by cunning. The animals were astonished at the proposal and asked how he meant to carry out such a desperate enterprise.

" 'I want nobody's help,' said the jackal. 'I will do everything myself.' "

(There follows a story within a story in which the jackal demonstrates his cunning. He then dismisses the animals and goes alone to the lion's den. But on the way he comes to a well, sees his own reflection there, and ponders awhile.)

" 'Here,' he said to himself, 'is a good way of getting rid of the lion.' He thought out his plan, and appearing before the lion with a dejected air, he said, 'I am come to serve as your meal for today because it is my turn. But before I die I want to tell you some news so disquieting that I hardly dare.'

"The lion was troubled no less than astonished at these words and asked him to explain frankly. 'Well,' replied the jackal, 'since it is your command I must warn you of your danger. A little way from here there is another lion who is trying to supplant you and to kill you; the better to keep his plans secret, he is living at the bottom of a well and is only waiting for an opportunity to take you by surprise, to kill you and to be king in your place.'

"On hearing this unexpected news the lion flew into a great rage. 'Now,' he cried, 'I know the truth of the old saying: *As insult punishes the wise, as ignorance kings, as infidelity the wife, so does the existence of rivals punish the powerful.* Show me at once the place where my rival is hiding that I may be revenged upon him.'

"The jackal led him to the edge of the well, told him to look in and see his enemy. The lion, with bristling mane and lashing tail, went up to the well in a fury and, looking in, saw his own image in the water. He thought it was in truth another lion, and with a terrible roar sprang in to the well to fight his rival. The jackal at once called the other beasts, who rolled great stones into the well and crushed their enemy. From that time on they lived in peace in their forest."

20 The Golden Jackal

IF ONE WERE TO TRY to describe the dozen or two local variations in jackals, this section would be confusing and lacking in interest, except to anatomists and mammologists. Moreover, until quite recently the four types were placed in separate genera. Today there is general agreement that the four varieties all belong to the genus Canis, although one, the Abyssinian Jackal is placed in a sub-species.

The best known, and the most widely distributed of all the jackals is the Golden Jackal, Canis aureous. Its range is from Southeastern Europe into Southern Asia, including the northern section of India, south even to Ceylon (now Sri Lanka) and Africa. It ranges from the Asian mountains to the sea coast, and it prefers thorny thickets and grassy savannas. These provide cover and easy escape routes. It also likes low, sometimes wet areas. In mountainous areas it ranges as high as 1500 feet where it lives in ravines and among rocks. On the whole, it avoids rain forests and deep jungles.

The Golden Jackal is not a large animal and it prefers to run rather than to fight. This is perhaps due to its habit of rushing in upon a lion's kill to grab a morsel of meat, then to dodge and run away. Yet in South Africa the writer once watched Borzois course jackals on an open veldt. When nearing capture, the jackals turned and fought viciously, and it required two of the dogs to make the kill.

In Asia and in the southern part of the Soviet Union the Golden Jackal has three major enemies—man, the wolf and the striped hyena. To them should be added a fourth which preys upon the young pups. These are hawks. Adults watch skyward, and try to protect their pups by jumping into the air in an effort to bite the hawks. This habit of watching the sky seems to be written into the jackal's genes, just as it is for chickens and birds. In Africa the spotted hyena is also an enemy.

Yet many observers have noticed that, on occasion, two jackals will combine forces to route a hyena. This they do by rushing in and biting at the hyena's rump. That is, one diverts the hyena by simulating a frontal attack while the other attacks from the rear. The hyena is a vicious fighter itself, but it is unable to cope with a double attack and must try for a kill against a single jackal. The attack by two jackals appears not to be an inbred characteristic but a learned one.

A similar learned procedure has been noted in southeastern Europe and the Soviet Union. There jackals pair up to attack sheep, particularly newborn lambs. Muskrats were introduced into Great Britain to be bred in captivity for their fur. Some escaped. They spread with alarming speed. And as so often happens when a non-native creature is introduced into a foreign environment, muskrats became a serious pest. They dug holes in dams, thus draining ponds for instance. Golden Jackals worked out a method of capturing those which lived along river banks. They work in pairs, one on each side of the stream. In this way, they would cut off the escape route for a muskrat which had wandered away from the under-water entrance to its house.

Golden Jackals are of major importance in Africa in keeping down the locust populations. At the time the locusts are ready to swarm, they form an important part of the jackal's diet. They also are expert at capturing snakes which they devour. But they are best known as scavengers. Jackals gather near lions which have made a kill. They wait patiently until the lions have finished eating, then rush in to clean up the remains. They may also gang up to capture new born antelopes. However, these animals are able to run quite swiftly a few hours after birth, so that the jackals have only an occasional success. They also eat herbs and other vegetarian matter.

Golden Jackals, in common with the other varieties, have what one might call personal problems. They suffer from heavy infestations of ticks and fleas. And they have internal parasites such as heart worms and other types of worms. All of these have an inborn mechanism which keeps them from killing their host. But if the host is weakened by disease or injury, death from parasites is often the result.

Golden Jackals are rust-gold in color, and when seen in bright light have a shimmering gold color. Most of the foreface, frontal area of the skull and the neck are ochre in color. There are small black areas above the eyes. The flanks are rust brown and the legs are ochre. Mountain jackals have a more grayish color. Golden Jackals are said to resemble wolves very closely, more so than the other members of the genus. However, they have shorter legs in proportion to body length and size, and the foreface narrows much more so than in the wolf. They have rounded eye pupils like the wolf. Although they have the so-called 24 hour eyes, they are chiefly nocturnal. They prefer to hunt in the early evening, but often go on a second hunt just before dawn. They seldom hunt in packs though as mentioned above, they may hunt in pairs.

Golden Jackals have a very strong pair bond and apparently mate for life. However, if one of the pair is killed, the other may take a second mate. The bitches come in season only once a year, and the heat period is short, being six to eight days. Mating comes in the January to March part of the year. It will be earlier in hot climates, and later in the northern range. At mating time, the male's testicles will triple in size. Gestation is about the same as that of the domestic dog, being 62 to 63 days. Litter size is up to eight pups. When the bitch is nursing, the male will hunt for food for her. The pups are born with their eyes closed. When the pups are approaching three weeks old, both parents will hunt for food which will be regurgitated for the pups.

Bitch pups are sexually mature before they are a year old, usually at 11 months. For those living in mountainous areas, maturity will come at about a year. Males do not become sexually mature until 20 months to two years of age. Again, climate seems to delay maturity.

Jackals may elect to have litters in secluded, rocky areas where there is protection. They may also dig dens. The den will be a quite small tunnel leading into a larger chamber. Jackals do not dig an escape tunnel as so many animals do, for instance, the American woodchuck or groundhog. The parents keep the dens scrupulously clean until the pups are weaned.

In times of stress, such as scarcity of food, parasites may kill many of the pups before they reach maturity. This occurs in most of the wild canids. Both parents teach their pups to hunt, and how to avoid danger. Golden Jackals have thrived even in southeastern Europe where they have been hunted and trapped by man. In those areas, they are blamed for extensive sheep losses, as the wolf and coyote are blamed in North America.

In North America, the various signal calls of wolves have been carefully studied. But this has not been done with jackals. While a number of their calls have been described, they sound different to different races or people. Ivan Sanderson once described one of the calls of the Golden Jackal in northern India as "Dead Hindoo, where, where, where."

It is fitting to quote part of which Lt. Col. Charles Hamilton Smith wrote about jackals 130 years ago.

"Jackals form a group of crepuscular and nocturnal canines, never voluntarily abroad before dusk and then hunting for prey during the whole night; entering the streets of towns to seek offals; robbing the hen roosts; entering out houses; examining doors and windows; feasting upon all dressed vegetables and ill secured provisions; and digging their way into sepulchers that are not carefully protected against their activity . . . They unite the cunning of foxes, and the energy and combination distinguished in the best trained dogs, with a tenacity of purpose surpassing both."

Syrian Golden Jackal, Canis aureus Syriacus. *San Diego Zoo photo*

Black-backed Jackal, Canis mesomelus. *San Diego Zoo photo*

21 The Black-backed Jackal

THE BLACK-BACKED JACKAL (Canis mesomelas) differs so greatly from the other members of the family it is hardly surprising that it was once given a separate genera status. Its black back makes it appear to be a short haired animal wearing a fur piece on the forward part of its back. But it differs also in being highly vocal, by its tendency to pack up, an irregular breeding season, and a tendency to live in family groups as well as in packs. It is also credited with having the finest eye sight of all the canids, and senses of smell and hearing far superior to most.

It ranges from Egypt to South Africa and to the southwest African deserts. It lives for the most part on grassy areas of the veld, and it shuns both thorny areas and deep forests. The black peoples of Africa credit it with being the smartest of all animals. Thus, in the chapter on The Lore of the Jackal, the South African stories can be said to deal with the Black-back, rather than the other species.

The basic color of the belly and most parts of the body is rust red, bright rather than brownish red. The base of the tail is red, varying from gray to yellow red. But the rest of the tail is black. The back ranges from slate gray to nearly black. It is the contrast with the belly that gives the animal its name. The slate-black begins at the shoulders, about at the withers, extends about half way down the body but narrows rapidly to the tail. Thus, it is triangular, with the base of the triangle being at the withers. In some cases, the tail may have the body's red as a sort of stripe on the sides. Maximum body length is about two and a half feet, and the average weight is about 22 pounds. The tail is about 12 inches long and is thickly furred.

Its omnivorous diet does not differ greatly from that of the other jackals. It catches small mammals, birds, enjoys insects, takes the eggs of birds, and of course eats carrion and the leavings of lions and leopards. Black-backed Jackals gather in family groups, or in a pack around lions as they feed. They wait patiently to grab what the lions leave, though an occasional one will rush in and try to seize a bite. They have to fight over the leavings with hyenas, vultures, and the African marabou stork. The black-back also eats vegetable matter and fruits. It is expert at killing snakes which it also devours.

Black-backed Jackals are adept at killing young lambs and newly born antelope and gnu babies. In order to save their lambs, South African farmers have tried to fence out the jackals much as the Australians have tried to fence out the dingo.

Other than the fact that breeding can occur at any time of the year, the statistics for gestation and litter sizes are the same as for the Golden Jackal. Death from parasites takes many of the pups, so that when nearing maturity, a family group may consist of the parents and only three pups. Black-backed Jackals apparently summon other members of the pack or family by a loud scream, followed by short barks. They utter long, mournful screams when they have captured food. A peculiarity of their shedding is that the black back disappears, or is shed, and then grows back again.

Col. Hamilton Smith's drawing of a Black-backed Jackal which he called "Cape Thous Dog," 1839–40.

Cheetah pursues a Black-backed Jackal. *Time-Life photo by John Dominis, 1965*

Black-backed Jackal. *Courtesy of Roger Caras*

Side-striped Jackal, Canis adjustus. *San Diego Zoo photo*

22 The Side-striped Jackal

THE SIDE-STRIPED JACKAL is known to naturalists as Canis adustus. It is about 17 inches tall at the withers, but its legs are longer in proportion to its total height than is true with other jackals. Its ears are shorter, and its tail is bushier. It is brownish gray with a brighter reddish sheen on the back. There are light stripes on each side which usually have a black edge at the bottom.

It is very shy and nocturnal so that it is rarely seen by people. It is also, in contrast to the others, a forest dweller. It is also found on the mountain slopes. Its range is not as large as that of the other species being in Ethiopia, parts of West Africa and extending only to the northern edge of the Republic of South Africa.

It is also less social and probably hunts almost entirely singly rather than in packs. For this reason, it never attacks sheep or other farm animals. Nor does it seize the calves of antelope. It is known to be much more of a vegetarian than are the other species.

Side-striped Jackals are seldom seen in zoos. This is partly because of their shy and nocturnal nature, and partly because they are difficult to keep. They are not good exhibition animals in zoos because of their shyness. They have seldom been mated in zoos. Both Golden and Black-backed Jackals mark home territories, and both sexes do this by raising their legs. It is presumed that the Side-striped Jackals do also, both because they are jackals and because they are canids. But their shyness has made proof of this difficult to obtain.

In The Lore of the Jackals, we have included an ancient legend which tells how this jackal got its stripes.

Col. Hamilton Smith's ''Painted Thous Dog'' (jackal) 1839-40.

23 The Abyssinian Jackal

THIS ANIMAL, Canis simensis, has sometimes been called a wolf and sometimes a fox. It certainly has some fox-like features. Once it was placed in the genus Thos. Now it has been given a sub-species recognition as the Abyssinian Jackal. Almost nothing is known about it, and very little more is likely to become known. It is close to extinction. It has been relentlessly hunted and trapped, both because its pelt is highly prized in Addis Ababa and because it is accused of attacking cattle.

However, from what is known about it, it feeds almost entirely on rodents. It is not even certain that it attacks sheep. Longlegged, it has a maximum shoulder height of 19½ inches. Its head is fox-like with a sharply narrowing foreface. Its upper carnassial tooth also seems fox-like. But its general appearance and behavior tend toward the jackal.

It has reddish brown hair, tending toward yellow on parts of its body. The upper lips, chin and throat are white. Two reddish stripes, separated by a dingy band, extend down from the neck across the nape. It hunts day and night, may live alone or in pairs, and catches rodents by running them down.

The Magellan Fox, now believed extinct. Eugene
Gayot in *Le Chien Histoire Naturelle*, Paris 1867.

24 The South American Canids

THE GREAT MOUNTAIN SYSTEM which men call the Cordilleras begins in Alaska and extends all the way to Cape Horn at the end of South America. It erupted during the Tertiary, the interval between the close of the Mezozoic Era and the Quaternary. It was also the beginning of the great Age of Mammals evolving some 160,000,000 years ago. North and South America are separated by what we call Central America whose mountains are made up of igneous, volcanic rock. Its low lands are often steaming, heavily forested jungles and swamps upon which heavy equatorial-type rains fall almost daily, and the year around. Central America is sometimes called a neotropical environment, and sometimes a zoogeographical one.

Archaeologists are no longer certain that the great family of the canids developed in North America, but at least they were present during the early Tertiary. Sometime during that period, but before the mountains erupted, some of the canids migrated southward into South America. After the eruption of the Cordilleras, Central America became an almost impenetrable barrier for most of the animals of North America. No modern North American canid has been able to overcome that barrier.

The isolation of South America forced it to develop its own animals. They included the New World monkeys with prehensile tails; a flightless ostrich-like bird, the rhea; the tapir; and distinct canid families. Father José de Acosta was one of the first educated men to reach the New World and to write about it. He found the

native animals so different that he was forced to speculate in a way
which could have got him burned at the stake as a heretic.

In his *The Naturall and Morall Historie of the East and West Indies,*
Chapter 36, he wrote: "It were a matter more difficult to shew and
prove what beginning many and sundry sorts of beasts had, which
are found in the Indies, of whose kindes we have none in this
continent (Europe). For if the Creator hath made them there, wee
may not alleadge nor flie to Noah's Arke, neither was it then
necessary to save all sorts of birds and beasts, if others were to be
created anew. Moreover, wee could not affirme that the creation of
the world was made and finished in sixe days, if there were yet other
new kindes to make, and specially perfect beasts no lesse excellent
than those that are known unto us. . . . It may be God hath made a
new creation of beasts."

Since many readers will be interested in domestic dogs, it is
worthwhile to add some other observations made by Father Acosta.
"At the first, there were no dogges at the Indies, but some beasts like
unto little dogges, the which the Indians call Alco, and therefore,
they call all dogges that go from Spaine by the same name by reason
of the resemblance that is betwixt them."

I have used Edward Grimston's 1604 translation. Father Acosta
left Spain in 1570, spent 15 years in Peru and two in Mexico. He
went home in a fleet which carried 1200 pounds in gold and 11
million pieces of silver.

Those canids which managed to migrate to South America
before the mountains erupted evolved into the various species of
foxes, and into the Bush Dog, the small eared Zorro, and the
Falkland Islands Wolf. Very little is known about them. They have
not been studied to the extent given to North American and other
canids. Some have lived in dense jungles and among hostile people.
Some of these canids have been placed in a subgenus,
pseudalopex—false foxes. This they are, being neither true foxes
nor true dogs, but simply strange canids.

Felix de Azara was a Spanish soldier and cartographer who
spent many years in the hostile Indian country trying to work out
with the Portuguese and the Spaniards a boundary between Portuguese Brazil and Spanish South America. So far as is known, he
had little training in biology, and yet his name will be forever

associated with the quadrupeds and birds of southern South America. Felix had an older brother whom he never met until he was a grown man, and whom he met only occasionally and for very brief periods after that.

Azara would assemble a large number of horses and dogs, gather together huge quantities of brandy, beads, cloth, knives and ribbons for the "savages," and then set off into previously uncharted areas never before visited by white men. The Indians were hostile. After each day's journey, Azara would have to obtain a guide from the next tribe.

At each camping place, the horses were used to stamp over every inch of space as a protection against venomous snakes. Horses were lost occasionally from snake bites. Each camp site had to be surrounded by fires to prevent jaguars and pumas from seizing the men. The dogs were used to alert against both the animals and the attacks of hostile Indians.

Given such circumstances, it is astounding that Azara could have made the studies of both the animals and birds which served for his books. His two volume *Natural History of the Spanish Provinces of South America* was sent to his brother Nicholas. Felix wanted it to be submitted to a European trained naturalist before making corrections. But Nicholas had it published immediately—and in French, not Spanish.

Azara's three volume set on ornithology was published later. There was great confusion. Nicholas, a sort of ambassador to the Catholic Church at Rome, was named in some editions as the explorer-naturalist, and Felix the diplomat. Much of what English speaking people knew about Felix de Azara comes from a memoir of him written by Lt. Col. Charles Hamilton-Smith, a great naturalist in his own right and the greatest authority of his day on canids. Hamilton-Smith was a great admirer of Azara. But even he could find nothing about Azara's later years, nor even be certain whether he died in 1804 or in some other year.

Hamilton-Smith was a contributor to *The Naturalist's Library,* a great multi-volume work edited by Sir William Jardine, Bart. He was the author of Volume 10, *Mamallia—Dogs,* subtitled "Canidae or Genus Canis of Authors, including also the Genera Hyaena and Proteles." It was published in Edinburgh, Scotland, in 1839–1840, and it is the greatest book of its day on domestic dogs and wild canids. It was also a part of the greatest set of books on natural history since the time of Aristotle.

Today our knowledge of all canids is far greater than it was in the days of Azara and Hamilton-Smith. Yet we know little more about the South American canids than they did. The work which perhaps most nearly matches Sir William Jardine's library is *Grzimek's Animal Life Encyclopedia*. It was edited by Bernhard Grzimek, whom I believe to be the greatest animal authority of our time, particularly on African animals. Grzimek selected unquestioned authorities in their specialties to write each section.

Here we quote directly from Hamilton-Smith. We cannot know, however, how much he owed to Felix de Azara.

"Canidae of South America.—All, it seems with a tendency to elliptical pupils, but not perfectly as in true foxes. Dentition invariably less powerful.

"Section VIII. Chrysocyon Aguara Wolf. Stature nearly equal to the wolf; head smaller; legs long, slender; mane on neck and shoulders; tail straight, bushy; pupils round? mammae six. Habits subdiurnal and nocturnal; solitary, campestral. (Campestral probably means "related to fields or open country." M.R.)

"Chrysocyon jubatas, Canis jubatus, Desm; Canis campestris, Wied.; Aguara Guazu, Maned Aguara."

(Five Spanish dictionaries do not list the word Guazu at all. One does not list Aguara. The other four give four different definitions: maned dog, maned wolf, Argentine fox, Argentine dog.)

"Section IX—Dusicyon, Aguara Dogs. Forms between the wolf and fox; body bulky; legs short; tail medial, tip white; eyes oblique, pupils round? burrow; more social, more placable; eat fish, crabs, birds, etc.; swim well, subdiurnal.

Dusicyon canescens, Nob, Hoary Aguara Dog; Canis thous: Linn.

D. Antarcticus, C. Antarcticus, Auct.; Falkland Island Aguara.

D. silvestris, Nob., Aguara of the Woods; Chien des bois.

D. fulvipes. Vulpes fulvipes, Martin; Culpew molina.

"Section X—Cerdocyon, Aguara Foxes. Form of foxes; very large brushes; rather low on the legs; nose very pointed; pupils vertically contractile, with difficulty; fur soft, abundant; livery mixtures of greys, buff, white, and black; tip of tail black; subnocturnal; placable. (It is difficult to know what Hamilton-Smith means by 'placable.' An archaic meaning was—peaceful, quiet—and another meaning was—tractable—which hardly seems to fit. M.R.)

Cerdocyon mesoleucus

C. Guaraxa

C. Azarae, C. cancrivorous is the young.

C. Magellanicus

"All the foregoing sections present species more or less liable to intermix with domestic dogs."

On the last point, Hamilton-Smith was obviously wrong, as will be explained in the chapter: Thoughts on Canid Reproduction. But I think that the above will do much to explain what follows. There were many variations of the chief species. But they defy individual description without becoming confusing.

In concluding this introduction, we have seen that it is the fox which is the sly and cunning animal of Europe; that its place is largely taken by the coyote in North America; and by the jackal in Asia and Africa. It is strange then to find that the false foxes of South America appear to be sly and cunning in native folklore but that, for the most part, they are worsted in battles of wit with the other animals. This will be shown in the Lore of the South American Foxes.

25 The Lore of the Argentine Foxes

THE BRITISH NATURALIST, W. H. Hudson, was born near Buenos Aires, Argentina in 1841. He wandered the pampas until he was 33, observing wildlife, taking notes, and living with Gauchos and Indians. His most famous books are *Green Mansions* and *A Hind in Hyde Park,* published after his death in 1922. But one of his most fascinating works was *A Naturalist in La Plata,* published in 1891. In that book appears his Biography of the viscacha. This is a small rodent, weighing about 15 pounds and about 20 inches in length. It belongs to the same family as the chinchilla.

The viscachas built villages which are called viscacheras. They are of interest to us here because the viscacha allowed its underground homes to be shared with various other creatures, among them a fox. To understand the fox's place in the story, it is necessary to know something of the viscachera which was a permanent town or settlement for the rodents. (Hudson spelled the animal Vizcacha; the village, vizcachera.)

"The village is composed of a dozen to 15 burrows or mouths; for one entrance often serves for two or more distinct holes . . . the entire village covering an area of from one hundred to two hundred square feet of ground.

"The burrows vary greatly in extent; and usually in a vizcachera there are several that, at a distance of from four to six feet from the entrance open into large circular chambers. From these chambers other burrows diverge in all directions . . . A vast amount of loose earth is thus brought up, and forms a very irregular mound, fifteen to thirty inches above the surrounding level . . .

"It will afford some conception of the numbers of these vizcacheras on the settled pampas when I say that, in some directions, a person might ride five hundred miles and never advance half a mile without seeing one or more of them."

Hudson goes into fascinating detail on the vizcacheras, and then lists all the other creatures which join the vizcàchas—several varieties of birds, a weasel, and a number of insects. But it is the fox which interests us, as it did Hudson.

"The fox takes up his residence in a vizcachera, and succeeds, after some quarrelling (manifested in snarls, growls, and other subterranean warlike sounds) in ejecting the rightful owners of one of the burrows, which forthwith becomes his. Certainly the vizcachas are not much injured by being compelled to relinquish the use of one of their kennels for a season or permanently; for, if the locality suits him, the fox remains with them always.

"Soon they grow accustomed to the unwelcome stranger; he is quiet and unassuming in demeanour, and often in the evening sits on the mound in their company, until they regard him with the same indifference they do the burrowing owl. But in spring, when the young vizcachas are large enough to leave their cells, then the fox makes them his prey; and if it is a bitch fox, with a family of eight or nine young to provide for, she will grow so bold as to hunt her helpless quarry from hole to hole, and do battle with the old ones, and carry off the young in spite of them, so that all the young animals in the village are eventually destroyed. Often when the young foxes are large enough to follow their mother, the whole family take leave of the vizcachera where such cruel havoc has been made to settle in another, there to continue their depradations. But the fox has ever a relentless foe in man, and meets with no end of bitter persecutions; it is consequently much more abundant in desert or thinly settled districts than in such as are populous, so that in these the check the vizcachas receive from the foxes is not appreciable."

Hudson gives us an unforgettable picture of the fox which we call the Crab-eating Fox, but which was known in his day as Azara's dog (Canis azarae).

"Amongst mammals our common fox (Canis azarae) and one of the opossums (Didelphys azarae) are strangely subject to the death simulating swoon. For it does indeed seem strange that animals so powerful, fierce, and able to inflict such terrible injury with their teeth should also possess this safeguard, apparently more suited to weak inactive creatures that cannot resist or escape from an enemy and to animals very low down in the scale of being.

"When a fox is caught in a trap or run down by dogs he fights savagely at first, but by-and-by relaxes his efforts, drops on the ground, and apparently yields up the ghost. The deception is so well carried out, that dogs are constantly taken in by it, and no one, not previously acquainted with this clever trickery of nature, but would at once pronounce the creature dead, and worthy of some praise for having perished in so brave a spirit. Now, when in this condition of feigning death, I am quite sure that the animal does not altogether lose consciousness. It is exceedingly difficult to discover any evidence of life in the opossum; but when one withdraws a little way from the feigning fox, and watches him very attentively, a slight opening of the eye may be detected; and finally, when left to himself, he does not recover and start up like an animal that has been stunned, but slowly and cautiously raises his head first, and only gets up when his foes are at a safe distance. Yet I have seen gauchos, who are very cruel to animals, practise the most barbarous experiments on a captive fox without being able to rouse it into exhibiting any sign of life.

"This has greatly puzzled me, since, if death-feigning is simply a cunning habit, the animal could not suffer itself to be mutilated without wincing. I can only believe that the fox, though not insensible, as its behaviour on being left to itself appears to prove, yet has its body thrown by extreme terror into that benumbed condition which simulates death, and during which it is unable to feel the tortures practiced upon it.

"The swoon sometimes actually takes place before the animal has been touched, and even when the exciting cause is at a considerable distance. I was once riding with a gaucho, when we saw, on the open level ground before us, a fox, not yet fully grown, standing still and watching our approach. All at once it dropped, and when we came up to the spot was lying stretched out, with eyes closed, and apparently dead. Before passing on my companion who said it was not the first time he had seen such a thing, lashed it vigorously with his whip for some moments, but without producing the slightest effect."

Alas for both the foxes and the viscachas, by the time of the third edition of his book in 1912, massive attempts had been made to wipe out both the foxes and the viscachas. Today, nearly one hundred years since Hudson wandered the pampas, both are extremely rare.

In her book, *Latin American Tales,* Rand McNally, Genevieve Barlow has charmingly retold two stories of the Argentine foxes. These stories indicate a different conception of the intelligence of the foxes from that in Europe. In Europe, the fox was the slyest, most cunning of all the animals, always outwitting them. But in South America, the fox only thinks it is cunning. And in a battle of wits, it is the fox which is outwitted.

But, as in the great fables of Asia and India, of the Panchatantra and Aesop, the stories are meant to carry a moral lesson for people. Genevieve Barlow has written those lessons for children. But moral lessons are really designed never to be forgotten during all the stages of our lives.

The Lazy Fox
A Tale Told in Argentina

There was once a fox who was known throughout the land for being a lazy scamp as well as a scheming rascal. He was too lazy to work on his own little farm, and he was so scheming nobody would work for him. The fox was as full of tricks as a fig is of seeds.

One morning he looked at his barren fields and sighed, "Unless my fields are planted, I shall go hungry. But what can I do?"

He sat on his haunches and thought and thought. Finally, an idea popped into his head.

"I'll get this slow, stupid armadillo to plant my fields for me, and I'll promise him a share of the crops. Of course," he added slyly, "it will be a very SMALL share."

So the fox hurried down the path to the home of his neighbor. He found him sitting under a quebracho tree, telling stories to his children.

"Good day, friend armadillo," the fox called. "I have been thinking about you this morning, and I want to help you."

"Help me?" asked the armadillo, not able to believe his ears.

"Yes, indeed. Your ground is rocky and poor. Why don't you plant on my good land? I will ask only a small share of the crop as payment."

"That is very generous of you," the armadillo replied.

Now the armadillo knew he was no match for the cunning fox, and suspected a trick, but he did want to grow food on that rich soil.

"You may choose whatever you want to plant," urged the fox, "and I will take only half of it."

"That is fair enough," said the armadillo slowly.

"Better yet," suggested the fox, swishing his bushy tail, "I'll take only the part of the crop that grows beneath the soil. You may have all that grows above the ground."

"That is more than fair," the armadillo agreed.

Early the next morning, the armadillo and his family got busy in the fields. By the time the fox sauntered past, they were well along with their work. The fox was pleased to see how well his scheme was working, but he never bothered to ask what crop was being planted.

Raindrops fell on the dark, thirsty earth. Warm fingers of the sun reached down to the fields, caressing the new plants. How they grew! At last it was time to harvest the crop.

The armadillo brought his entire family to help him. And what a fine field of wheat they harvested! By the time the lazy fox went out to get his share, all that remained were the tasteless roots.

He was not only very angry, but he was very hungry too. Hurrying over to the farm of the armadillo, he found him resting under his favorite tree, looking sleek and contented.

"You made a terrible blunder," the fox shouted at his neighbor. "I cannot eat roots! Surely you know that the good part of the wheat grows above the ground. But I forgive you. Next season we will work together again. Then what is below the soil will by yours, and I shall take what grows above."

"It seems a fair bargain," the armadillo said. "Do you want to choose the crop?"

"No, but you must choose it wisely. Just let me know when the food is ready to eat."

The next season the armadillo planted potatoes. Again the crop was large, but the fox could not eat the tops, which were above ground and lay withering in the sun.

He went to the farm of his neighbor. "Last season I thought you made a stupid mistake. But now I believe you are tricking me. I cannot eat the vines of the potato plants."

The armadillo squirmed in his suit of armor, and remained silent.

"I have made a great sacrifice to help you," the fox continued, "but you never think of me when you plant your crop. See how thin and weak I am."

"It is true that you are thin, but your coat fits you much better that way."

The fox glared at him. "We are going to try another plan. Next season, I shall take the tops of the plants as well as what grows beneath the soil. You may take what grows in the middle of the plants."

The armadillo remained silent.

"It is only right," added the fox, "That I have a larger share next year, because I have had nothing of the first two crops."

At last the armadillo replied. "Well, it seems a fair enough bargain." And he agreed.

The fox went happily up the path, sure that he could not be tricked again.

When planting time came again, the armadillo planted corn. The crop was large, with ears full and tender, but they grew in the middle of the stalk. There was nothing left for the fox but roots and husks.

The armadillo and his family were munching on the tempting ears of corn when they saw the fox running down the path toward them. His bushy tail trailed straight out behind him.

"You are just in time for a feast," greeted the armadillo. "Sit down and have a roasted ear and we shall talk of next season's crop."

"We shall not! For three seasons, you have tricked me."

The armadillo blinked his heavy eyelids. "I am sorry, but I gave you the part of the crop you asked for."

The fox looked hungrily at the corn, but he didn't sit down with his neighbors. Instead he stared at the armadillo, wondering why he had ever been stupid enough to call him stupid.

"Next year I shall plant my crop and keep all of it." With that the fox went back up the path, his tail dragging in the dust.

The armadillo reached for another ear of corn, and seated himself under the quebracho tree. He was laughing so merrily that he had to hang on to his bony armor to keep it from cracking.

The Fox Who Wanted to Whistle
A Tale Told in Argentina

More than anything else in the world the fox wanted to whistle like the partridge. Every day he leaned back against his den wall to practice. He pursed his lips together and blew his breath between his sharp teeth. Out came a whooshing sound from the front and sides of his mouth. Again and again he tried, often taking such deep breaths that his chest bellowed out like a furry balloon.

Now, although the sound he made was not at all pleasant, the fox smiled to himself broadly and exclaimed, "How well I am learning!"

One day as he was giving himself a whistling lesson, a puma passed by.

"Good day, friend fox," he said, "What is wrong? Are you sick?"

The fox was highly indignant.

"No, I am not sick!" he fairly shouted. "Can't you see I am only practicing?"

"What are you practicing?" asked the puma, who had meanwhile climbed a nearby tree.

"Whistling," replied the fox. "Listen to this."

He took a deep, deep, breath and opened his mouth, so one could barely see his teeth. He lifted his sharp muzzle skyward and let loose such a horrible sound that the puma lay back his ears and hunched in his head.

"You are a creature of many talents . . ." began the puma tactfully. Then from the safety of his perch, he laughed at the fox and added, ". . . but whistling isn't one of them!"

The hair on the fox's back bristled. As soon as he regained his composure, he answered the puma with a confident air, "Oh yes it is!

Some day I am going to whistle like the partridge. She has the most beautiful whistle of any bird in the forest."

"Then why don't you ask her to teach you?" asked the puma. "But you'll have to promise not to eat her," he warned. "You know how much you like partridge meat."

The fox nodded. "Yes, I am most fond of the bird—especially if it's in my stomach—but this time I have something more important on my mind than food. I must learn to whistle."

Without another word, the fox left the puma and went off in search of the partridge.

As the fox stalked the woods, the partridge saw him coming through the thicket and flew into a bush to hide. However, the fox saw her and called in the most gentle voice he could muster. "Don't be afraid, little partridge. I promise never to harm you or your family again if you will teach me to whistle as beautifully as you do."

Now the partridge was proud of her whistle and pleased that anyone—even a fox—would want to imitate her. Nevertheless, she was cautious, remembering the many times he had tried to catch her.

"I'd gladly teach you, Mr. Fox, if I were sure you would keep your promise," said the foolish bird.

"Indeed I will," replied the fox. "Now let's begin the lesson at once."

The partridge flew several circles around the fox's head before she gained enough courage to land next to him. She peered at him closely for the first time.

"Well," she exclaimed, "no wonder you can't whistle! your mouth is much too long. I'll have to sew it closed along each side to make it the right size for whistling."

"Sew up my mouth!" shouted the fox.

The bird flew back into the bush. She called in a quaking voice, "It will only hurt a little."

"Come back then and do it!" commanded the fox, "for I must learn to whistle."

"Will you be patient and hold still?" she asked in a frightened voice.

"I'll do just as you say," answered the fox meekly.

Using a feather from her underwing for a needle, and a strong shoot of grass for thread, the partridge began to sew. She darned carefully with cross-stitches, making them small and tight. When only a ring-sized opening remained, she bit off the thread with her sharp beak and said, "Now I think your mouth is just right for whistling. Try it Mr. Fox."

The fox released his breath. Such a fine, beautiful whistle came forth that he leaped and danced for joy.

"Good! Good!" cried the partridge happily. "Soon you will be able to whistle as well as I do!"

"I can do that already," mumbled the fox through his clenched teeth, for he was unable to speak very well with such a small mouth. And he continued his whistling.

The partridge was dismayed by the fox's vanity and hurt by his ingratitude. "If you are doing so well by yourself," she said bravely, "you no longer need me around." And she started to fly away.

Immediately the fox forgot his promise. All he could see was a bird on the wing. Without thinking, he grabbed for the partridge with his mouth. Rip-rip-rip went all the stitches. Not a single one remained.

The partridge escaped unhurt, but not so the fox. His mouth was sore and bleeding. Worse yet, his hope of learning to whistle was gone forever.

He crept back to his den and lay in a dark corner. All he could think about was his puffy lips and empty stomach. He was miserable.

He covered his mouth with his large bushy tail and heaved a mournful sigh through his nose.

Never again did the fox try to whistle, and never again did a partridge go close to a fox.

There are two world renowned brothers named Durrell—Lawrence the novelist, and Gerald the wild animal collector, great wildlife authority, and the author of some fascinating books dealing with his adventures. But Gerald's wife, Jacquie, is an equally capable author. It is from her book, *Intimate Relations* that we take this story of a pampas fox. The scene is Puerto Casada on the Bolivian-Brazilian border. Stein & Day published the book.

"The next addition was a small grey Pampas Fox, whom we called, not very originally I regret to say, Foxy. He again had been found by an Indian and kept as a pet. When he came to us he could

not have been more than about three months old. These little foxes
are charming and not only look like dogs, being the size of a terrier,
but behave very like them. Foxy certainly displayed none of the
more unpleasant characteristics of the fox family. Neat and slender
in build, he had a most ingratiating grin and, when anything
obviously pleased him, would fold back his top lip and show his teeth
in the most idiotic manner. Here again, we decided to keep him on a
lead rather than put him into a cage, for he was perfectly tame and
friendly. We used the old-fashioned method of a ring threaded on a
wire stretched between two posts, for in this way, he would get a
tremendous amount of exercise and have a large area to roam in. At
night, we kept him in a box which we filled with dried grass.

"Every morning, when released from the box, he would greet us
with delight, leaping, bounding, and wagging his tail. We had to be
careful how we held him, because he was so overcome with seeing us
again after all that dreadful length of time that he could not really
contain himself, and we were quite likely to be inundated by a
deluge of saliva at one end and steaming urine at the other. His two
passions in life, we soon discovered, were chickens and cigarette
butts. The former addiction was quite natural, of course, in a fox or
indeed in a dog. If, as happened on several occasions, one or two of
Paula's fowls happened to come by our enclosure, he would crouch
down ready to pounce on them, ears back and tail swishing from
side to side. The stupid hens, of course, did not realize that a
possible enemy was close by and often came too close, whereupon he
would leap at them and send them scurrying hysterically back to
where they should rightfully be. He was obviously amused by all this
uproar because he would turn around, look at us, and give us one of
his fatuous grins.

"The cigarette butt addiction was more worrying. I did not
smoke but Gerry and all the Indians did and were apt to dispose of
their cigarette ends wherever they happened to be when they
stopped smoking. Not thinking that an animal would crave cigarette
butts, they took no precautions to keep them away from Foxy. On
finding the butts Foxy would devour them with great eagerness but
also with a weird expression of distaste on his face. Then would
follow what could only have been a most uncomfortable half-hour of
violent coughing, at the end of which he would have a very long
drink of his water and be ready for any other butt that might fall.

"Nothing we could do could break the habit until, on one dreadful day, Nemesis struck. Carelessly Gerry, who was making an intricate bird cage, put down his cigarettes, not realizing that Foxy could quite easily get at them. Before we could do anything, Foxy indeed not only found them but had polished off the whole packet. I think by this time Foxy's poor stomach had decided that it really must do something drastic to prevent this constant invasion of tobacco, and so it reacted with appalling violence. Seemingly every shred of tobacco was regurgitated, as indeed was everything else that Foxy had eaten that day. The poor animal was so weak and exhausted by this eruption that even chickens would walk right past him without the slightest twitch of his nose. We starved him for the rest of that day but relented sufficiently by the evening to offer him a bit of meat and two raw eggs. Then by way of an experiment, Gerry offered his cigarette packet to Foxy. The cure was dramatically effective; he backed hurriedly away, sneezing madly. Never again was Foxy tempted by the dreadful weed."

26 The Biology of the South American False Foxes

Crab-eating Fox

In the 1700s, a famed Spanish naturalist went to South America to study and catalog the plants and animals of the continent, especially that portion belonging to Spain. His name was Felix de Azara. In time, one of the foxes he described became known as Azara's fox, or Azara's dog. However, the animal is closer to the true fox than to a wild dog. Its scientific name is Cerdocyon thous, but it is generally known as the Crab-eating Fox. According to one tradition, the first of the foxes to be dissected had a crab in its stomach. Another story is that foxes living along the sea shore have been seen digging up crabs, or capturing those moving along the shore. The shore living foxes are also known to dig up turtle eggs and to prey upon the newly hatched turtlets as they struggle to reach the comparative sanctuary of the sea.

The Crab-eating Fox has an average head and body length of about 25 inches. Its bushy tail is about 11 inches long. Weights range between 11 and 17 pounds. The predominant color is gray with black stripes across the middle of the back, and with cheek areas darkening. The upper side of the tail has black stripes and the tail tip is black.

C. thous has a very great range. It can be found in the rain forests and jungles of Colombia and Venezuela, in the jungle areas

Crab-eating Dogs, Dusicyon thous. *San Diego Zoo photo*

Andean Wild Dog or Culpeo Fox. *San Diego Zoo photo*

Loveliest of St. George Mivart's drawings is this picture of ''Azara's Dog,'' now called Cerdocyon Thous.

of Brazil, in parts of Bolivia at high altitudes, and in the northern parts of Uruguay, Paraguay and Argentina. Despite its name, it feeds chiefly on small rodents, insects, lizards, eggs and fruits. Its adaptability to a wide variety of environmental conditions has helped to make it the most populous of the South American canids.

The Crab-eating Fox is thought by some to be solitary, by others to live in pairs. Whether a true pair bond is ever set up is not known. In northern Argentina, mating takes place in late winter. After a gestation period of about 62 days, litters of four to six puppies are born. Whelping usually takes place in the abandoned den of some other animal. In Venezuela and the low lands of Colombia matings often take place in either summer or winter. Puppies are born either in the spring or the fall. It is not known, however, whether a female comes into heat twice a year, or whether there is simply a variance, with the heat period in some coming in winter and in others in summer. Nor is it known to what extent both parents raise the pups and teach them to hunt. Mortality among the pups is high. The fox is nocturnal, and spends the day in dens or among rocks. The fur is of no value, but none the less, the animal suffers from intense hunting.

Paraguayan Fox

This fox is known scientifically as Dusicyon gymnocerus. It is closely related to the Culpeo fox, and it has an even greater range. It has been found at the Strait of Magellan and as far north as the Equator, on the pampas, the deserts, in forest areas, and as high on the mountain slopes as 13,000 feet. In some respects, it is reminiscent both of the American Red Fox and the Arctic Fox. Its skull and foreface are similar to the Red Fox, and whereas the Arctic Fox lives on lemmings for the most part, the Paraguayan Fox finds the cavy to be its primary food source. Americans know the cavy as the guinea pig. However, the Patagonian cavy is a very large guinea pig indeed, reaching a maximum length of two and a half feet. Since guinea pigs breed the year around, they normally supply the Paraguayan fox with plenty of food. Both hunter and prey are nocturnal.

When the supply of guinea pigs fails, the Paraguayan Fox falls back upon mice, rats, and other creatures which live near cultivated areas. In tropical areas, they eat fruits, berries, insects, and sometimes are able to catch fish. In the chapter, the Lore of the South American Foxes, W. H. Hudson tells some fascinating facts about the habits of this fox.

Its coloration is gray, with some hairs being black tipped. Some have a medial black stripe on the back, others not. The legs are red-yellow, and the paws are yellow to white, turning to brown at the pads. There are gray-black facial markings, particularly on the cheeks. There is a black spot at the base of the tail and the tail tip is black.

The gestation period is about 62 days. The female either digs a den or moves into the den of other animals. She gives birth to litters of four to five, sometimes more. They are born at the end of the southern spring, in November or December. At about two months of age they are large enough to begin short hunts near the den. The mother is the teacher. The father takes no part in rearing the young. And, except when she is nursing and training her litter, the mother is solitary. The young foxes, however, stay near the mother during the first year, and learn the mating code from older foxes.

The Andean Wild Dog—Culpeo Fox

This animal demonstrates the confusion that surrounds so many of the South American animals. Scientists call it a fox (Dusicyon culpaeus) for want of a better name for it. But within its range—the foothills of the Andes—it is known as a wild dog. It is found at elevations as high as 15,000 feet in Argentina and Chile. Except for the Maned Wolf, it is the largest of the South American canids.

It may reach a total body length of three feet, and its tail is correspondingly long, being up to 16 inches. A weight of about 28 pounds has been found in a full grown male. It is an extraordinarily hardy animal, since it ranges from Ecuador south to the Straits of Magellan and is found in both the hostile deserts of Chile and Tierra Del Fuego.

In the sheep grazing areas its diet includes sheep and rabbits, the latter having been introduced from Europe. Before the sheep and rabbits came it lived on small rodents, as it still does in the wilder ranges of its territory. The major body color is gray with black stripes on the middle of the back. The gray turns slightly reddish on the flanks. There is a black spot at the base of the tail. The muzzle is unusually long, slender and fox-like.

The gestation period is about 62 days. Litters average five or more, and are born in the southern spring between October and December, depending upon how far south the fox is living. As with other wild canids the pups are heavily parasitized, and pup mortality probably reaches 50 per cent. The species is heavily hunted by sheep herders. It is nocturnal, and is able to survive in heavy snow areas where it is possible for it to find animals killed or dying in the snow.

Two other members of Dusicyon are the Peruvian Fox, D. sechurae; and the Pampas Fox, D. griseus. They are somewhat smaller than the Culpeo fox. The Peruvian Fox lives on the western slopes of the Andes along the cliffs overlooking the Pacific. Its hunting range is small, from the sea coast inland. The Pampas Fox has a fairly wide range, from the beaches of the South Pacific to those of the South Atlantic. Its diet includes crabs, small fish caught in tide pools, and small rodents which can be found on the grasslands.

The Maned Wolf

People who have seen most of the world's wild canids are apt to claim that the Maned Wolf of southern South America is the most beautiful of them all. To be sure, it is neither wolf nor dog. And though its head and ears are quite fox-like, it differs so greatly from all the foxes that one is at a loss to give it any but a very distinctive name. This it has, at least in some parts of South America, where it is called the aguará guazu. However, its scientific name is Chrysocyon brachyurus. Since it is so generally called the Maned Wolf, that is what it shall be called here.

What makes the Maned Wolf so distinguished a canid, apart

from its beautiful color, is its long legs. They are nearly twice as long as its body depth. And this is so even though the bottom of the chest reaches the elbows. Mature Maned Wolves weigh about 50 pounds. They are 32 inches tall at the withers. The head and body length is about 42 inches, and the tail, which reaches to the hock is more than 15 inches. One should qualify this by saying that the long hairs on a very bushy tail reach the hock joint. The tail tip is white.

The dominant color is a red-brown on the back and sides, though there is a blackish mane which gives the animal its name. In some the red is nearly a bright yellow, but there is always a beautiful sheen to the long coat. The legs darken about midway from the elbows, and are quite black at the feet. The muzzle is dark but lightens as it approaches the skull at eye level. There are lighter patches (eyebrows), and then the skull becomes reddish. The throat has a pure white patch. The large ears are carried erect or slightly to the sides. They are triangular with slightly rounded tips, white on the insides and red on the backs. The tail is bushy, has a white plume for about a third of its length, and the long hairs reach to the hock joints.

The Maned Wolf's gait is also remarkable. It paces. That is, it moves both feet forward at the same time on each side, instead of the more normal one-three-two-four gait. Many domestic dogs move in this way when walking slowly, but then switch to the other gait when moving faster. However, the Maned Wolf maintains the pacing gait even when moving swiftly. In galloping, its long legs permit the hind legs to hit the ground in front of the forelegs, as is the case with domestic dogs of the greyhound family. The long legs also give it remarkable agility in leaping over shrubs and bushes when chasing or being chased.

When moving at a fast pace, the Maned Wolf lowers its head until it is carried level with the top line of the back or even lower. It may also carry its head at that angle when studying the landscape. At other times the head is carried erect. The big ears help to give it great hearing powers, and it is believed to have very highly developed scenting powers as well.

The Maned Wolf is solitary, both in the wild and in zoos. Since it is a savannah animal, it has no enemies other than man. And man hunts it relentlessly, presumably because it is supposed to attack and steal calves and lambs. However, its dentition is peculairly altered so

Maned Wolf puppy. *Los Angeles Zoo photo by Gib Brush*

Maned Wolf. *Los Angeles Zoo photo by Sy Oskeroff*

that it approaches the fruit or vegetable eater in at least part of its molars. It is nocturnal in hunting habits.

During the mating season, a male and female come together and mate after an elaborate sex play. Copulation is much like that of the domestic dog. The pair stay together until the pups are at least partially reared. Gestation is 62 to 63 days, and four or five pups are whelped. The pups are blackish-gray at birth, and their legs are not especially long. Neither are their ears. Both legs and ears develop rapidly. As with the domestic dog, the muzzle is compressed at birth. Unlike the dog, the muzzle does not reach its full length until the pup is about a year old. As with all other wild canids, maned wolf pups are heavily parasitized. But since the pups have no enemies, other than man, mortality is less than with other wild canids, being only 30 to 40 percent.

There is little evidence that Maned Wolves actually are a threat to calves and sheep. Their diets in the wild are chiefly small rodents, insects, lizards and fruit. Surprisingly enough their long legs are not used for coursing, and at high speed they have little stamina. At a slow pace, they seem tireless. Men hunt them from horseback, partly as a sport. They are therefore in danger of extinction, and partly also because exploding population brings an intense demand for cultivated land, thus robbing the Maned Wolf of its habitat.

Many wild species face extinction unless they are saved by zoological parks. Yet the breeding and rearing of wild animals in captivity is very difficult, and in some cases has been a total failure. The San Antonio, Texas, Zoological Society has an excellent zoo, and enjoys unusual participation in its activities by its members. Its difficulty in rearing Maned Wolves is an excellent example of the frustration which so often accompanies attempts to breed wild animals.

Between 1971 and 1977, there were three whelpings. But only two pups from the last litter survived. However, two extensive Maned Wolf breeding and behavioral studies project are having more success. One is at San Diego's great wildlife park, and the other is at the National Zoological Society's endangered species facility at Front Royal, Virginia.

But now let us pick up the story as written by Jan Strother, supervisor of the Animal Health Center, for the Zoological Society's *News from the Zoo* publication.

"Then on October 31, the rains came . . . and the wind . . . and the cold . . . and the Maned Wolf den was flooded. Only one baby could be seen on the TV screen, so the mother was removed, and—the first good news all day—two cold, wet, but very much alive babies were found shivering in the wet hay. They were immediately transferred to the Animal Health Center.

"After a warm water bath and massage to get temperature and circulation back to normal, the two pups, both females, were placed in an infant incubator, and feedings were started with a formula of goat's milk with vitamin and mineral supplements. At five days of age each pup weighed five grams. Their eyes were closed as well as their ears. Their fur was a solid black except for white tips to their tails. To tell the truth, they looked for all the world like any mixed breed shepherd or Border Collie type of puppy—so much so that nightmare thoughts of fence-jumping feral dogs momentarily occurred to us, but we really knew it couldn't be. Could it? No one, for some reason, has ever mentioned in any literature that baby Maned Wolves are black with white tail tips. For the record, they are!

"After virtually accusing our poor youngsters of being hybrids, we compounded the indignity by naming them 'Blackie' and 'Brownie' to distinguish one from the other. Brownie was brownish-black, and Blackie was plain black, so we gave in to the temptation and named them accordingly. Besides, it's a nice common touch for such rare and special animals.

"By two weeks of age, both pups had doubled their weight, had eyes and ears open and were beginning to teethe. At three weeks they were moved to a large, roomy incubator (2½ feet by 3 feet by 5 feet long). The extra space allowed them to begin normal puppy rough-housing and vocalizing. Each began to develop distinct personality characteristics. Soon they were eating Zupreem carnivore diet in addition to the milk formula and were losing their puppyish features. They were beginning to be little Maned Wolves. By six weeks of age Blackie and Brownie graduated to a nursery pen outside the incubator which could better accommodate their energetic 'rassle and chase' activities. At this stage, although they were friendly and affectionate to Health Center personnel, our Maned Wolves would flatten their ears and growl menacingly if approached by strangers.

"At almost three months, Blackie and Brownie each weighed

approximately 14 pounds. They had now exchanged their fuzzy baby fur for sleek chestnut and black coats, their ears were large and pointed and alert, and the long slender legs that so readily distinguish the species from any other were very evident. Their luxuriously furred tails wagged incessantly for their friends, but they showed the characteristic shyness of their breed toward strangers.

"Soon they will leave the nursery for a home down in the zoo, and after that, one or both will probably go to another zoo on loan or trade so that we may improve our breeding potential by introducing an unrelated animal into our group."

(In August of 1978, an exchange of females was made with Lincoln Park Zoo of Chicago, Ill.—M.R.)

The Bush Dog

If the Maned Wolf is the most beautiful of the South American canids, then the Bush Dog is its opposite. The former has a beautiful red coat and black mane, the latter a rather dull brown and short coat. The Maned Wolf has extremely long legs, the Bush Dog remarkably short ones. The Maned Wolf has a long, fox-like bushy tail, the latter the shortest tail of any canid. The Maned Wolf has a long, sharp, fox-like muzzle and large fox-like ears; the Bush Dog a short, very powerful muzzle, and very short ears. The Maned Wolf is a solitary hunter; the Bush Dog hunts in packs. The former is nocturnal; the Bush Dog has eyes adapted for 24 hour hunting, and often hunts day or night.

The Bush Dog is an excellent swimmer and an accomplished diver. It can catch coypus, or other swimming creatures, as well as those which try to escape by taking to water. Females come into heat twice a year whereas most other canids, except for domestic dogs, have an oestral cycle only once a year. Its scientific name is Speothos venaticus. It has only 38 teeth, and thus differs from all other South American canids.

Much of what is known about Bush Dogs comes from their lives in zoological parks. That is because they live in inaccessible places, in

Bush Dog puppies (Speothos venaticus). *San Diego Zoo photo*

Guiana Bush Dog. S. venaticus venaticus. *San Diego Zoo photo*

deep jungle areas, along the edges of swamps and rivers, from
Panama to the coastal areas of Venezuela and Brazil. The head and
body length of mature animals is about 26 inches, but the tail is less
than six inches long. Bush Dogs weigh between 11 and 15 pounds.
Their bodies are brown, darkening on the legs starting at the elbows.
Their heads and necks are a lighter, reddish brown.

Bush Dogs live in packs of about a dozen, and are led by a
dominant male. Even though they do hunt during the day in areas
where there are human beings, they are apt to hide underground in
dens during the day. For this reason, they are seldom seen unless
one goes deep into the jungles.

It is believed that they mark out territory for themselves as do
other canids. Males urinate and mark territory in the usual canid
manner. But females, particularly when in season, back up to trees,
climb upward with their hind legs until they are virtually standing
on their heads, and then urinate on the tree. Meanwhile an
interested male will simply raise his leg and urinate as dogs do.

At least in zoos, Bush Dogs have a strong pair bond. At first it
was difficult to breed them in captivity and even more difficult to
keep them alive. Then it was discovered at the Frankfort, Germany,
Zoo that the mother would not take proper care of the pups unless
the male was with her. The first litter born there in 1969 did not get
proper care from the mother. Five of six survived but were weak
and sickly, and one of them was raised by a keeper.

Of six born the next year, only one survived. When the father
was allowed to be in with the mother, the remaining pup thrived. It
was found that the male took a part in raising the pup by bringing
both mother and pup bits of food. After this experience, other zoos
kept the mated pair together, and the pups had a normal survival
rate. This is the only evidence available to indicate pair bonding in
the wild. But it does seem to show that the bond is very intense. The
gestation period is about 62 days and litters average six.

The Small-eared Zorro

The rarest of all the world's canids is probably the Small-eared
Zorro, Atelocynus microtis. Zorro is the Spanish word for fox. In

Brazil the animal is known as Cachorro-de-ma-de-orelhas curtas which, in Portuguese, means the short-eared bush dog. It is so little known that a mammologist who recently went to South America to try to collect some told me that he had difficulty finding anyone who had even heard of the animal. His mission was therefore a failure.

Since 1882 when the London Zoo first displayed one, a dozen or more have been on exhibition. Yet almost nothing is known of the animal's life in its native environment. By far the best study ever made of the Small-eared Zorro was made by Philip Hershkovitz, curator of mammology at the Chicago Zoological Society's Brookfield Park. Mr. Hershkovitz's study was published in February, 1961 in *Fieldiana-Zoology* by the Chicago Natural History Museum. Mr. Hershkovitz had the benefit of notes made by Señor Jorge Hernandez macho, a Colombian mammologist.

Señor Hernandez sent a Small-eared Zorro to Brookfield in 1957. This one was a male, and a female arrived the following year. So far as is known no other zoo in the world has been able to exhibit or study a pair. I am grateful to the Chicago Natural History Museum for permission to quote at length from Mr. Hershkovitz's report.

Specimens of the Small-eared Zorro have been captured in Brazil, and in most of the Amazon basin, which includes Peru and Ecuador. The northward range extends into Colombia, and probably Venezuela. It is found at near sea level to slightly more than 3000 feet on mountain slopes. The body, including the head is up to 35 inches in length, and the tail in large specimens is nearly 12 inches long. Average weight is about 20 pounds. This means that the zorro has a long body and proportionately short legs. The tail is curved at the tip and is curved back against the outer side of a hind leg.

The tail deserves special mention because the animal seems to wag only the latter half of it. Moreover, it can erect the hairs when excited. Thus, some of the natives have named it the "flag-tailed wild dog." The hair is gray to brown with black stripes on the back and tail. The gray turns to dark brown or black on the lower part of the limbs. The dog's sleek pelage caused Hershkovitz to suggest that it may spend a great deal of time in the water, or that it is especially adapted to life in rain forests.

The Small-eared Zorro has the smallest ears of any canid. Hershkovitz writes "the upper canines are impressively long, their

Small-eared Zorro, Atelocynus microtis. *San Diego Zoo photo*

St. George Mivart's drawing of a Small-eared Zorro.

tips projecting outside the closed mouth for about half a centime-
ter . . . Another feature . . . is the remarkably bright glow of his
eyes in dim light. In the bright beam of a hand torch the eyes shine
with a pale green brilliance. The normal color of the iris is hazel."
The tapetum is the brilliant layer, or reflection blanket, which
gathers light and which makes the eyes of nocturnal animals visible
by reflected light at night. The Small-eared Zorro may therefore be
unusually well adapted for night hunting, and it may also have
better vision than other canids in the comparatively dim light in the
daytime on the jungle floor. Hershkovitz believes the animal to have
a more lithe, graceful, catlike gait than any other canid.

The Brookfield female was one third larger than the male, her
body was more lithe, and her head heavier, with the muzzle
proportionately thicker and longer. However, at least with this
captive pair, the male dominated. He became quite tame and
playful, did not bite, and eventually rolled over so that his belly
could be scratched. This caused him to squeal with delight. But the
female was always hostile and would snarl continuously when being
observed. The male had a strong musk odor which he seemed able
to emit from his anal gland when frightened or excited. This was not
observed to the same extent in the female.

Nothing is known of the mating habits of the Small-eared
Zorro. The Chicago pair never mated. She was believed to have
come into heat but neither animal showed any real interest in
mating. So there is no available information as to the period of
gestation, the number of offspring in a litter, and the rearing habits
of the parents.

In concluding his report, Hershkovitz wrote:

"The Small-eared Zorro cannot be confused with other known
canids. It bears no close resemblance to any variety of domestic dog
or to wolf- or fox-like types of wild dogs. Its short ears and coat
pattern are unique; certain of its cranial characters, taken singly,
others in combination, are diagnostic; in the live animal the gait and
relaxed stance or posture are distinctive . . ."

In response to the author's request, Donald J. Kuenzer, curator
at Cleveland's Metroparks Zoological Park, asked the International
Species Inventory System for a list of zoological parks which
presently have Small-eared Zorros. He received this reply, dated
April 4, 1978: "There are currently *NO* specimens listed by any ISIS

participants." This, then, is another indication that A. microtis is close to extinction.

The Brazilian Fox

This Brazilian Fox has been given an individual genus, Lycalopex vetulus. It is found in the great farming areas of Brazil where it enjoys capturing an occasional chicken. It also eats small rodents, insects, fruits and berries, and such birds as it is able to catch. It has a body length of about 25 inches, and a bushy tail of 11 inches.

The basic coloration is gray, turning to light yellow on the legs. The throat is white. There is a black spot above the anal gland and the tip of the tail is black. Gestation period is about 60 days. Litters are small, two to four being average. The species is solitary, and unlike most foxes, active during the day. Males take little or no part in raising the litter. The mother whelps usually in dens deserted by other animals. The pups leave the den at about six weeks, but remain close for several weeks longer. They then begin short hunting forays led by their mother. It is believed that they mature at about ten months, but they probably do not mate until nearly two years of age. One litter a year is born, usually in September.

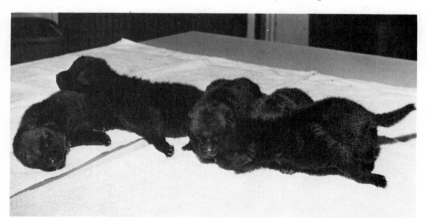

Newly whelped Maned Wolf puppies.
Los Angeles Zoo photo by Gib Brush

Raccoon Dogs (Nyctereutes procyonoides), Tama
Zoological Park, Tokyo, Japan. *Photo by Masaru Saito*

27 The Lore of the Raccoon Dog

THE RACCOON DOG plays a large role in Japanese folklore. As explained in the biology of Nyctereutes procyonoides, this canid and the badger have often been confused, even by people who should have known better. At least one English-Japanese dictionary translates anaguma, tanuki, and mujina all as badger, whereas a more concise dictionary translates tanuki as Raccoon Dog, and mujina as being the name for the animal in some parts of Japan.

If one is working with English translations, therefore, there is some difficulty in guessing whether the animal called a badger in the story is truly a badger or a Raccoon Dog. But we have seen from the translation of J. Ohno's work by Junko Kimura that both tanuki and mujina refer to the Raccoon Dog. Miss Kimura who grew up hearing the tales from older people, says: "Those old fairy tales which I heard as a girl all refer to the Raccoon Dog, the tanuki." Another writer also says that most of the folklore and fairy tales deal with the tanuki.

All authorities agree that the animal is a "humorous prankster, seldom doing evil, occasionally doing its human friends a good turn." One of its pranks is to wait until there is moonlight, and then to assume the shape of a moon on earth. Another is to sit up and beat a tattoo on its chest. When very fat, the booming of its big chest can be heard at a great distance. Another trick for a moonlight night was to squat by the side of the road. It then lowered its head between its black legs, and open its mouth. Passers by were thus startled into thinking they were seeing the pubic triangle and opened vulva of a partial woman. As they approached, the Raccoon Dog disappeared in the dark, presumably laughing all the way home.

Miss Kimura has retold for us here the famous story of one such prankster.

The Prank of the Mujina (Raccoon Dog)

Many years ago, there was a road along a stream in the city of Edo (the old Tokyo). There were no houses at all in the area. In those days, there were no street lights along the road. At night, very few people walked there because people said: "Don't walk along the road at night. A mujina lives there."

One night, an old man was walking along the road. In his hand he was holding a chochin (paper lantern). The man was on his way back to his home in Kyobashi. Then, by the stream, he saw a woman. She was crying. "Why, a woman at such a late hour of the night!" The old man could not understand it.

He went up to the crying woman and spoke to her. "What's the matter with you? What are you crying for?" The woman did not answer him, covering her face with a part of her beautiful kimono. "Oh, don't cry! Is there anything that I can do for you?" the man asked. But she did not say a word, still crying. Patiently the man went on. "Oh, listen to me. What's wrong with you? It seems to me that this is no place for a young lady like you at this late hour."

Now the woman slowly stood up, yet turning her back to the man. She still seemed to be crying. The old man gently put his hand on her shoulder and spoke to her encouragingly. "Now listen to me. Don't cry." Finally, the woman slowly turned to the old man, slowly taking away the kimono from her face. It had no eyes, no nose, and no mouth. He exclaimed and ran away. His paper lantern (chochin) went out.

The old man ran and ran, never looking back. At last in the darkness, he saw a light far away. He ran to it.

The light he saw was from a soba (noodle) stand by the road. The old man ran up to the stand and fell down at the feet of the soba man. Trembling nearly to death, he could not say a single word. The soba man, without looking at the old man, asked: "What's wrong with you, old man? Is anyone running after you?"

"N-no!"

"Oh, what surprised you so much, then?"

"O-only . . ."

"Well, some bad men?"

"Oh no. I . . . I saw a woman . . . by that stream . . . But I can't tell you!"

"Well, was her face like this?" said the soba man.

He turned his face to the old man. It looked like an egg. Just then the light went out.

One of the most famous stories is that of "The Accomplished and Lucky Tea-kettle." In 1871, A. B. Mitford (Lord Redesdale) recorded it. He, however, translated "tanuki" as "badger." Here we tell the story as he wrote it, but correcting it to Raccoon Dog as, according to our Japanese authorities, it should be. The text is from *Tales of Old Japan* as published by the Charles E. Tuttle Co, Rutland, Vt. and Tokyo, 1966. It begins, as all fairy stories, the world over, begin . . .

A long time ago, at a temple called Morinji, in the province of Joshiu, there was an old tea kettle. One day, when the priest of the temple was about to hang it over the hearth to boil the water for his tea, to his amazement, the kettle all of a sudden put forth the head and tail of a tanuki. "What a wonderful kettle, to come out all over fur!" The priest, thunderstruck, called in the novices of the temple to see the sight; and whilst they were stupidly staring, one suggesting one thing and another another, the kettle, jumping up in the air, began flying about the room. More astonished than ever, the priest and his pupils tried to pursue it; but no thief or cat was ever half so sharp as this wonderful tanuki-kettle.

At last, however, they managed to knock it down and secure it; and, holding it in with their united efforts, they forced it into a box, intending to carry it off and throw it away in some distant place, so that they might be no more plagued by the goblin. For this day their troubles were over; but, as luck would have it, the tinker who was in the habit of working for the temple called in, and the priest suddenly bethought him that it was a pity to throw the kettle away for nothing, and that he might as well get a trifle for it, no matter how small. So he brought out the kettle which had resumed its former shape and had got rid of its head and tail, and showed it to the tinker. When the tinker saw the kettle, he offered twenty copper coins for it, and the priest was only too glad to close the bargain and be rid of his troublesome piece of furniture. But the tinker trudged off home with his pack and his new purchase.

That night, as he lay asleep, he heard a strange noise near his pillow; so he peeped out from under the bedclothes, and there he saw the kettle that he had bought in the temple covered with fur, and walking about on four legs. The tinker started up in fright to see what it could all mean, when all of a sudden the kettle resumed its former shape. This happened over and over again, until at last the tinker showed the tea kettle to a friend of his, who said: "This is certainly an accomplished and lucky tea kettle. You should take it about as a show, with songs and accompaniments of musical instruments, and make it dance and walk on the tight rope."

The tinker, thinking this good advice, made arrangements with a showman, and set up an exhibition. The noise of the kettle's performances soon spread abroad, until even the princes of the land sent to order the tinker to come to them; and he grew rich beyond all his expectations. Even the princesses, too, and the great ladies of the court, took great delight in the dancing kettle, so that no sooner had it shown its tricks in one place than it was time for them to keep some other engagement. At last the tinker grew so rich that he took the kettle back to the temple, where it was laid up as a precious treasure, and worshipped as a saint.

We can only presume that since the lucky tea kettle-raccoon dog had reached sainthood, it lived happily ever after in true fairy tale fashion.

Two other stories which Lord Redesdale found deserve mention, one because it is so tender a story, and the other because it shows one aspect of the Raccoon Dog combined with the code of ethics of the ancient Samurai.

In the first, a poor priest "famous neither for learning nor for wisdom" lived alone in a small cottage, spending most of his time repeating the famous Buddhist prayer: "Save us, Eternal Buddha." Friendly people in the area gave him food and repaired his cottage when it began to fall apart.

One winter night, he heard a voice outside the door saying: "Your Reverence, Your Reverence." He found an old Raccoon Dog outside. It bowed in reverence and begged to be allowed to come in by the fire.

"Hitherto, sir, my lair has been in the mountains, and of snow or frost I have taken no heed; but now I am growing old, and this severe cold is more than I can bear. I pray you to let me enter and warm myself at the fire of your cottage, that I may live through this bitter night."

The priest allows the animal to enter. After that, it returns nightly until spring. Then it returned to the mountains. This was repeated for 10 years and the priest got to enjoy its company. But the tanuki asked how it could repay the priest for his hospitality.

At first, the priest says he needs nothing, and that the tanuki will always be welcome. But then he says he would like to have three gold pieces that people can pray for him after he is dead. But then he changes his mind again. "Posthumous honors after all, are the wish of ordinary men. I who am a priest ought not to have such thoughts."

But the Raccoon Dog goes away and is gone for three years. He has gone to the famous gold mining island of Sado and has managed to get the gold from the sands. He brings it to the priest, and begs him not to tell where he got it. But the priest replies that he must because since he has no income, people will think he has stolen it. He decides he will add that the tanuki gave him the money and has disappeared.

"You need not fear being waylaid, and can come to my hut as of old and shelter yourself from the cold." To this, the Raccoon Dog assented, and as long as the old priest lived, it came and spent the winter nights with him.

And as all good fairy tales should, this one ends: "From this, it is plain that even beasts have a sense of gratitude."

In the other story, a 14 year old prince has a passion for fishing. He goes with a retainer, and they make a large catch. But they are driven home by a violent rainstorm. On the way they see a girl of extraordinary beauty, crying by the wayside. The retainer instantly falls in love with her. She tells a sad tale. Her mother is dead and her father has married a shrew who continually beats her. Now the shrew had driven her from the house. Now she is lying in the rain. Her father is away on a trip. She suffers from stomach spasms. And she has nowhere to go.

The retainer is now hopelessly in love with her, but the young prince draws his sword and beheads her. He orders his retainer not to mention this. But that night the retainer cannot sleep, he awakens the prince's parents and tells them the story. The father gets his own sword and goes to the bed of his son.

"Oh! dastardly cut-throat that you are! How dare you kill another man's daughter without provocation? Such unspeakable villainy is unworthy a Samurai's son. Know that the duty of every Samurai is to keep watch over the country, and to protect the people. . . . Grieved as I am that I should take away the life which I gave you, I cannot suffer you to bring dishonor on our house; so prepare to meet your fate."

But the son begs his father to wait until morning and then to send his retainers to find the corpse. If it is indeed a woman then he will disembowel himself. In the morning, the servants find only a beheaded giant Raccoon Dog. How, wonders the father, could his son have known that this was only a tanuki masquerading as a woman. The ending is one to make Sherlock Holmes proud.

"Here was a young girl, at night, far from any inhabited place. Stranger still was her wondrous beauty; and strangest of all, though it was pouring rain, there was not a sign of wet on her clothes. And when my retainer asked her how long she had been there, she said she had been on the bank a long time and in pain from her spasms. . . . So I detected and killed her."

The old prince was so proud of his son's wisdom that he promptly abdicated and the boy became the Prince of Tosa.

28 The Biology of
the Raccoon Dog

T HE VERY NAME of this queer little member of the canid family indicates the confusion that surrounds it. To Americans it looks startlingly like a raccoon. Europeans have often mistaken it for a badger, and so have some of the Japanese themselves. One European writer, for example, has said that there are three kinds of badgers in Japan and includes the Raccoon Dog as one of them.

Zoologists do not make this mistake, nor do the more informed Japanese who have endless stories about them. To the zoologist, the Raccoon Dog is Nyctereutes procyonoides, with the second half of the name meaning raccoon-like. To most Japanese, its name is tanuki though in some areas there has been a tendency to call it a badger, anakuma (ana-hole, and kuma, bear). It has been introduced into the Soviet Union, and thence into Eastern Europe where it has sometimes been known as the Ussuri raccoon.

Zoologists consider it to be the most primitive of all the members of the canid family. For one reason, it is the only member of the family which hibernates. It lives at higher mountain altitudes during summer, gets very fat, descends to a lower range, and then selects a burrow, often a badger den, where it gets its winter sleep. Since it might use a badger den, it is understandable that some people might mistake it for a badger.

We quote here parts of a translation, made by Junko Kimura from the works of the Japanese authority, J. Ohno.

"Raccoon Dogs are very humorous and amiable animals, and they are heroes of our old folklore legends such as 'Kettle' and 'Temples.' (See the "lore" section, M.R.) In some places Raccoon Dogs are called 'Mujina' and raccoon dogs are sometimes mixed up with badgers. . . . As Raccoon Dogs have small black areas under their eyes, and also above their eyes, they look like badgers."

The Raccoon Dog is about eight inches tall; has a length of two and a half feet, and weighs slightly more than 16 pounds when it is ready to hibernate. It has a heavy body, ridiculously short legs, and a short tail. Its coat is a brindled brown, gray, and yellow. It has black on the throat, belly and legs, and the black about the eyes gives a "spectacles" appearance, such as the Keeshond dog has.

The dark brown tips are particularly prominent on the back and shoulders. This is particularly so after a change of coat. But as the season progresses, the tips grow lighter. There is a brownish-black band which crosses the shoulders and reaches to the forelegs. The lower legs and paws are nearly black.

Raccoon Dogs originally had an extended range which included the Amur-Ussuri region. Since they were trapped for their fur, and were sometimes eaten, the Soviets introduced them into eastern Russia. There they have prospered to the extent of becoming pests, and a danger to native animals. They became a particular danger to pheasants, other upland game birds and even to water fowl. They proved to be voracious fish eaters. One report indicates that they also eat toads, a creature which few other creatures will touch. Their fur is less valuable than that of other northern fur bearers.

They have excellent eyesight, since they have the "24 hour vision" of wolves. Like the other canids, they have a highly developed sense of smell. They are not known to bark, but they do growl and whimper. They are expert at hiding in the dens of other animals, in swamps and among rocks. Despite their small size, they have no problem in defeating medium sized dogs. They have been known to dig dens of their own. They cannot climb trees.

They breed once a year in February or March, depending upon the area in which they are living. Those farther north breed later than those in a more southerly area. The gestation period, though similar to that of dogs, also varies with weather conditions. It is roughly 59 to 64 days. The average litter is six, but occasional litters of as many as 12 have been recorded. The pups are born black and blind, but with a well developed, thick coat of hair. Weaning takes place at about six weeks. Both parents help in educating the pups and in bringing them food. The growth of the pups is extremely rapid. By November, they are mature.

Raccoon Dogs do well in captivity, and they are bred in fur farms in some parts of the Soviet Union. The fur is used to line military garments and cold weather attire. The fur is only prime during cold winter weather. In the southern parts of the Soviet Union, where Raccoon Dogs have spread, shedding takes place during most of the year, and so the fur has no value. Raccoon Dogs adapt very well to conditions in zoos, particularly those in the north.

A very primitive canid, the Raccoon Dog. Tama Zoological Park, Tokyo, Japan. *Photo by Masaru Saito*

Dingo and puppy. *Courtesy Australian News and Information Bureau*

29 The Lore of the Dingo

"A warrigal will pick your bones within six moons."
Aborigine curse.

THE WHITE SCIENTISTS of Australia may study and speculate as to how and when the Aborigines got to Australia, whether by some ancient land bridge or by water, but the Aborigines themselves have no doubt about it. While men were still animals, they say, the starfish engaged the whale by agreeing to pick off its lice. The animals then stole the whale's canoe. When the whale discovered its loss, it swam after the canoe. But the koala helped to paddle so fiercely that the canoe reached land. In revenge, the whale then so damaged and scared the starfish that it has become a hider ever since.

Australia boasts the longest fence in the world. It is 6000 miles long, starting at Eucla in Western Australia and ending in Queensland. Some 377 miles of it cross a corner of New South Wales and have high netting on top. The fence is to keep out the Dingoes, and it permits 8,000,000 sheep to be grazed in New South Wales. Farm owners pay for the upkeep of the fence.

An unknown author wrote "The Border Fence Song" which is sung by the men who keep the fence in repair. One verse of the song, as it appeared in *Singabout* in Oct. 1964, reads:

"And the station owners say they can get no sleep
Instead they're chasing dingoes that are killing sheep.
They brag about the holes they find, where the dogs just gallop
    through
They go to report to the Sydney heads, and half of it's not true."

Tucker is an Australian word for food, and the drovers, the pioneers and the fence menders keep their food in tucker boxes. Australia's most famous dog statue is at Five Mile Creek near Gundagai. The story behind the statue is a "blue" one. One of the earliest versions of a poem about the dog ends with this verse:

"For Nobby Jack has broke his yoke
Poked out the leader's eye
And the dog sat on the tucker box
Five miles from Gundagai."

In this poem, "sat" is an Australian euphemism for "shat" which is a euphemism easily guessed.

In 1904, Constance Campbell Petrie published the accounts of her father under the title of *Tom Petrie's Reminiscences.* They go back to 1837 in Queensland. Under the heading of Native Cat And Dog, Petrie had this to say:

"Native cats were caught and eaten. Dingoes, however, so far as my father's experience went, were not eaten; but the natives would capture the pups for taming. Often all around a hollow log tracks would be seen where the youngsters had come out to play, and so the natives knew where to look. A native dog was called 'mirri' and a native cat 'milbur.' "

The stories which follow will have more meaning if one knows something about the Aborigines themselves and their culture. They are as intelligent as other people. But the poverty of the land, and the total lack of both domesticated grains and meat animals has held them back technically. Yet they have a highly developed and rich culture in music, dancing, poems, tribal stories, ritual and religion. They have creation stories which seem to parallel Genesis.

After the animals and the first man have been created, the man is lonely. One night he sleeps under a flowering tree. When he awakens, all the animals have gathered, and the lovely flower turns into a beautiful woman, to the cheers of the animals. There is a flood story, and an attempt by the spirit people from heaven to mate with the daughters of earth.

As with all ancient people, they were very close to nature. They had totems, or totemic animals, so that a given group or clan would be named for an animal. Lest readers forget how close to these

Aborigines we are ourselves, consider our sports world. We have the Chicago Bears, the U. C. L. A. Bruins, the Michigan Wolverines (there are no wolverines in Michigan), the Miami Dolphins, the Detroit Lions and the Washington Cougars. Men dressed as their totem animals attend sports events. The Army mule and the Navy goat are paraded at games.

An Aborigine clan totem might be a wombat or a kangaroo. And sometimes there would be a dual totemic organization divided between two animals. Great respect was given to the totem animal. It was believed it would befriend the clan, appearing in working life or in a dream, and often helping to predict the future and to warn against evil. One can cultivate dreams, can teach one's self to remember them upon awaking. And since the Aborigines believed so thoroughly in dreams, it is not surprising that dreams played a great part in their lives.

The fundamental doctrines are pre-existence of the soul, reincarnation and dreaming. The latter is a creative, timeless condition which always has been, is now, and always will be. And so to be in the "dream time" is a very real condition for the people. Members of each group believe they belong to a given area in which they live, or have hunting and food gathering rights, not because of occupancy but because their spirits pre-existed in that particular spirit center.

If one understands this, then perhaps the following stories will have greater meaning. The first has been selected from *Myths & Legends of Australia* by A. W. Reed. The first concerns a cannibal, named Newal, his wife and his Dingo. They lived in the wilderness in a great hollow tree. To enter it they walked up a log and dropped through a hole. Newal and his Dingo would ambush hunters, kill them and drag them back to the hollow tree. They became highly successful at this.

Tribes for miles around grew frightened and puzzled as some of their finest warriors simply disappeared. But Newal and his dog grew overconfident. They were seen by hunters and bady beaten. The Dingo, in fact, lost his tail. But they escaped. However, they could no longer get human flesh. Then the Dingo—playing the part taken by the fox in Europe, the jackal in Asia and Africa, and the coyote in North America—suggested a solution. Newal would hunt alone. When he found a tired hunter, he would invite him to come to his home where, he said, a marvelous spring of cold water bubbled up in the heart of the tree. He would say to the hunter:

"You look tired. Have you come a long way?"

"You can see that for yourself," the hunter answered shortly. "A man does not catch kangaroos easily or quickly."

"You have a long walk before you reach your camp?"

"Yes."

"Then come with me to my home. It is only a little way off. You can rest there and enjoy the coldest water you ever drank. It bubbles from an underground spring inside a hollow tree, and there I live with my family."

The hunter was curious, never having heard of such a thing before, and accompanied Newal to the tree.

"Stay a moment," Newal ordered. He ran up the log and put his head through the entrance.

"Here is our supper," he whispered excitedly. "Are you ready?"

"Ready," growled the dog. "Ready," grinned his wife.

Newal returned to the hunter.

"All is well. Leave your burden here. Go up the sloping log and put your head through the hole in the tree and look down. There you will see something you will never forget."

The hunter climbed the log, put his hands on the tree trunk, and thrust his head through the hole. The dog sprang at him and sank his teeth in the man's neck, while Newal's wife struck him heavily on the head with her club. His body slid down and fell lifeless at the foot of the tree.

"See how simple it is," the dog barked as he bounded out of the tree and scampered down the log.

The experiment had been so successful that it was repeated many times. Once more word went from tribe to tribe that some hidden danger lurked in the bush; but no one was able to discover what form it took until one day two strangers arrived in that part of the country. They were tall men and walked with dignity. Everyone made them welcome and they talked to their hosts until far into the night, telling of the wonderful sights they had seen in their travels. No one dared to ask their names though there were some who whispered to each other that they might be the Winjarning brothers who had come to do justice.

It was an old man nodding over the fire who discovered the

truth. He was dreaming of sights he had seen many years before when a memory rose out of the past. He stood up and in a quavering voice, said, "This is Buda Gooda, and this is his brother."

"Other men sprang to their feet looking expectantly at the strangers.

"Yes, said the older brother, "you have guessed aright. We have heard of your troubles and have come to see whether we can help you."

Tongues were loosened. The visitors were told of the many hunters who had been lost, and how no man knew what had happened to them.

"We will go out tomorrow and will see what will befall," Buda Gooda and his brother promised . . .

Newal met them some miles from the encampment.

"You look hot and tired," he said.

"Yes," Buda Gooda replied, not knowing that this was the man he was seeking. "We did not bring water bags with us and we are thirsty. Do you know where we can find a water hole?"

"I can do better than that," Newal replied. "My home is not far away. It is in a hollow tree in which there is a spring of pure water that bubbles up from the depths of the earth. You are welcome to come and satisfy your thirst."

The brothers went with him.

"Wait here," Newal said to the younger brother. "My wife is a little nervous, and will be afraid if two strangers enter her home at once."

Buda Gooda accompanied Newal. In his bones he felt that there was something curious and a little sinister about the man.

"Wait by this tree," Newal said to his guest. "My home is in the hollow tree over there. I will tell my wife that you are coming."

He walked over to the tree, climbed the log, and went inside to prepare his wife and dog to receive two separate meals. As soon as he was out of sight, Buda Gooda tiptoed forward and looked round the camp fire. The ground was covered with skulls and human bones. His brother followed him and hid behind a tree. Newal returned.

"All is ready," he announced. "Come, climb up the log, and put your head inside the opening. You will see something you will never forget as long as you live."

Buda Gooda went slowly up the log ramp. Before he put his head through the hole he held his parrying shield in front of him. Inside the tree the dog saw the man's head appear. He sprang at his throat, but his teeth sank into the wood of the shield, and he could not let go. Newal's wife struck at Buda Gooda's head, but he caught the club, wrenched it from her hand and brought it down with such force that her skull was crushed. The dog was still hanging on to the shield. Buda Gooda dashed it against the side of the tree, but as he was doing this, Newal sprang on to the log and swung his nullanulla in a terrific blow directed at the base of Buda's skull.

The nullanulla was poised high above Newal's head when a searing flash of light seemed to pass through him and he fell lifeless from the log. Buda Gooda's brother had fitted a spear to his woomera and sent it whistling through the air to lodge in the heart of the last of the eaters of human flesh.

Tom Petrie remembered an ancient story which he had heard by a campfire. It was told to him by the clan's story teller. Here it is as Constance Campbell Petrie wrote it. It is called The Dog and the Kangaroo. The dog is a Dingo, or, as perhaps that tribe in Queensland called it, a mirri.

"An old man who lived with his tribe on a little island possessed a dog which he was exceedingly fond of. One day this dog, wandering round, perceived a kangaroo over on another island, and swimming across began to chase it. Of course the kangaroo made off, and the dog followed. Now, the old man missed his dog, and picking out his tracks, got into a canoe and crossed over after him. And this is what he saw: His dog was chasing the kangaroo, and every now and then the animal would tire and lie down to rest, and the dog, being tired as well, also laid down, and the two would look at one another. The old man thought that in these intervals he could catch up to the pair, but whenever the kangaroo saw the man approach he made off again and the dog followed, in spite of many calls and entreaties from his master.

"This sort of thing went on till many, many miles had been traversed, and the old man often stood stockstill and scratched his head, wondering what had come to his dog. He did not blame his favorite, however, but all the time heaped curses upon the kangaroo, saying it was certainly his fault. At length the kangaroo and dog both got into the water, one after the other, and started to swim to yet another island. Landing, they were both so exhausted that they died.

"The old man could not see this, however. When he saw them swimming he stood helplessly watching and crying, and at length turned back again, and seeking his canoe, went home to his island, wailing all the way, for had he not but one dog, and that one surely lost to him now?

"Time passed, and one day some strange men from the distant island, visiting friends, told the old man that they had seen the dead bodies of the dog and the kangaroo."

Tom Petrie also remembered how the Aborigines (he often called them "blackfellows") treated their dogs. His daughter took down the following account.

"Sometimes old men (never young ones) would carry puppies too young to walk, but it was mostly women who did this also. Aborigines were 'awful fond' of their dogs—they were the only pets they had. They would never by any chance kill a puppy, but would keep every one, and this, no doubt, accounted for the poor condition of these followers. Father says that even in the old days they were a mangy lot.

"Probably they did not get sufficient food, but had to live on the scraps and bones thrown to them. However, a gin (an Aboriginal woman, M.R.) would nurse a puppy just as carefully as any baby; all dogs would sleep with their owners, and they would drink from the same vessel. Children—in spite of their parents' fondness for them—if they dared ill-use a dog, would call down torrents of abuse upon their little black selves, and they would be smacked soundly. Dogs would be taught to hunt; they were always native dogs in the old times, but those of the white man soon got amongst them, and my father knew one blackfellow who carried a domestic cat about with him."

As said earlier, the white men may argue as to when the Aborigines first arrived in Australia, and when and how the Dingo got there, but the Aborigines have their own traditions. In *The Blood of Marindi* as told by G. Aistan in *Savage Life In Central Australia* and collected by Roland Robinson in *Aboriginal Myths And Legends*, the story-teller begins with "In the old days before there were men . . ."

In the story a jecko lizard challenges the big dog, Marindi, to fight. The lizard grabs the dog by the throat, its blood spurts out and dyes the rocks an ochre red. Ever after, "dog-blood ochre" is obtained at that spot. However, once when the tribe was digging the ochre, dogs-blood jumped out and smothered the diggers. And in a sense this is true. Tribesmen digging there more than a hundred years ago were smothered under a landslide.

Roland Robinson tells another story first collected by Edwards and Shaw, in *Legend And Dreaming*.

In this story, which we will quote in part, the Dingo-man Barwal and his wife, the Dingo-woman Durandurar make a bark canoe and start for the sea shore. On the way their children are born and they place them in the canoe, which they carry over their heads. They see an encampment of Maccassars (people from across the Maccassar Straight-M.R.) on a headland.

"This is the place of the crocodile dreaming," Barwal says to his wife. "This country belongs to you and me."

The two load their children in the canoe and push off. But the canoe sinks, the children drown, and only Barwal and his wife get safely back to shore. "They sat down on the beach and howled for their children." Two big stones sit down on the beach at that place. Barwal and his wife talked: "These stones are our bodies. Our spirits go on to another place."

They walk to the camp of the Maccassars who make them welcome, and offer them cooked meat. But they refuse it and demand uncooked meat, which they eat. They are offered shelter, but they refuse, saying they will sleep in the grass, even though a great rain storm is coming.

"No matter," says Barwell. "You see that rock and that ant-bed? That is where I and my wife will sleep. This is my country. *It is better that you go back to your country*, you see that fire a long way off in the country Yoormanga? That is your country. It is better that you load your boat and all your things. Pull down this house, and take everything back to your country."

Barwal and his wife watch as the Maccassars load their boats, pull up their gardens and their bamboo plants, and sail away. "Go back to your country and stay there," Barwal says. "This is my country. I sit down here."

Charles P. Mountford tells another story of a cannibal and man-eating Dingoes in *The Dreamtime, Australian Aboriginal Myths*. In this story, a woman named Yirbaik-Baik trains a pack of Dingo puppies to attack people. She would lure hunters near her home, and the Dingoes would surround and kill them. Yirbaik-Baik and her pack then feasted on the dead. Eventually, Yirbaik-Baik and her savage pack were killed. She was turned into a small brown bird, the dogs into deadly tiger snakes.

Native children were kept from wandering off into the darkness by another story, also collected by Mountford. A woman, who was hated by the tribe, had a white Dingo. However, she loved children. But in planning revenge on a woman, she was responsible for a child's death. Tribal members killed the woman and her dog, and buried them very deeply. But their spirits escaped and live in a tree. Every night at dusk their spirits wander, hoping to seize children.

The Dingo or Warrigal. *San Diego Zoo photo*

Bruce Jacobs, founder of the Australian Native Dog Foundation poses with three of his purebred Dingoes, Sheba, Lobo and Ben.
Photo by John Hart, courtesy of THE AGE, Melbourne, Australia

30 The Dingo or Warrigal

"If it moves, shoot it; if it doesn't, chop it."
Australian pioneer saying.

TASMANIA and the Tasman Sea are named after Abel Janszoon Tasman, greatest of the Dutch navigators. He was the first to circumnavigate Australia. He makes no mention of the Dingo. But another Dutch navigator, Jan Carstensz, explored the land about the Gulf of Carpentaria. On April 25, 1623, he recorded seeing the tracks of men and great dogs. All the South Pacific lands were first called Terra Australis. But by the time of William Dampier, Australia was called New Holland. Dampier also reported seeing the tracks of men and dogs in 1688. In 1699 he made another record, published in 1703. We give it here, since it is the earliest report of what was probably a Dingo that we have.

"There are but few Land Animals. I saw some lizards; and my Men saw two or three Beasts like hungry wolves, lean like so many skeletons, being nothing but skin and bones. Tis probable that it was the Foot of one of those Beasts that I mentioned as seen by us in New Holland."

Let us now skip 101 years to the description which Sydenham Edwards made in 1800 for the "Dingo, or Dog of New South Wales." In Edwards' time, it was called Canis Antarcticus. Today we call it C. dingo.

"He adds to the general appearance of the fox and wolf a considerable degree of elegance; is near two feet high; coat short; somewhat rough about the neck and haunches; muzzle pointed;

eyes piercing; ears short and erect; tail bushy and hanging down-wards; of a pale brown colour; darkening on the upper parts and lighter beneath the muzzle; cheeks, breast, insides of the legs and feet, nearly white."

If the Dingo is just another feral dog—a domestic dog gone wild—then we might dismiss it with just a few words as so many students of wild canids have done. But the Dingo is more than that. Embodied in it is the mystery of early Australia and its people. Dingo .bones have been found in association with those of giant marsupials, such as the marsupial lion, thylacoleo; the giant kan-garoo, polarchestes; and the hippopatamus-like, euryzygoma. Yet no human artifacts exist to indicate that man lived in Australia at that time. These giant marsupials existed during the late Pleis-tocene, the Ice Age, which affected even Australia. They failed to survive the warming climate which made deserts of large areas of "the driest continent."

Time, or history, is being pushed farther and farther back in Australia as more and more discoveries are made. It is now assumed that the Dingo reached Australia during the period from 9000 to 15,000 years ago. Some have suggested that it arrived earlier. But, since it is assumed that it had to cross water to reach Australia, the question then becomes: How did it reach the continent? Who brought it?

It is then necessary to consider the Australian natives themselves—the people we call the Aborigines. They differ in so many respects from other races that some anthropologists have called them Australoids. The respected *Encylopaedia Britannica* quotes the speculation that the Australoids might have arisen independently from some long gone Pithecanthropus of the Java type. Another question arises. Were the Australoids the first people to reach Australia?

In our own North American Arctic, traces have been found of human habitation by a race which preceded the present Eskimos. Nothing more than that is known about them, not who they were, when they arrived, nor where they went. In their recent book, *Origens,* Richard Leakey and Roger Lewin state that there is no good reason why man could not have reached Australia 200,000 years ago.

There is evidence that there once existed a land bridge between

New Guinea and Australia. This is deduced primarily from the fact that many of Australia's animals appear to have radiated from New Guinea. And since they could not have crossed water, then they must have come by a land bridge. It is not likely that the Dingo came with them. For there must also have been a land bridge to Tasmania, and the Dingo has not been found there.

The same puzzle exists if it is assumed that the present Aborigines brought the Dingo with them in their canoes, rafts or other sailing vessels. For if they thought sufficiently of the Dingoes to carry them to Australia, why did they not take them also to Tasmania? Or, were the Tasmanians and the Aborigines ethnically different races?

One possibility is that early migrants crossed the shortest water route from New Guinea and reached the inhospitable northern coast near Darwin. They brought Dingoes with them. But, finding the area too difficult, they returned. They may have left their Dingo dogs behind, or the Dingoes may have escaped, multiplied, and begun their own radiation through the continent.

In Australia today, a group called the Dingo Study Foundation is attempting to show that the Dingo is really not a feral dog at all, but a small wolf. It is supposed to be a smaller and lighter variety of the Asian wolf, Canis lupus pallipes. But it seems unlikely that early migrants would have added wolves, even if semi-domestic, to their crowded canoes. Still another group would like to make of the Dingo a family dog, and one which might eventually be recognized by the Kennel Council for breeding and show purposes.

Anatomically, the Dingo is a pure dog. It has been known as C. antarcticas, C. familiaris domesticus, and simply C. dingo. Its behavioral traits are also those of modern dogs, even though the Dingo is a primitive dog. It shares with the Basenji, Sinhala Hound and other primitive dogs certain physical and mental traits. Both males and females seem to have a heat period only once a year. Dingoes do not bark, but they are not silent or mute. They have "24 hour eyes" and share with all domestic dogs a love of chasing and capturing small game.

There are two varieties of Dingo, the Alpine and the desert. The former is the larger of the two. Males are 20 to 22 inches tall at the shoulder. Females are slightly smaller. Although the chest is not deep, Dingoes are otherwise strongly built. The ears are erect with rounded tips and the tail is moderately furred. The predominant colors are red to fawn, but there are other colors, including pure black and pure white. A male and female will pair for life. Mating occurs during the winter months. The gestation period is 63 days, and litters of five to nine pups are born. Probably half or more of a litter will die before maturity because of heavy parasitism. The surviving pups mature, except possibly sexually, at about a year. They are not permitted to mate but help to take care of their mother's next litter. They then pair and mate the following year.

Before the coming of the white man, the natural food of the Dingo was the kangaroo, wallaby, wombat, opossum, and similar animals. But Europeans destroyed the natural ecology in many ways. The words which started this chapter: "If it moves, shoot it, if it doesn't chop it" were not taken lightly. Countless milllions of the native animals were destroyed, including the Dingoes' food. And vegetation suffered a similar fate. But the white man also brought in sheep, cattle and rabbits. They also brought their dogs, countless numbers of which were dumped into uninhabited areas where they, too had to become feral dogs to survive. The Dingo had to change its food habits. It turned to the rabbits which had become a national pest. But, according to sheepmen, it also preyed upon the new-born lambs.

Dingoes hunt in pairs or in family groups. To save themselves, kangaroos would try to find a tree. They would back up to the tree, balance on their tails, then try to grasp the Dingo with the front paws, and then disembowel it with their terrible hind claws. A single Dingo would have no chance in such circumstances. But one of a pair could circle behind, bite at the tail and attempt to knock the kangaroo off balance.

The facts about the modern Dingo are tragically like those which surround the coyote. They are that Dingoes are being poisoned, trapped and shot as noxious vermin who are wanton killers of sheep and young cattle—killing both for food and pleasure. But, as with the coyote, these "facts" seem not to be true. The Dingo faces extermination only because the sheepmen refuse to face the truth.

Thus, Dr. Alan Newsome of the Commonwealth Scientific & Industrial Organization, Division of Wildlife Research, has made a thorough study of Dingo food habits. So has Robert Harden of the

New South Wales National Park and Wildlife Service. They report that Dingoes survive almost entirely on wallabies, wombats, opossums and rabbits. They will eat carrion before they attack sheep and lambs. Even then, they perform a service by killing the weak animals, many of which could not survive anyway. Both men estimated that Dingoes' diet is only four per cent sheep or calf meat. Both men agreed, however, that upon rare occasions, Dingoes may kill for pleasure.

While Dingoes hunt in pairs, or sometimes in family groups, as noted, Corbett and Newsome reported that 73 per cent of Dingoes which they saw were alone. They therefore appear to be less social than are domestic dogs or most other canids. Males, as well as bitches, appear to have mating cycles, and may have actual aspermous periods during summer. Thus, they might eagerly mate a domestic bitch in heat during fall or winter, but would ignore her in summer.

Corbett and Newsome concluded that Dingo vocalizing is for the following purposes: warning signal when coming in to water; warning signal of danger; an expression of alarm; to locate and avoid strangers; to locate family members; and finally to attract a mating partner.

The Alpine Dingo is very close to extinction. In 1976 only about a dozen purebred Alpine Dingoes were known to be in captivity, and these were all descendants of one pair. The desert Dingo is less menaced.

Mountain trappers report that only one of four animals trapped by them is a Dingo. The others are feral dogs. Or they are hybrids. Domestic dogs dumped in the mountain area have a greater survival possibility than would the same dogs dumped in desert areas. Dingoes are territorial, and tend to remain within the territory they have staked out for themselves. But the wild dogs, dumped into the wilderness, do not have territorial instincts. They wander over vast areas, and of course, they destroy the food supply of the Dingoes. Finally, the shooting of parent Dingoes leaves young dogs and puppies without a family head, and as a result they may not survive against the competition of the domestic dogs. The latter also breed twice a year, so that under natural circumstances, they outnumber the Dingoes in a very short time.

In North America much opposition to the leghold trap has

arisen in recent years. Animals caught in such traps may suffer agony for days before being shot. And many animals will chew off their legs to escape. So will the Dingo. To avoid this, trappers will lace their traps with poison so as to kill the Dingoes if they should try this method of escape. A common poison is 1080, as it has been in America until President Nixon put restrictions on its use. Until recently, poisoned 1080 baits were dropped from airplanes in Australia. While these killed the Dingoes and the feral dogs, they also killed countless numbers of other animals, including lyre birds.

In ending this chapter, one should note that the Dingo appears in the background of two of Australia's famous cattle dogs. To be successful, a cattle dog must be silent. Constant barking will disturb and tend to stampede cattle. In the early part of the last century, drovers had to take their cattle overland for long distances to get them to market. But the drovers' dogs were all barkers.

The Dingo does not bark. It also likes to creep up behind its prey and bite it from the rear. A drover named Timmins conceived the idea of crossing barking cattle dogs with Dingoes. Timmins lived in New South Wales. His dogs were called Timmins' Biters. They were silent, but they were also enthusiastic biters. So further crosses had to be made to dull some of this enthusiasm. Timmins is believed to have begun his cross breeding in 1830.

The two Australian breeds are the Australian Cattle Dog and the Stumpy-tailed Cattle Dog. The latter is now somewhat rare, but the former is now catching on the United States and Canada. The writer once had the privilege of judging the Australian Cattle Dogs in Australia. There was an entry of 35, and they were all dogs which had been brought in off the range. They were thus hard-as-nails working dogs who were used to ducking the kicks of angry wild cattle, while giving an occasional nip at the heels. One Australian judge warned: "They like to bite anything that moves in front of their faces, and they are miraculously fast in doing so." However, they gave me no trouble, and those which have appeared in America are sweet tempered and remarkably intelligent.

31 The Lore of the Dhole

THE SUB-CONTINENT OF INDIA abounds in ages-old folklore which deals with animals. The chief actors are the jackal, the crow, and an animal which probably no longer exists there—the lion. In a search of more than a thousand of these stories, the writer could find only two which deal with the Dhole, or Asiatic red dog. In one, an Indian deer, called sambar or sambhar, makes a contract with a fish for mutual protection against their enemies.

The sambar has a mortal fear of the Dholes. The fish counsels the sambar to rush into the water of the swamp and get as far from shore as possible. The fish will roil up the water, and splash it onto the deer's tracks until its footprints are obliterated. In return, the sambar is to root up and destroy the fish poison vine. This is a vine which the people dig up. The roots are crushed. They release a poison which when put into the water stuns or kills the fish.

The second story we quote as Stanley Rice translated it from the ages-old Panchatantra, written at least 600 years before the Christian era.

"In the forest of Nemicha dwelt a lion in whose service were a jackal, a wild dog, and a crow. They were living happily together when an old camel, tired out with work and ill-treatment, escaped from his master and took refuge in the jungle. One day when the lion and his companions were out walking, they met the camel. They were surprised at such an extraordinary meeting, and the jackal began to lay plans for killing the stranger, and consulted his friends who entirely approved.

"But it was impossible for them to destroy so strong an animal by themselves, and they began to cast about for a plot to induce the lion, their master, to kill him. The jackal had a plan ready at once, and suiting the action to the word, he went up to the camel, showed surprise that he should be wandering alone in the jungle, and asked what had brought him there. The unsuspecting camel told him frankly why he had escaped and complained especially of the ill-treatment he had received from his master for the numberless services he had done him.

"The jackal pretended to praise the camel's escape, and with a few words of sympathy, he said: 'The place you have chosen to come to is the domain of the lion; so it would be better for you to appear before him to do him homage and to ask for his protection.'

" 'But why,' asked the camel, 'do you advise this? What can there be in common between a lion-king and a wretch like myself whom all the world has cast off? And how can a miserable creature such as I dare to appear before such a mighty monarch?'

" 'The weak,' answered the jackal, 'always need the protection of the great and should try to gain their favor by a humble submission. Follow us. We will take you to the lion's abode and will introduce you to him.'

"The camel, not suspecting treachery, followed this advice and went with them to the lion. The jackal introduced him and told his master why the stranger had taken refuge in the wilds, where he hoped to end his days in the shadow of his powerful protection.

"The lion received the camel kindly, treated him affably, and became familiar with him. So pleased was he with his good qualities that he trusted him entirely, and made him his chief minister. But the three friends who introduced him, seeing the influence that the stranger had acquired, did not know what to do to carry out their plan of inducing the lion to kill him.

"Meanwhile the lion fell sick, and as his illness left him very weak, for a long time he could not hunt. One day, being very hungry, he called his three servants, told them his needs, and commanded them to bring him some animal to eat in order to appease the cravings of nature.

"The three animals made excuse that they could not do the impossible, for they knew quite well that none of them was strong enough to attack and kill the kind of animals on which the lion used to feed.

" 'However," added the jackal, 'if you really are so desperately hungry, you can satisfy your pangs without going far. All you need do is to kill the camel who lives with you. Considering your necessity, you can do this without scruple and he ought to submit cheerfully to his fate, as the saying has it: To give one's life for the life of one's master brings for ever the favor of Sri-Narayana. Or, again, if it pains you too much to sacrifice the life of the camel to save your own, kill us three; we shall die happy in the thought that we are laying down our lives for our master.'

"This speech made the desired impression on the lion. He could no longer bear the pangs of hunger, sprang upon the camel, killed him, and fed full on the flesh. Then the jackal, the wild dog, and the crow lived on the rest for many days."

Red Dog of Asia, the Dhole, as seen by Col. Hamilton Smith, 1839-40.

32 The Biology of the Dhole or Asiatic Red Dog

THE DHOLE has been called the Siberian wolf and the Indian red dog. But because of its range, it is correct to call it the Asiatic red dog. It has the widest range, as to environmental habitat, of any of the wild canids. It exists along the sea coast, at sea level, on the plains, in the forests and jungles, in mountains far above the tree line—as high as two and a half miles or more—and in the mountains of China, Tibet and the Himalayas. Its range extends in a mainland area of Siberia, as far north as Okhotsk, on the Sea of Okhotsk, and southward to the tropical islands of Borneo and Sumatra. Oddly, it is not found on Sri Lanka (formerly Ceylon).

Its hardiness is so great that it normally scorns digging dens. Even in rocky mountain areas, it prefers to live among the rocks and crevices. It does, however, use dens for whelping and the early rearing of pups. At high altitudes, and in winter, in northern climates, it grows a tremendous coat of hair. Outer guard hairs are as much as six inches long. The undercoat is dense wool. In tropical areas, guard hairs are shorter and the undercoat thinner.

Dholes look more like domestic dogs than do some of the other wild canids. The planes of muzzle and skull are roughly parallel. There is very little stop, and this is quite remarkable in an animal which lives in high altitudes and great cold. In such climates one would expect to find a deep stop and large sinuses, so that cold air could be warmed before reaching the lungs, and being warmed, could in turn help to warm the inner side of the skull and eye sockets as it is being expired. It seems obvious, therefore, that the head of the Dhole is generalized to permit it to exist in both hot and cold climates and in desert or steppe areas and humid tropical forests. As one would expect of an animal which could live on rocky mountains above the tree line, it has 24 hour eyes.

The Dhole also differs from most other canids in having only 40 teeth, and in having 12 to 14 nipples, although as will be seen later, it hardly needs that many feeding stations. The maximum length of the Dhole is 36 to 39 inches. The shoulder height is about 19½ inches. The average weight is 33 to 44 pounds. The legs are short in proportion to body depth.

The Dhole gets its "red dog" appellation quite deservedly. It is orange red to red-brown on the head, neck and shoulders. The belly, breast and other under parts are grayish, but with yellow hair tips to give coppery sheen to the coat. Hair turns to grayish white on the toes, but there is a brownish-black strip on the front of each foreleg. The last third of the tail is a very dark brown.

Dholes were originally divided into three species, with some 11 sub-species. Two, Cuon alpinus, and Cuon alpinus hesperis, lived in Siberia, Sinkiang and along the edge of the Gobi Desert. C. a. hesperis also was found in Tibet, the Himalayan mountains and Indian forests. C. a. dukhunensis, is an Indian species. The sub-species were considered to live in Sumatra, Borneo, etc.

Today it is considered that all species and subspecies belong to the single genus. C. alpinus. The differences are those mainly brought about by living conditions in a given area. That is, the differences are insignificant and not sufficient to warrant separate classification.

It is believed that Dholes, like so many other canids, mate for life. Certainly they live in pairs during the mating season and during the rearing and training of the pups. Dens are used for whelping. A number of investigators have noted that the fibrous remains of rhubarb plants are always found in these dens. Dholes appear to have a great passion for rhubarb. The parents chew, masticate and swallow parts of the stems and blossoms, then regurgitate the now partially digested mass for the pups.

Mating season varies with the climate, being fairly early in winter in warm climates, and much later in colder areas and at higher altitudes. Gestation period is 63 days. Litters of four to six

New Guinea Wild Dog, member of the Dhole family. *San Diego Zoo photo*

pups are average, although ten have been recorded. The pups are well furred with dark brown hair at birth. Their eyes open at 10 to 14 days.

Most Dholes do not appear either to bark or growl, but they do make whimpering sounds. However, some researchers have reported that Dholes in the Soviet Union do sometimes howl. Others have reported growling sounds.

Since the Dholes range over such vast territories, it follows that their diet differs according to the range, and the available prey animals on that range. In Siberia, musk ox and reindeer fall prey to Dholes. In the high mountains, ibex and mountain sheep are hunted; at lower altitudes, various deer including the sambar. Those moving along the sea coast in Sumatra have been known to capture turtles. Their jaws are strong enough to bite through the shells.

As a rule, they hunt in packs of from four to six to 30, with the smaller groups hunting in mountainous areas and often above the tree line. The latter groups are highly skilled at driving prey animals over cliffs. However, like any social carnivore, hunting pairs and lone animals are not uncommon.

The hunting packs have highly developed procedures, according to the prey. They will split up and fan out to cut off escape routes. They appear to hunt more by wind borne scents rather than by trailing or sight coursing.

Because of their relatively short legs, Dholes cannot run as fast as wolves. But they make up for it by showing great stamina and perseverance in continuing the hunt. It is usual for the lead Dhole to seize the prey by the hind quarters. This may slow down, but not fell the animal. In that case, others try to eviscerate the animal. It may continue staggering along while pack members are already disemboweling it and feasting on the viscera.

As is true with all other predators, Dholes have been persecuted by man to the extent that they are becoming very rare in many areas where once they were abundant. They are not known to attack cattle. They appear to have an inborn understanding that they must not kill off all of the prey animals in a given area. Thus, they will take one animal and then move to a new territory. They therefore lead a nomadic life. And this may account for the fact that they are not primarily den dwellers.

33 African Wild Dog

T HE AFRICAN WILD DOG has also been called the Cape Hunting Dog and the African Hunting Dog. Since, according to *The Cambridge Natural History,* its skeletal remains have been found in England, its arrival in Central and Southern Africa presents a great puzzle. How did it reach the British Isles, and then how and when did it get to Africa? It has been considered a recent arrival as millenia go in Africa.

It is named after a mythical king of Arcadia, Lycaon. I have given one version of the story in the section on wolves. Another is that Lycaon prepared a meal of human flesh for Zeus. Zeus was not deceived and in wrath caused the deluge which devastated the earth. In another story, a man's entrails were mixed with those of other sacrifices. Any man tasting them would be turned into a wolf. He could return to human form after nine years, provided he had not again tasted human flesh.

Apparently the Wild Dog was thought to be so cruel that no better name could be given to it. So it is officially named Lycaon pictus. Pictus is the past participle of the Latin word "pingo" to paint. So in this usage it means the painted or various colored canid. It is the most brilliantly colored of all the canids.

It is from 24 to 29 inches at the withers and weighs 35 to 66 pounds. It has a bony skull with very strong zygomatic arches. This makes one think that it has retained some of the characteristics of the hyena type animals of North America from which all the canids have sprung. It is not, however, related to present day hyenas.

The first molar is unusual in having a cutting edge, and the last lower one is poorly developed. The dental formula for the premolars and molars is PM $\frac{4}{4}$, M $\frac{2}{3}$. Like other canids, it has a caecum. But it differs from most canids in having a relatively short small intestine, averaging one foot three inches, and a relatively enormous large intestine, some nine feet long or more. The stomach has a very large capacity and can expand at least double its empty size. This is the visceral tract of the pure meat eater, but it is more than that.

The last step in digestion is to store unused waste food in the large intestine until water can be extracted from it. This means that L. pictus can store more water than can most canids. Or, to put it another way, it can derive more water from the food it eats, and can consequently go for much longer periods without drinking. This is a remarkable adaptation to life in areas where there will be long dry spells. It also indicates a rather special kidney. A noted biologist has stated that, were it not that the soft parts disappear, a study of the kidneys of prehistoric animals would tell more about evolution than do the bones. The African Hunting Dog would be an excellent animal for such a study.

Among other physical differences between L. pictus and other canids are the following. It has no lytta—the fibrous, cartilaginous rod which lies horizontally under the tongue of other canids. It has only four toes on each foot. Its ears are large and very wide at the base. They stand upright on the skull, and are so rounded as to be almost cylindrical above the base. The colors are best described as tortoiseshell and white, or calico cat colors.

Another color description is ochraceous gray ground color with black markings. It might be better to say "mottled yellowish-orange, black and white." Variations in the mottling are so great that rarely are two dogs marked alike. However, an occasional pure black Wild Dog does appear. The tail is very short, reaching only about half way to the hock joint, and often not more than 12 inches long. There is a white plume on the end of the tail, and this seems almost certainly to be useful in communication. Pups are black with irregular white spots when born. The yellowish-orange color appears at about seven weeks.

As with most wild canids, but including the now fully domestic Basenji and the feral Dingo, African Wild Dogs come into season only once a year. However, there seems to be no clearly defined period of the year for this. Normally, the female mates only with a

African Wild Dog or Cape Hunting Dog paces restlessly. *San Diego Zoo photo*

selected male, so that observers are always able to tell the sire of a given litter. But Hugo Van Lawick and Jane Goodall have recorded a strange case in which a female within two weeks of whelping accepted a mate. As a rule, a dominant pack male will mate with a dominant female.

When the bitch comes into heat, she marks various spots with urine, and the selected male does also, even sometimes while she is still urinating. The Van Lawick-Goodalls noted that the male often stood on his forelegs while urinating on the spot used by, or still in use, by the bitch. This should be compared with the actions of the South American Bush Dog, as related in another chapter.

The gestation period is 70 days on the average. C. E. Cade, director of the small zoo at the entrance to the Nairobi National Park, kept careful records for one bitch and found the gestation period to be 72 days. This is exceptionally long for a canid. Average litter size is six to eight. But as with all canids, much larger litters have been recorded. In the wild there is an average mortality of 50 per cent before maturity. This is due to heavy parasitism, and to losses to hyenas or accidents, some involving other animals such as wild boars, leopards, and lions. The pups open their eyes at from 10 to 14 days, and may be brought out of the den between two and three weeks of age.

There is evidence that the African Wild Dog once lived in Egypt some 3000 years ago. But in the last few centuries, until quite recently, their range was from the desert edge south to the Cape of Good Hope, and in all areas except jungles. They are primarily sight hunters and may have the finest vision of all the canids. For this reason they prefer to live on the plains, or on mountain slopes up to about 3000 feet.

Unfortunately, African Wild Dogs suffer from the same merciless enmity, the lack of understanding—and the refusal to understand—which have been the fate of the wolves, coyotes, Asian wild dogs, Dingos, and jackals. Their role in the ecology of the great African plains, in killing off the weak and the sick, is now well known, but is usually ignored.

Hugo Van Lawick wrote that great story *Solo, the Story of an African Wild Dog*. His wife, Jane Goodall, wrote an introduction to it. She suggests that part of man's enmity toward L. pictus is the way in which it kills. A zebra, for example, may be brought to bay, and then disemboweled, with the pack feeding on the entrails while the animal is still alive. This may be for a period of not more than three minutes.

She says that she was sickened the first time she witnessed this, and that though she has seen the kills countless times since, she is still sickened by the "ghastly" sight. Yet in fairness, she points out that nature gave to the Wild Dog this method of killing; that it is quickly efficient; that the animal may be in shock and feel nothing during that three minutes; and that this can be no worse than the slow strangling method used by the lion.

African Wild Dogs live in packs—usually from half a dozen to 15 to 25. Sometimes a single pair may wander off, mate, raise pups, and then rejoin a pack. Sometimes, packs may have 50 to 60 members, though this would be rare. The packs are nomadic, and a single pack will wander over tremendous distances—a thousand square miles or more. They will, of course, follow migrating herds of prey animals.

They do, however, cease their wandering when a female is about to whelp. The usual den will probably have been constructed for her by an aardvark. Aardvarks seem to dig dozens of dens. Some may have been used by other animals for hundreds of years.

The expectant mother will clean out the den, then may change her mind and move to another one. After the pups are born, she may move them two or three times, and may return them eventually to her first choice. This is a behavioral trait common to many of the canids. Those canids which tend to pack up also seem to take a great interest in puppies. The African Wild Dogs are highly specialized in this.

When two litters are born about the same time, the two mothers have been known to suckle each other's puppies with seeming pleasure. Moreover, pack members can take over all the other duties of the nursery. One observer, Goddard, noted that a bitch had her litter in late February. On April 3d, she apparently died in the den, and Goddard watched as the males dragged the body out. The pups were still trying to nurse. Although the other pack members were males, they took over for the dead mother.

One male would be left to guard the den. (Hyenas have a passion for wild dog feces, will take great risks to get it, and if nosing about an unprotected den, would devour a few puppies as well.) The others would hunt, gorge themselves with food, and then bring it to the puppies. There were nine puppies and only five adult males. They would regurgitate the food—predigested as it were—and the puppies would feast. Often there would be no food left for the hunters, who would have to hunt again to satisfy their own needs.

So strong is the pack bond that a member may make submissive gestures and whimper, and be rewarded with some disgorged food. Also, pack members often seem to gorge themselves, then make presents of the food to other pack members, actions which I myself have witnessed. Having eaten, the animal would then regurgitate the food in front of another. That dog might even repeat the ceremony in front of a third.

In zoological parks, officials often separate mammal pairs as the time approaches for the female to deliver because the male may kill the infant. Also, the female may desert the infant which must then be raised on a bottle with formula. But this procedure cannot be followed with L. pictus. The family bond is too strong, and the canid instincts are equally strong. If separated, the female becomes very restless, and the male almost equally so. After whelping, the female delights in showing her "husband" the children.

African Wild Dogs have a variety of calls. They twitter like birds and whimper. Another call is actually a howl while lips are closed. The hunting call sounds like distant bells—much more so than George Washington's description of the hounds sent to him by Gen. Lafayette; "hounds with voices like the bells of Moscow." If frightened, they will give sharp barks and even growl.

An autonomic nervous system reaction of most animals, from snakes up, is to urinate or to defecate when frightened. Lycaon is no exception. It gives forth a particularly foul smelling stench, both from feces and from gas. Many say that the animal always has a foul odor about it. But, in the case of the orphan Solo mentioned earlier, the Van Lawick-Goodalls did not detect such an odor when she was not frightened. The African Hunting Dog's large intestine serves as a storage area for water, which would be absorbed into the body as needed. When large amounts of water were being carried, a certain amount of fermentation would take place. If expelled at such times there would be a foul odor.

Competent observers, who have spent years in studying animals in the wild, do not always agree on their findings. Thus, the observations of Van Lawick-Goodall on dominance relations are in conflict in some respects with those of Goddard, Kuhme and Estes. Lockwood has suggested that this may have been an artifact of the close proximity of the Van Lawick-Goodall team to the pack, and the disturbances caused by this.

In the short section that follows, I should like to explode some of the misconceptions held against L. pictus. But here I would like it to be understood that the African Wild Dog is not a primitive canid, regardless of its tooth arrangement. It is, in fact, the most highly developed socially of all the canids.

Col. Hamilton Smith's drawing of Lycaon pictus, the African Wild Dog.

34 Exploding Misconceptions About African Wild Dogs

IN RESEARCHING African native folk lore, I have been unable to find any stories or fables which deal specifically with the animal we know as the African Wild Dog, African Hunting Dog or Cape Hunting Dog. But there are so many vicious and untrue stories about Lycaon pictus that I feel it needs some support before it is destroyed in its rapidly diminishing territory.

On my first visit to Africa, I was assured that it was the most vicious of all animals, and that it was the only one in all of Africa which was not protected. This was not true even then. At least as early as 1936, Lycaon pictus was being protected in some areas.

It was said that once an African Wild Dog set out after prey, the prey animal was doomed. There could be no escape. This was said to be true even if only one dog was chasing it. To start with, even if only one dog starts a chase, it is likely to call the pack which quickly joins.

African Wild dogs have excellent hearing as their huge ears suggest. And they probably have an excellent sense of smell. But they are not "nose brain" animals as, for example, domestic hounds are. They are supreme sight hunters, which is why a single dog might lose the prey animal and call upon the pack to help.

It is not true that once the chase begins, the prey animal is doomed. Hugo Van Lawick and Jane Goodall have estimated that at least two out of three escape.

Nor is it true that the Wild Dogs hunt in relays. It is true that antelopes and gazelles, when hard pressed and tiring, begin to zig zag in an effort to elude their pursuers. This is a fatal mistake. It permits the slower dogs to cut corners. There simply is no evidence that these slower dogs lag behind in order to be able to cut the corners.

It has been said that certain dogs are designated to attack the throat. This is not necessarily so. But some dogs have been noted for their method of attack, for instance springing to grasp the lip of a zebra—the lip, mind you, not the throat. This can only be done when other dogs have slowed the animal by biting at the rump or in other ways.

African Wild Dogs are credited with being able to run at a speed of 30 miles per hour for three miles. Presumably such tests are made by following in Land Rovers, and checking the car's speedometer. In testing this method with running horses, I have found it to be totally unreliable. But that they do have excellent speed and great stamina is undeniable.

It has been said that L. pictus has never been known to drink water. But this is untrue; both on the African plains and in zoological parks. It is true that in their natural environment they can go for extraordinarily long periods without drinking. The amount they drink depends upon many factors—climate, the length of a chase, the nursing of puppies, etc.

In the previous chapter it was pointed out that African Wild dogs are nomads, wandering over vast areas. This was brought out rather pathetically at Cleveland Zoological Park. Director Dr. Leonard Goss, knowing of my long time interest in Lycaon, decided to get a male and a female. Two zoo directors who had once been at Cleveland, and who had remained my friends, donated a male and a female. They were placed in a new section which carried a name plate dedicated to me. The pair were promptly named Max and Marty, Marty being my wife Martha.

They did not do well in the Cleveland winter climate. The bitch died in whelp. The male was restless. He literally wore his feet off to the pastern joint by his ceaseless walking. Finally he was given merciful death.

Most observers believe that, as wolves do, African Wild Dogs study a herd, note the sick and weak, and then deliberately cut them

African Wild Dog, Max, named after the
author of this book. *Cleveland Press photo*

African Wild Dog, Marty, named after
author's wife. *Cleveland Press photo*

from the herd. In doing this, they are preventing the unworthy animals from perpetuating their kind, and they are removing animals whose continued life only destroys valuable forage.

Death In The Long Grass by Peter Hathaway Capstick (St. Martin's Press) is one of the most fascinating animal books of early 1978, or for that matter, any year. In it, Capstick recounts his adventures as a big game hunter in Africa. But Capstick is something more than that. He is also, now at least, a conservationist, and he has a remarkable flair for writing. Here, in part, is what he says about the African wild dog.

"I find it interesting that any visitor who has seen African wild dogs kill is invariably affronted, revolted by them basically because of their extreme, somehow detached skill and the heart-wrenching violence of their methodology. Of course, this is just another example of humans labeling animals with supposed virtues or faults we value or despise in ourselves. On this reasoning lions are 'noble,' elephants 'wise,' Koala bears and bushbabies are 'cuddly.' Wild dogs are 'evil.' Well, so it goes.

"In actuality, wild dogs have an extraordinarily complex and formal social structure, rich in elaborate behavior mechanisms and abstract ceremony. They are unquestionably very intelligent and much of their ritual has to do with submission and dominance of individuals arrived at by nonviolent means. They are one of the only wild mammal predators that will permit young pups to feed on a kill before adults do. Yet, for all their brightness, unless they have been shot at or molested, they display almost no distrust of man, which has led to the out-of-hand slaughter of untold thousands of them at the judgment of rifle-wielding idiots who believe they are saving other soft-eyed creatures from horrible death and thereby, through some hazy logic, assisting the balance of nature.

"It is good news for man that there has never been a confirmed case of man-eating among wild dogs. This strikes me as singularly strange because their diet includes any meat they can catch, even adult lions according to reliable sources in various parts of Africa. This being the case, what is it about man that incurs this gastronomic snub? It might just be that one of the oldest theories of the success of man, who has no natural physical weapons, is true: he simply smells too bad to eat to a sensitive creature like a wild dog. We're ripe enough from any animal's viewpoint, but you can bet that the early protypes of our model were surely no bunch of lilacs . . .

"The wild dog, because man in his infinite wisdom has declared him unworthy of life, is much reduced in numbers all over Africa. Over the past ten years, however, a few people have seen the light, and protection has been provided in many countries. That's good news. For my money, he's one of the great reminders of the facts of life in Africa: life feeds on death in the exact ratio that death feeds on life. One is the other and it is only one's viewpoint that varies."

In the section on wolves, Pimlott has suggested that wolves do not attack man because they have never considered man to be a threat to their own food sources. Both are predators. But there has also been sufficient food for both, so that the two species did not truly compete against each other. Perhaps this also has been true of the wild dog-man relationship in Africa where the vast herds of game animals made it possible for the two predators to live peacefully side by side.

Hugo and Jane Van Lawick-Goodall reported that in East Africa prey animals do not flee at the first sign of Wild Dogs, but treat them as they do the lions. That is, they recognize that the Wild Dogs, or the lions, are not hungry, and so do not flee. Peter Capstick, living, hunting, and working in a different part of Africa more heavily forested, found the exact opposite to be the case. He decided that the open plains of East Africa offered great sight distance, and great running room. But in the thick "miombo" and woodlands of Central Africa, sight distance was short and flight was more difficult. The prey animals could not keep a watchful eye on the Wild Dogs. And therefore, the mere scent of one, sent the herd into flight.

Hugo Van Lawick's *Solo, The Story of an African Wild Dog,* is one of the truly great stories of all time. Aside from its writing, it represents months and months of watching the Genghis pack of African Wild Dogs and a dozen others. It meant watching the pack day and night, following it on its nomadic wanderings in search of food, water and whelping dens.

The pack had a dominant bitch, Havoc, who assumed leadership of the entire pack, including the males. Havoc had a litter of pups, and shortly afterward so did Angel. Havoc had a violent hatred of Angel and managed to kill all but one of Angel's pups. She also prevented other dogs of the pack from feeding Angel, so that she and her remaining pup, Solo, nearly starved. As the blistering summer heat began, the Genghis pack had to trek the Serengheti, toward distant mountains in search of food and water. The nearly dead Angel and Solo, had to accompany the pack. But they were weak and lagged behind. At this point, we take excerpts from the story.

"The dogs rested until nearly seven p.m. and then set out on a trek of fifteen miles, a trek that taxed Solo almost beyond endurance. Right from the start she lagged behind, and her calls of distress became more and more frequent as that gruelling night wore on. Quite often she stopped altogether, crying again and again, whilst the following hyenas moved ever closer.

"Several of the dogs turned back in response to Solo's calls, but for the most part they hindered rather than helped the distressed pup. Meaning well, perhaps, an adolescent would bend down to lick Solo, and this invariably bowled her over so that she lost even more time. Jezebel and the male adolescent Apollo carried her quite frequently, and occasionally one of the adults picked her up also. But mostly she was on her own. The dogs did pause, from time to time, so that the pups could rest briefly, and it was particularly distressing for us to see that almost every time, just as Solo finally caught up during these short respites and collapsed wearily to the ground, the adults would set off again and Solo missed her rest.

"The hyenas were very numerous that night. We counted no less than twelve skulking shapes, never very far from the dogs, often terrifyingly close to Solo.

"Eventually, at two o'clock, the pack stopped. Even the older pups seemed almost exhausted, and when Solo finally stumbled up to where they lay she did not have the strength to clamber amongst the others, searching for a comfortable resting place. She simply collapsed beside the older pups and lay completely still.

"Even now, however, Solo could not have the real respite that she needed. The restless hyenas prowled closer and closer, their presence a constant menace to the uneasily sleeping dogs. Each time one of them whooped the pups would leap up, terrified, race forward a few yards, and then settle down once more.

"Suddenly a lion roared. It made us jump for it was very close, and the entire pack was startled. All the dogs leapt to their feet and raced from the spot, as though in panic. Solo had been unable to keep up during this wild flight, but eventually she joined the other youngsters. Now the hyenas approached more closely until we could hear the stealthy rustling of the vegetation as they walked by, looking toward the pups.

"We feared that there would be a tragedy, until all at once, out of the darkness, one dog bounded. It was Yellow Peril. He ran at several of the nearest hyenas and chased them off, and then lay close to the pups, until the rest of the adults appeared some ten minutes later.

"The sun rose to show that the dogs were resting in gently rolling country that was no less hostile and barren than the flat plain they had left the night before. A strong wind swept the land, blowing great billows of dust from the hills to engulf the dogs. Twice we were almost caught in huge whirlwinds that raced across the country with a roaring sound. They were black with dust and pieces of vegetation torn out of the ground and seized by the fierce air currents, spiralled high into the air.

"The pack moved off more than an hour before sun set even before the cool evening set in. They were heading straight for the distant Gol Mountains which floated, like magic islands, above the heat haze on the horizon. On they travelled in single file, a small caravan crossing a hostile semi-desert. The ground, when I felt it with my hand, was red hot to the touch. Probably it was burning Solo's small paws which had had no chance to become hardened during her short life. The dust stirred up by the pack floated behind, carried on the hot air above the ground until gusts of dry wind blew it away or sent it spiralling into the blue sky. Solo panted as she stumbled on, breathing the dust kicked up by the dogs ahead of her and which she stirred up with her own dragging feet. She was obviously exhausted and finally she stopped altogether and cried.

"Angel was amongst the rear dogs of the procession. As soon as she heard her pup, she turned back and went to her. She stood for Solo to nurse, although, in her emaciated condition, it was unlikely that her shrunken teats yielded much nourishment. The pack waited, staring back. The brief refreshment over Angel started after the pack, and then she paused, turned back and picked Solo up in her mouth. But Havoc noticed, and accompanied by Rasputin ran back and briefly threatened Angel. The subordinate bitch, even now, was not permitted to treat her pup in that way. Cringing, she accepted her rebuke with a quick jerky wagging of her half tail. Havoc did not offer to carry Solo in place of her mother, but amazingly even that short drink seemed to have revived the little pup and she managed to catch up by herself.

"The dogs stopped early that night and, after resting for a while, the adults went off to hunt. As before, the pups were constantly harrassed by hyenas and we felt sure that, unless they soon left this barren country where the hyenas were starving, there would be a number of casualties. Once again, however, the Genghis pack made a kill, and thus the hyenas were kept busy.

"All the next day the dogs rested. They were, by this time, close to the foothills of the Gol Mountains and when they set out again in the coolness of evening, it took them only an hour to reach the hilly country. When the pack stopped again to rest Solo collapsed and lay motionless. That she was still there at all was a tribute to the amazing vitality and determination of the dog herself, for although Jezebel and Apollo and occasionally an adult had carried her several times, she had travelled for most of the way on her own four weary legs.

"After a couple of hours the dogs were on the move again. The moon cast deep dark shadows where tumbles of rocks were piled here and there on the hill-side, and amongst the rock shadows, were the moving shadows of the hyenas, still present. We reckoned that there were twelve of them.

"As the dogs passed one of the rocky outcrops a dark form emerged from the shadows and followed closed behind them. It was a gaunt long-legged hyena, probably half starved. After a few minutes, it quickened its pace until it was not far behind Solo. If there was any conscious thought in the mind of the little pup, which is doubtful, it must have been a desire to keep up, somehow, with the pack. Her limbs moved almost automatically, one after the other.

"She did not notice that there was an animal behind her, an animal who at all times was getting closer and closer. The hyena was not more than two or three yards behind Solo when Brutus happened to turn: instantly he was racing back, darting for the hyena's rump, sinking his teeth in its buttocks. With its shrill giggling call the hyena turned and ran.

"The pack had come to a halt on hearing sounds of combat, and the dogs stood waiting until Solo, followed by Brutus, caught up. Then they continued on their way. But the hyena did not give up. Hyenas can be incredibly patient and persistent, following sick animals for days, and Solo, already lagging again, must have seemed a certain meal. And behind that hyena there were others.

"Several times again during that long night a hyena almost caught Solo. Mostly one or other of the adult dogs noticed in time to race back and rescue the small pup, but on several occasions James and I ourselves protected Solo, moving the car between the predators and their intended prey. Normally we obey the rules, we observe nature as she is in all her beauty, her tenderness, her cruelty. Our task is to record, as accurately as we can, selected episodes from the endless story. But, rightly or wrongly, we had become involved with the life of this small scrap of dog. It had been so easy to view her actions through human spectacles and to admire traits in her which, had she been a member of our own species, we should unhesitatingly have labelled determination, resilience, and above all, pluck. And so, when her own kind failed her, we stepped in.

"As the night wore on, however, we became increasingly certain that we were wrong to give Solo this protection. The pack, while it was attentive to the small pup, was still aware of her. Every so often one of the adults would turn back to wait for her, or carry her for awhile. And so the progress of the whole pack was slowed down by our interference: but for us Solo would no longer be following and the dogs would have been free to hasten onward in search of fertile country where half starved hyenas would no longer threaten the lives of all Havoc's pups.

"The Gol Mountains were as barren as the plains. Wearily the dogs headed up one of the small foothills. They had travelled forty miles since leaving the den. When they reached the brow of the hill Solo was left far behind, way down at the bottom. As the dogs paused, the faint calls of the lost, exhausted pup could be heard. Angel turned and stared back, then very slowly moved towards her daughter. The others watched. Angel called to Solo and, some ten minutes later, Solo appeared. She was tottering with exhaustion and when she stopped for a moment she swayed from side to side. When the pack moved on again Solo remained standing, crying, unable to move. This time it was Rasputin who returned. He picked her up and carried her for awhile. But probably he was tired too, and presently he put her down and she staggered along behind the pack.

"It was clear that she could not continue much longer. The dogs had been circling the eastern slopes of the mountains, and now they looked out over the plains on the far side. There were a few trees here, amongst the rock piles. It would be hard to follow the dogs. Suddenly the pack quickened its pace: we chose to stay with Solo. She staggered another few steps, then collapsed and lay down. She uttered a few calls of distress and was silent.

"We were sure the other dogs had gone, and I got out of the car to examine Solo. But even as I did so there was a sudden explosive bark and, from the shadows, a dog came racing up. Solo had staggered to her feet at my approach, and now Yellow Peril ran up to her and stood, barking in threat at the car. He picked Solo up and moved on with her to where the pack waited.

"Once more we followed, but almost at once Solo was left behind again. This time she did not even call: she just collapsed and lay still. She seemed a very small object in the moonlight. After a long time two shapes appeared, moving towards Solo through the shadows. We thought they were hyenas, come to claim their meal at last, but they moved off without ever noticing the small, still pup. Through binoculars, we could see that they were two adult dogs, apparently searching for Solo. They moved out of sight, and did not reappear. Solo was very fast asleep. Possibly she was in the coma that precedes death . . ."

The Van Lawicks took Solo to their home, and there began the process of nursing her into good health. They decided to keep her only for a month. Meanwhile, they fed her well, gave her calcium to strengthen her already deformed front legs, and took her for walks on a long string. But she was not happy, and as she gained strength she began to make the distress calls which might have brought the pack to her.

They searched for the Genghis pack but without success. However, they did discover Lotus and her mate, Rinogo, who had left the pack half a year before when Lotus was in heat. Now they discovered that she had five pups, obviously whelped at least four weeks after Solo, but about her size. A week later, still unable to find the Genghis pack, they decided to try to get Solo into Lotus' litter. They built a small wire cage with a door which could be opened by pulling a string from a distance. Then they drove to the den area. When Jane Van Lawick put Solo into the cage, the frightened dog defecated over everything. And the strong smell probably killed the human smell which must have clung to her.

To continue Van Lawick's account:

"At first the two adult dogs did not notice the cage and its frantic occupant; Lotus and Rinogo were lying on the ground and the pups continued to play. But suddenly, probably as she heard Solo's calling, Lotus stared in the pup's direction and leapt to her feet, uttering a gruff bark of alarm. This sent the pups scampering back into their den and brought Rinogo to his feet. Cautiously the two adult dogs approached, craning their necks forward and taking quick jerky steps with frequent pauses. In this way they gradually came closer and closer until they were able to put their noses down and sniff towards Solo through the wire. Then they jumped back and this time Rinogo gave a bark. Were they responding to the strangeness of the cage, or to the pup inside? We had no means of telling.

"Solo, meanwhile, was becoming more frenzied every minute. She made every submissive and greeting gesture that a wild dog puppy can make, flattening her ears, pulling back her lips into a smile, whining, twittering, rolling on her side, waving her tail, crouching. It certainly looked as though she was desperate to escape her prison, for she began to dig furiously at the floor of the cate. But what did Lotus and Rinogo, on their part, feel about things?

"At this moment the five pups emerged from their den and, somewhat hesitantly, began to approach their parents and Solo. They were half way there when Rinogo turned his back on the whole situation and slowly and deliberately began to wander back in the direction of his den. It looked as though he had no interest in this stranger. His pups, meeting him, turned round and went gamboling back beside him.

"Lotus continued to look agitated. She made a half-circle around the cage, still taking short quick steps and stopping every few moments. Once more she approached and, with stretched neck, sniffed towards Solo. Then she also turned and began to move after her pups and her mate. What should we do? Solo, twittering incessantly, was still frenzied in her attempts to dig through the floor of her prison, pausing only repeatedly to stare after the retreating Lotus.

"Looking over towards Jane and James I hesitantly gave a 'thumbs up.' Slowly Jane pulled on the string; slowly the trap door lifted. The movement gave Solo a fright, and for a few moments she pressed herself to the far end of the cage. Then suddenly, she seemed to see the open door to freedom and, without a pause, darted out and raced after Lotus.

"It was a tense moment. One bite and all would be over—all Solo's struggles, all our efforts to help, all Angel's sufferings, would have been in vain. Havoc had killed Solo's siblings, born actually within the pack. Had we been foolish to imagine that a bitch might tolerate a completely strange pup amongst her own?

"Now Solo had reached Lotus. Her whole body seeming to wriggle in ecstasy, her tail wagging almost off, she jumped at Lotus's face and then lay flat on her side, smiling. Lotus had stood and watched the pup's approach, looked down at the very tiny wild dog lying submissively at her feet. Suddenly she lowered her head and briefly licked Solo's face. Seldom have I experienced more intense relief.

"Solo leapt up, still wriggling all over, licked Lotus's face and then raced on towards the den. Just before she reached it the five pups emerged and Solo stopped, looked at them, and then darted down a nearby burrow. The pups immediately bounded over to investigate this stranger. A couple of them went down the burrow and, after a few moments, Solo, followed by her new companions, emerged and stood while the other pups sniffed at her. One jumped up at her, either playfully or aggressively, we could not tell. Solo ran from them then, and, like a homing pigeon, vanished into the nursery den of the Lotus family, closely followed by the other pups. Lotus stretched out on the ground near Rinogo, who, throughout Solo's release, had remained totally aloof. From below ground there was silence."

That is the story of Solo. The Van Lawicks watched for a few days as she adjusted and learned to play. Then they moved on to other duties. The ultimate fate of Solo is unknown.

I have reprinted these excerpts from the book for several reasons. They show the remarkable social development of the African Wild Dogs. They show their gentleness; their willingness to share all of the pack's responsibilities; their concern for little Solo. But they do not hide the villainy of the black bitch, Havoc, who ruled the Genghis pack. Finally, the story of Solo is a plea, above all others and yet without making it, to save the African Wild Dogs from extinction.

African Wild Dog, Lycaon pictus.
Drawing by Eugene Gayot, *Le Chien
Histoire Naturelle, Paris, 1867.*

35 Neither Wolves nor Dogs: Falkland Islands Wolf, Aardwolf, Prairie Dog

IT MAY SEEM STRANGE that this chapter should be concerned with a now extinct canid; one which is neither extinct nor a canid; and with one which is, in fact, a rodent. Yet they have a place here, both because of history, and because of the need to clarify their position in the animal world. The three are the extinct Falkland Islands wolf; the Aardwolf of Southern and Central Africa; and the so-called Prairie Dog.

Interest in the Falkland Islands Wolf is based upon two considerations. It is said to be the only canid totally exterminated by man—a claim which may not be true. And it presents a great puzzle. How did it reach the Falkland Islands which lie 250 miles east of the nearest point on the mainland of South America?

The Falkland Islands themselves are of interest for two reasons. In a great naval battle fought on Dec. 8, 1914, the British battle fleet totally destroyed a German fleet, thus giving England total command of the South Atlantic seas. The second is the current diplomatic battle being waged by Argentina to gain sovereignty over the islands. The people on the islands are of British descent.

First, the Falkland Islands Wolf was not a wolf at all. It belonged in the South American fox group of Dusicyon. Its head and body length was about 36 inches, and its tail length 12 inches. Its dominant color was a brownish red, or yellowish brown, sprinkled with black. The tail was white tipped. These "wolves" were the only quadrupeds ever found on the islands, although Charles Darwin suspected that there might have been a native mouse.

There is no evidence that the islands ever knew human habitation before 1764 when L. A. de Bougainville established the first settlement there. His men found the so-called wolf to be so tame that they could tempt it with a bit of meat in one hand and kill it with a knife in the other. This argues that the animal had been separated from any knowledge of man for a very great period of time, perhaps thousands of years. Otherwise, it seems unlikely, as one early writer said: "They will run up to any person they see, and show no fear of man."

I can do no better than to quote Charles Darwin, who visited the Falkland Islands during the Cruise of the Beagle. Darwin was the naturalist aboard the Beagle from Dec. 1831 to Oct. 1836. Here is what he wrote after his return, and based on his notes carefully taken during the voyage. We are raising his foot note on the possibility of the field mouse.

"The only quadruped native to the island is a large wolf-like fox (Canis antarcticus) which is common to both East and West Falkland. I have no doubt it is a peculiar species and confined to this archipelago; because many sealers, Gauchos, and Indians, who have visited these islands, all maintain that no such animal is found in any part of South America. Molina, from a similarity in habits, thought that this was the same with his 'culpeu' but I have seen both and they are quite distinct. (A footnote states: 'The culpeu is the Canis Magellanicus brought home by Captain King from the Strait of Magellan. It is common in Chile.')

"These wolves are well known from Byron's account of their tameness and curiosity, which the sailers, who ran into the river to avoid them, mistook for fierceness. To this day their manners remain the same. They have been observed to enter a tent and actually pull some meat from beneath the head of a sleeping seaman. The Gauchos also have frequently in the evening killed them, by holding out a piece of meat in one hand, and in the other a knife ready to stick them.

"As far as I am aware, there is no other instance in any part of the world, of so small a mass of broken land, distant from a

THE ALCO

Extinct Canid which the Indians called Alco, and the
Spaniards dog. Drawing by Col. Hamilton Smith.

continent, possessing so large an aboriginal quadruped peculiar to itself. Their numbers have rapidly decreased; they are already banished from that half of the island which lies to the eastward of the neck of land between St. Salvador Bay and Berkely Sound. Within a very few years after these islands shall have become regularly settled, in all probability this fox will be classed with the dodo, as an animal which has perished from the face of the earth."

Darwin was right. Extinct is forever. And so we are permanently denied the pleasure of seeing an aboriginal animal, and almost the only one which has no fear of man. This is man's tragedy as well as the animal's, and it is another indication that mankind has a duty to protect the animal species.

Darwin also mentions another fox which is perhaps extinct. At least I cannot recognize it from the scientific name which Darwin gave to it. He mentions reaching Caylen, called "el fin del Christiandad" (the end of Christendom) on Dec. 6th. And that evening "we reached the island of San Pedro, where we found the Beagle at anchor. In doubling the point, two of the officers landed to take a round of angles with the theodolite. A fox (Canis fulvipes) of a kind said to be peculiar to the island, and very rare in it, and which is a new species, was sitting on the rocks. He was so intently absorbed in watching the work of the officers, that I was able, by quietly walking up behind, to knock him on the head with my geological hammer. This fox, more curious or more scientific, but less wise, than the generality of his brethren, is now mounted in the museum of the Zoological Society."

It is possible that this fox is now extinct, although it may not have been exterminated by man as was the Falklands Islands wolf.

The Aardwolf is another animal that is very close to extinction. At the International Convention at London in 1933, it was given Class A protection, that is, the most complete protection that it is possible to give.

The Aardwolf is given the scientific name of Proteles cristatus. But African natives have given it many names, including earth wolf, erdwolf and Inci. In the idiom of the Dutch Boers, or Africaaners, it is the maanhaarjakkals, or maned jackal. It has a head and body length of from 22 to 32 inches, with an average tail length of eight to 12 inches, proportionate to head and body length. Mature males are 18 to 20 inches at the shoulder. The dominant color is a yellow-gray.

There are verticle black stripes, and the legs below the knees and hocks are black. The animal is double coated. The underfur is long and soft. The outer coat is made up of coarse guard hairs. The tail is black tipped. The hair from near the junction of the skull and muzzle to the tail is carried erect, thus giving it the name of the maned jackal.

It is hyena-like rather than wolf-like. It is less stocky than the hyena, and it has five toes on its forefeet whereas the hyena has only four toes on all feet. As one description has it, it is hyena-like but one which has adapted to a different diet. Normally Aardwolves refuse meat, although it is believed they may eat mice, small birds and the eggs of ground nesting birds. They are known to hover around carrion where they feast upon carrion beetles, maggots and other insects.

There appears to be no particular family pattern. Some are solitary; some live in pairs; others live in small family groups. They are nocturnal. Dens are those deserted by other animals. They mate in September and October, and give birth two months later to litters of two to four. They are found from the Cape of Good Hope to Tanzania and in Rhodesia.

Manuel Orozco y Berra published his classic history of Mexico, *Historia Antigua y de la Conquista de Mexico,* in 1880 after a lifetime of work. In it he states: "The Aztecs had only three domesticated quadrupeds, all of which carried as root the word itzcuintli, which the Spaniards translated as 'dog' because of the similarity of them with that animal."

A great history of the conquest of Mexico was written by William H. Prescott. His *Conquest of Mexico* was published in 1843. Prescott wrote: "The resemblance of the different species of those in the Old World, with which no one of them, however, was identical, led to a perpetual confusion in the nomenclature of the Spaniards, as it has since done in that of better instructed naturalists."

The Spaniards spoke of a perro Chihuahua, or perro Chihuahueno which translates simply to Chihuahua dog or little Chihuahua dog . . . And some authorities have said that this was truly the dog we know by that name. However, the perro Chihuahua is not a dog. It is a gopher. And we have to forgive the Spaniards. For we Americans also call the gopher a "prairie dog."

To make matters worse, three different groups of North

Aardwolf. *San Diego Zoo photo*

Prairie Dogs. *Photo by Ron Garrison, San Diego Zoo*

American animals are called gophers. The ground squirrels, which we call chipmunks are sometimes called gophers. And there is a gopher tortoise. The word, gopher, is believed to come from an ancient French term, meaning to burrow. Both the gopher tortoise and the chipmunk are burrowers.

But the gopher which is called a Prairie Dog is properly known as the pocket gopher, of the rodent family, Geomyidae. Perhaps the Spaniards and early Americans called them Prairie Dogs because they have an almost dog-like, sharp bark. They have large front claws for burrowing, fur-lined cheek pouches, small ears and small eyes. They live in large colonies. Males are dominant and hierarchies are well established.

Since they compete with man's grazing animals, and because their burrows may form a hazard for the grazers and horses, great extermination projects have been carried out. As a result, they join the canids as creatures which face extinction.

Extinct Falkland Islands Wolf, drawing by Col. Hamilton Smith.

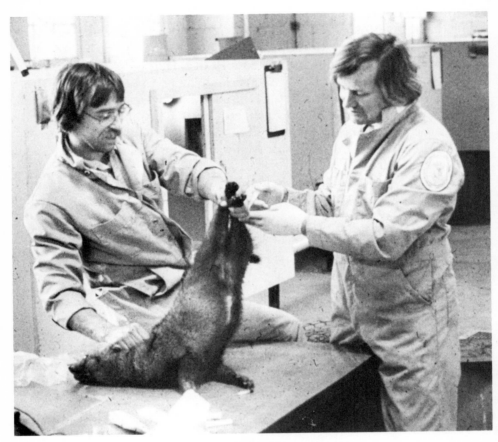

Dr. Stephen Seager (right) inseminates a
Bush Dog. The insemination did not "take."

36 Some Thoughts on Canid Reproduction

THERE ARE MANY REASONS why this chapter should be included in a book on wild canids. One is that many experienced dog breeders and—surprisingly—even some veterinarians do not know or understand important factors governing reproduction. This is also true of some animal keepers in zoological parks, although to some extent they are helpless even when they know and understand. Another reason is that superstitions die hard. Some of these have been around for thousands of years, and are still being told as absolute truth.

Recently, a dog breeder came to me with the following complaint. His stud dog was only eight years old, and had not been used at stud for about a year. A veterinarian twice checked it for spermatozoa. None had been found in the seminal fluid. What was wrong?

I referred the owner to Dr. Stephen Seager, probably the world's greatest authority on reproduction in animals, and possibly in people. Dr. Seager pointed out that sperm production is governed by a number of factors including stress, illness, lack of certain vitamins, etc. But he also pointed out that sperm are not stored in the seminal fluid, but move into it during sex play.

He suggested that the dog be placed with a bitch in season, but not yet ready to mate. The male courted his lady for two days. Then an ejaculation was obtained, and an adequate sperm swarm was present in the fluid.

Wolf born after artificial insemination performed by Stephen Seager, Institute of Comparative Medicine, Baylor College of Medicine.

Recently a man swore to me that his "friend" had a Foxhound which was trailing a fox. The fox, a vixen, stopped and waited for the hound, which promptly mated her. The hunter came up while the two were tied, and shot the vixen. Always such stories involve a friend or "a man I know."

In Canada, within the past year, a breeder of those remarkably intelligent and highly biddable Nova Scotia Duck Tolling Retrievers, told me that they were developed from a cross between the Golden Retriever and a red fox.

These stories are ridiculous, but they survive. It is necessary to explain why they cannot happen. One should understand that nature has set up many barriers to ensure that a species continues to exist; that hybridization (except rarely in plants) seldom if ever occurs naturally.

The Greeks and Romans were excellent dog breeders. They were chiefly interested in hunting, and they knew and wrote about many breeds of hunting dogs. Yet they reported crosses between dogs and a variety of animals, including lions, tigers, hyenas, civet cats, foxes and others.

For more than a thousand years, Aristotle was the absolute authority on most of natural history. Yet Aristotle reported that one breed of dogs resulted in India from crossing dogs with tigers. (Some writers also reported Indian crosses between dogs and, it is supposed, lions). Aristotle reported there was some risk in making the dog-tiger cross. The bitch when in heat and ready for mating was taken into the forest where a tiger was known to lurk. She was tied to a tree. The tiger was attracted. If amorous, he mated with the bitch. If not, he ate her. Aristotle gives no percentages, but one can guess that the bitch became a meal in 100% of the cases.

Both Aristotle and Oppian reported that fine hunting hounds were developed by crossing domestic hounds with one of some five breeds of wolves. And Zenophon, great general and great huntsman, reported that the Laconian hounds resulted from crossing dogs with foxes. Zenophon wasn't exactly enamored by the performance of those hounds.

Some ancient writers reported that crosses between leopards and wolves created the jackals, and perhaps the African hunting dog, *L. pictus.* In at least one text, the hyena was reported to be able to change its sex each year. And it, too, was said to have been used in some dog and wolf crosses.

I have no wish to write a highly technical treatise on genetics or ecology, even if I were capable of doing so. But I think it is necessary to note some things briefly even at the risk of over simplifying them. For example, unicellular organisms do not die unless they are killed by outside causes, such as being devoured by other organisms. They reproduce by division, and there are no dead ancestors. Each is part of the original of the species.

Death is the penalty which the higher animals and man pay for their bodies. We are programmed to die in our genetic inheritance. The life span of a given animal is based upon youth and a maturity which is long enough to allow it to reproduce its kind. For most, this is long enough to permit for several litters. In this way a new generation is always ensured.

In addition, there is some mysterious automatic adjustment between the length of life of the individual and the chances of survival of the offspring. Where the hazards of living are great, the number of offspring is high. In most canids, mortality among the pups may be as great as 50 per cent. Thus, many of the canids have litters of five to eight, or sometimes even a dozen. When the risks are small, as in human beings, one offspring at a time is usual. Even so, women have a long fertility period, and some women have had 16 or more children. (Benjamin Franklin was one of ten children by Josiah Franklin's second wife.) Men, too, have a long fertility period, although true maturity may be only from 18 to 25. This is perhaps nature's way for compensating for single births, and man's propensity for killing other men in wars. Male births are said to rise during wars.

Increases in food supply normally bring an increase in the survival rate. That is, if there is a sudden increase in the food of the lemmings, then the survival rate among lemmings will increase. And, in turn, more offspring of the Arctic fox and the wolf will survive. The reverse will also be true. If the food supply is poor for the prey animals, then there will be fewer to be captured for food, and the foxes and wolves will starve.

The anthropologist, Julius Lips, once explained to me his theory of the origin of our tradition of the June bride. Lips had

spent years in studying primitive tribes in Africa. They, too, had a
June bride tradition. Some tribes, in fact, prohibited marriage until
May or June. Asked why, chieftains explained that then nature was
at its optimum. The young men and women, too, were at their
healthiest, having feasted upon green things and fruits. Thus, they
were perfectly prepared for mating.

We, knowing more than they, but not wiser, would say that we
had prepared our bodies with plenty of vitamins and minerals. And
we now know that in animal nutrition, vitamins play a role in
preparing the body for conception. Yet we differ in an important
respect from the animals. It has been said that a majority of our
great men have been born in February and March, that is, from
conceptions which took place in late spring. But wild canids have
their mating season in late winter. They have a comparatively short
gestation period, and their young are born in the spring. Nature,
then has prepared their bodies for winter conception and, to quote
the Bible, "God tempers the wind to the shorn lamb."

We can qualify what we have said above to some extent. The
warmer the climate, the earlier in winter mating will take place. The
colder it is, the later it will occur. Since the gestation period is longer
in some species, for instance in the nomadic African wild dog, it is
possible that the longer period is in some way keyed to a nomadic
life.

It is believed that in biparental reproduction, the ova may be
preformed at birth. That is, within the genetic code of the individual, the number of ova to be produced is already determined. For
the human female, this has been estimated at well over 200,000 even
though only one ovum may mature at a time. The human male,
however, might produce 260,000,000 sperm at one ejaculation. In
many canids, a single ejaculation might contain 200,000,000 sperms,
while the female would produce four to 16 eggs. (Domestic dog
bitches have had litters of 18 to 19, and a Bloodhound owned by my
father had 17.) From the above, it is obvious that it is the female and
not the male which controls the size of the litter. Also, it should be
noted that, at least among the canids, the larger the animal, the
larger the litter it is likely to have. And, one should add, the shorter
its life span is likely to be. The St. Bernard illustrates both points.

Most of us learned in high school or college that in biparental
reproduction, the so-called chromosomes are paired. For example,

human beings have 23 pairs, or 46. The individual gets one of each pair from each of its parents. In reproduction, it is necessary that the final germ cell (gamete) has one of each kind of chromosome. For each carries special hereditary determiners, and plays its own role in the development of the individual.

If one of each kind of chromosome is not represented, then the developing offspring will show certain deficiencies. This will depend upon which of the single (haploid) set is missing. No two parts of a chromosome are the same, nor do different chromosomes have the same pattern. The genes are contained in the chromosomes.

Each cell is capable of reproducing itself. But the reproductive cells control the development of the entire organism. Meiosis is the process by which the chromosome number of a reproductive cell becomes reduced to half the diploid (2n) number to form the mature egg or sperm (the gamete). The failure of unlike chromosomes to pair during meiosis causes the gametes to be defective. This is the major cause of sterility in the offspring. For this reason, interspecies crosses are very rare, and when they do succeed, the offspring are incapable of reproducing themselves.

An example is the mule. It is a cross between a female horse (mare) and a male (jack) ass. It is stronger, tougher and meaner than a horse. But most are sterile. The reverse cross—a stallion and a female ass—is a hinny, also sterile, but no mule. It has too long a body, too short legs, but a gentler disposition. The chromosomal formula for a horse is 2n=64; for the ass, 2n=62. The result must be incomplete chromosomal pairings.

But one famous experiment using plants was made by the Russian cytologist, G. D. Karpechenko, as quoted by Eldon J. Gardner in his *Principles of Genetics*. Karpechenko used two distantly related plants, a type of radish and a cabbage. Each had nine pairs of chromosomes, and their diploid hybrid 18, or nine from each parent. But there was a failure of the unlike chromosomes to pair in meiosis, and sterility resulted.

In their 10 volume set, *An Atlas of Mammalian Chromosomes*, T. C. Hsu and Kurt Benirschke, give the pertinent chromosomal data on hundreds of mammals, including many of the canids. For the purposes of simplicity, we give here only the 2n=numbers for those canids which have been studied. The domestic dog, dingo, wolf and coyote have 78, that is, 76 plus the two sex chromosomes X (female) and Y (male.). In the totals given below, the sex chromosomes are included.

Bat-eared Fox (Otocyon megalotis) 2n=72.
Atelocynus microtis (Small-eared zorro) 2n=74
Lycaon pictus (African wild dog) 2n=78
Urocyon cinereoargenteus (American gray fox) 2n = 66
Alopex lagopus (Arctic fox) 2n=50
Vulpes fulva (American red fox) 2n=34
Vulpes vulpes (common red fox) 2n=36
Dusicyon griseus (South American gray fox) 2n=74
Nyctereutes procyonoides (Raccoon dog) 2n = 42

Although fertile hybrids of Vulpes and Alopex have been reported (Fox, *The Wild Canids*) it is obvious that for most of these animals the chromosomal and other differences are so great as to make the possibility of fertile offspring most unlikely. But, in addition, nature places other restrictions upon the hybridizing of species.

We think of sexual mating as being actions imprinted in our genes. A pair of animals is expected to "do what comes naturally." But this does not always happen. Human children learn about sex and how to perform it while still quite young. That is because they live in groups in which sex, birth, babies, nursing and rearing are major experiences for all. This will usually be so with animals because of social relationships within their groups.

But the zoo experience teaches us that if you remove a baby animal from its mother and group, the reproductive cycle may never be learned. It may, in fact, have to be taught within the social group. The Cleveland Zoo, for example, got a bongo, rarest of the world's antelopes, captured when only a few days old. Since she was the only bongo in captivity, world zoos and animal dealers agreed that if a male should be captured it would go to Cleveland. In time, a three or four day old male was captured and was sent to Cleveland. But no mating has ever occurred.

Washington got a panda. Great publicity resulted when a mate was found for it. But there have been no baby pandas. Chicago's Brookfield got a pair of Small-eared zorros. They never mated. Often when a zoo chimpanzee or orang-utan does give birth, the mother will show no nursing or care instincts. She may desert it, ignore it, be afraid of it, even kill it. Dozens of animal babies are rescued by keepers and raised by their wives. At one zoo, a mate was found for a gorilla. Efforts to bring them together failed. He tried to kill her. Even after years in adjoining cages, he would still try to kill her.

Earlier we cited the case of the domestic dog whose seminal fluids contained no sperm until sperm production had been stimulated by sex play, and the sperm moved into the ejaculate. And we must add some other factors. In some of the wild canids, both sexes have mating seasons. The season of the male might not agree with a female of another species. Wild canid species do not mix in the wild. Like Aristotle's tiger and bitch, when canids of different species meet, one or the other is likely to get killed.

Nature certainly does imprint sexual procedures in each species. But these must be nurtured and developed in the group. The sexual odors of the vixen in heat may not stimulate a male wolf. Even if the vixen could conquer her fear of the wolf, her sex play would stir no desires in him. Nor would she understand his, or be interested if she did.

If artificial insemination could be made, still other factors might prevent conception. For example, the pH of the uterine fluids in the fox might be fatal to the wolf's sperm. Or the sperm might not be able to live long enough to reach the mature eggs. Or, having travelled in an improper medium, the sperm might not be able to penetrate the egg.

Finally, even if an interspecies mating did produce offspring, they would be sterile. Thus, they could not reproduce their kind, and a possible new genus could not be made.

37 Alaskan Malamutes and Wolves

AUTHOR AFTER AUTHOR glibly states that the Alaskan Malamute is "half wolf" and was developed by crossing wolves with dogs. They maintain this despite the careful questioning of Eskimo and Indian breeders and drivers by old time Malamute breeders, and even by this writer. Sometimes the same authors will report the unsatisfactory results from crossing dogs and wolves, and then will still state as a fact that the Alaskan Malamute is half wolf.

Mr. and Mrs. Robert Russell of Sussex, Wisconsin, have had a closer relationship with both wolves and Alaskan Malamutes than most. They are among the most successful of Alaskan Malamute breeders, and Mrs. Russell is, at the time of writing, president of the Alaskan Malamute Club of America. Here is her story.

Wild canids should not be brought into the home, and efforts to hybridize them with domestic animals should be outlawed. I believe the experience quoted below shows the falsity of claiming dog breeds to be half wolves, and also shows why wild canids belong only in zoological parks.

My Personal Experiences With Wolves

I had always wanted a wolf and had read about them and had studied them as much as I could. We visited the wolf farm at Kare, Pa. each time we went east, and Mr. Lynch let us go in with his wolves. He also warned us about them, especially around children.

In 1974, my husband bought a wolf pup for me for Mother's

Daffney, a wolf puppy (third from left), is shown with a Basenji puppy (extreme left), an Alaskan Malamute puppy, and (far right) another Alaskan Malamute.

Daffney, when nearly grown. Malamutes came to fear her, avoided her even when she was in heat.

Day. She was three weeks old and was totally fearless. We kept her in the house and bottle fed her. She attacked the vacuum cleaner and would growl at the cats and at "Bear" (Alaskan Malamute Champion Glacier's Storm Kloud C.D.). At six weeks we put her out with a litter of Malamute pups who were just one month older than she was, and a Basenji pup who was two months older.

She was on the "bottom of the pack" and stayed there. I took her everywhere I could. She must have gone to at least ten schools and Scout programs and seemed to love every minute of it. This lasted until she was about four months old. Then a shyness of strangers began to appear.

Instead of coming up to the fence to meet people as the Malamutes and Basenji did, she would run behind the dog house and peek out. By the time she was five months old, I had to take the Malamutes out of her kennel as they were beginning to mimic her actions. To this day, the female who was with her for that time still reacts to sudden noises and unusual actions by trying to run—the same reaction as the wolf had shown. This surprised me.

However, the Basenji picked up none of the wolf's fears and remained her companion and "superior" until his death in January of 1977. She mourned his death for weeks by long vigils of howling at dusk and dawn. I wish we could have gotten movies of their relationship. He used to sleep curled up on her back in the winter to stay warm. He dominated the food dishes and her. Yet she tried to protect him from people by coming between him and approaching strangers. He would get furious at her for blocking his way to be petted, and he would growl and grab her ruff and hang on while shaking her. She would just walk away with him hanging on. It was quite a sight.

We had named her Daffney. She seems to like all of the Malamutes, but none of them has anything to do with her. They make a wide circle around her cage even though she is showing only signs of playfulness and submissiveness. Even when she is in season and calls for a mate, none of my Malamutes has responded. None has ever gone within ten feet of her cage unless I take them to her on a leash.

However, I had a female Malamute which tried to flirt with the male wolf we had and she nearly lost her leg. She stuck her paw through the fence and the two female wolves grabbed her and pulled the leg in clear up to the shoulder, and proceeded to try to chew it off. I heard the screams of the bitch and ran, grabbed a shovel, and went in and hit both female wolves over the head with one hearty swing. They let go and ran, and the Malamute bitch pulled her leg out. Not much but bone was left, but, since the major blood vessels hadn't been severed, our veterinarian was able to save the leg. The big male was so startled by the furor that he didn't charge me and I got out of the pen before he hit the wire in his usual manner.

Now I'll back track and tell you how we got the adult wolves. The nearby zoo where we got Daffney lost its director and also its financial backing. The wolves, two females and a male, were going to be put down because the zoo people had been unable to place them. These were Daffney's mother and father, and a black female Arctic wolf. Also there were two litter mates of Daffney's which were to come back from the Milwaukee Petting Zoo. To save them, we agreed to take them all until proper places could be found. We set up chain link fence with a safety entrance and we took the three adults and the two young ones in the fall of 1974. Their adjustment here was full of surprises for us.

First of all, I had asked Dr. Michael Fox, who was speaking at a local seminar, for advice about moving these adult wolves and he told me they should be put down. He said they would never adjust to their new surroundings. We found him to be completely wrong. Here is what took place.

We let out the small Arctic wolf first. She ran around sniffing and looking, quite upset. Next we let out Sheba, Daffney's mother, putting her in with the other. They greeted each other with much licking and tail wagging. Then together they investigated the pen. When we let in the male, Hunter, they literally jumped on him and showered him with kisses and affectionate gestures. He proceeded to check out the pen and made sure all the corners were secure and also the roof. He marked everything with his urine and then lay down on top of the house and took a nap. The whole adjustment period took less than two hours.

In a matter of days, Bob had them shifting pens on voice commands. At the zoo the keepers had always used prod poles to shift them. The interesting experiences we had with them and what we learned from them would almost make a book in itself. However, the one thing which we feel that we learned best was that every wolf is an individual just as every dog is, or every person. No general statements hold true for every animal. Just because this wolf reacts this way, the next one may not.

Hunter was raised in captivity and as a family pet. He lost his fear of man. He was dangerous. We had heard that he had killed a child. I am sure he would not have hesitated to do so again. He respected Bob. He hated me. And it was obvious in all his body actions. The two adult females were caught wild, and they were afraid of all people. I had no fear of them, except when with the male, forming a pack.

(I break into her story here to make the following comments. In Ceylon, trainers of work elephants told me that they never use elephants which have been born in captivity. They have lost their fear of man and are dangerous. The elephant keeper at Cleveland's Metroparks Zoo (then Cleveland Zoo) had been a circus trainer. And he told me the same thing.—M.R.)

Our wolf, Daffney, has her fears of man. Yet she likes her family. I have no fear of her. She does not realize she is a wolf either. She was terrified of all the wolves and would not go near them. She stayed with the Malamutes and the Basenji all the time they were with us. We kept the wolves through that winter and placed them with the State Game Farm in the spring. We could not afford to feed them, nor did we have proper facilities for whelping pups, etc.

As an example of their intelligence, a week before they were to be moved, the crates from the zoo came. These were the same crates that had been used to bring them to us. From that day on they announced their knowledge and displeasure of being moved with the most mournful howling chorus. The whole kennel, including the Basenji, would join them. Then it made it very difficult to send them away. The big male, Hunter, actually leaned against the fence and into Bob's hand and whined when Bob was trying to get him into the crate. It was really very sad. I often feel those wolves were more intelligent and more socially acceptable than many people I have known. They were certainly nothing like the story books portray them.

After studying the wolves for that short time, I do feel that the body language of wolves and dogs is much the same. But the Malamutes differ structurally. The pack instincts seem to be similar also. Having had the wolves has certainly helped me to read my dogs' body language better.

Bibliography and Supplementary Reading List

Acosta, Jose de. Naturall and Morrall Historie of the East and West Indies. Edward Grimston translation, 1604.

Aesop. Fables. Any one of a dozen translations.

Aistan, G. Savage Life In Central Australia (see: Roland Robinson)

Amory, Cleveland. Little Brother of the Wolf. Defenders of Wild Life News, Oct. 1973.

Anthony, Harold E. A Field Book of American Mammals, Putnam's, 1928

Arrian. Consult a major city library for a text.

Azara, Felix. Natural History of the Spanish Provinces of South America. (See also Smith, Col. Charles Hamilton, on Azara)

Barlow, Genevieve, Latin American Tales, Rand McNally.

Bartram, William. Travels, 1791. Dover edition, 1955.

Bayless, Clara Kern. Old Man Coyote, Crowell, 1908.

Baynes, E. H. My Wild Animal Guests, Macmillan, 1930.

Behme, Robert L. Shasta Rogue, a Coyote Story, Simon & Schuster, 1974.

Bekoff, Marc. Coyotes, Biology, Behavior, Management, Academic Press, 1978

Beowulf. J. M. Garrett translation, 1900.

Benirschke, Kurt and Hsu, T. C. An Atlas of Mammalian Chromosomes. Springer-Verlag, 10 volumes.

Brinton, Daniel G. The Myths of the New World, McKay, 1868, 1896.

Brown, J. G. and "Dot." Dogs of Australia, Kennel Control Council of Victoria.

Bueler, Lois E. Wild Dogs of the World. Stein & Day, 1973.

California, University of, Div. of Animal Sciences. The Effects of Control On Coyote Populations. Bulletin 1872 By Connolly, Guy C., and Longhurst, W. M.

Cambridge Natural History, Vol. 10, 1909.

Canadian Fur Council, Information Canada. Report on Status of Canadian Wildlife Used in the Fur Industry, 1975.

Capstick, Peter Hathaway. Death in the Long Grass. St. Martin's, 1977.

Caras, Roger. The Custer Wolf. Little-Brown, 1966. Bantam-Pathfinder, 1967.

Chamberlin, Basil Hall. Japanese Things, Tuttle, 1971.

Colorado, Division of Wildlife, Denver. Predator Control, personal letter to the author.

Corbet, L., and Newsome, O. A. Dingo Society And Its Maintenance: A Preliminary Analysis, Division of Wildlife Research, Commonwealth Scientific and Industrial Research Organization. (See Fox, The Wild Canids).

Crisler, Lois L. Arctic Wild, Harper & Row, 1956

Curtis, Edward S. The North American Indians, 1907–1930. 20 volumes.

Dampier, New Voyages Around the World, 1697; Voyages & Descriptions, 1699.

Dobie, J. Frank. The Voice of the Coyote, Little Brown, 1949.

Dorson, R. M. Folk Legends of Japan, Tuttle, 1962.

Dorst, Jean, and Pierre Daudelot. A Field Guide to the Larger Mammals of Africa, Houghton-Mifflin, 1970.

Durrell, Jacquie. Intimate Relations, Stein & Day.

Eckels, Richard Preston, Greek Wolf Lore, University of Pennsylvania Press, 1937.

Edwards, Lionel. The Fox. Charles Scribner's Sons.

Fiennes, Richard. The Order of Wolves, Bobbs-Merrill, 1976.

Fish and Wildlife Service, U.S. Dept. of the Interior, Office of Endangered Species. Letter to the author.

Fox, Dr. Michael. Behavior of Wolves, Dogs, and Related Canids, Harper & Row, 1971. Between Animals and Man, Coward, McCann & Geoghegan, 1976. The Wild Canids; Their Systematics, Behavioral, Ecological Evolution. Van Nostrand, Reinhold, 1975.

Gardner, Eldon J. Principles of Genetics, Wiley.

Gidley, Mick. The Vanishing Race, Taplinger, 1977. (Selections from Edward S. Curtis)

Goldman, E. A. The Wolves of North America, Part II, Classification of Wolves. American Wildlife Institute, 1944.

Grzimek, Bernhard. Animal Life Encyclopedia, Van Nostrand-Reinhold. Vol. 12, 1968.

Grzimek, Bernhard and Michael. Serengheti Shall Not Die, Dutton, 1960, Bantam paperback, 1973.

Hadas, Moses. Fables of a Jewish Aesop, translated from the Fox Fables of Berechiah ha-Nakdam, Columbia University Press, 1967.

Hale, E. R. and Kelson, K. R., Mammals of North America, Vol. II, Ronald Press, 1959.

Hall, Charles F. Narrative of the Second Arctic Expedition, U. S. Naval Observatory, U. S. Govt. Printing Office, 1879.

Hamilton-Wilkes and David Cumming. Kelpie and Cattle Dog. Angus & Robertson, 1967.

Harney, W. E. The Dingo. Walkabout, June 1, 1951.

Hearn, Lafcadio. Kwaidan. Stories & Studies of Strange Things. Tuttle, 1971.

Hopf, Alice L. Wild Cousins of the Dog, Putnam, 1973.

Houston, Douglas B. Ecosystems of National Parks. Science, Dec. 10, 1962.

Hershkovitz, Philip. The Small-eared Zorro, Fieldiana-Zoology, Chicago Natural History Museum, 1961.

Hudson, W. H. The Naturalist in La Plata, Dent, 1892–1928.

Hull, Deneson Bingham. Hunting In Ancient Greece. U. of Chicago Press, 1964.

Kalm, Peter. Travels in North America, 1770. Dover edition, 1937.

Kennel Control Council of Victoria. Dogs of Australia. (See Brown, J. G.)

Kuhne, Wolfdietrich. Communal Food Distribution and Division of Labour In African Hunting Dogs. Nature, Jan. 30, 1965.

Leach, Maria. God Had A Dog. Rutgers University Press, 1961.

Lewisohn, Richard. Animals, Myths, and Men. Harper Brothers, 1954.

Lopez, Barry Holstun. Giving Birth To Thunder; Sleeping With His Daughter. Sheed Andrews McMeel, 1977.

Lorenz, Konrad. Man Meets Dog, Houghton Mifflin, 1955.

Mech, L. David. A Recovery Plan For The Eastern Timber Wolf, National Parks and Conservation Service, 1976. The Wolves of Isle Royale, U. S. National Park Service. Fauna Series, No. 7., U. S. Govt. Printing Office.

Metelerkamp, Sanni. Outa Karel's Stories, Macmillan, 1914.

Minnesota Department of Natural Resources, LeRoy Rutske, Wildlife specialist.

Mitford, A. B. (Lord Redesdale). Tales of Old Japan, 1871, Tuttle, 1966.

Montana Department of Fish & Game, Helena, Montana.

Mountford, Charles P. & Roberts, Ainslie. The Dreamtime, Australian Aboriginal Myths, Rigby, 1965.

Murie, Adolph. The Wolves of Mt. McKinley. U. S. National Park Service, Fauna Series No. 5. U. S. Govt. Printing Office.

McCarley, Howard. The Taxonomic Status of Wild Canis (Canids) in South Central United States. Naturalist, Dec. 10, 1940.

McLean, Charles. The Wolf Children. Hill & Wang, 1972-1977-1978.

Murie, Adolph, Ecology of the Coyote in Yellowstone National Park. National Park Service, Fauna Series 4. U. S. Govt. Printing Office.

National Board of Fur Farm Organizations, Brookfield, Wisconsin

Niethammer, Carolyn. Daughters of the Earth; Lives and Legends of American Indian Women. Macmillan, 1977.

Ohno, J. Notes on the Raccoon Dog. Translated by Miss Junko Kimura, Tokyo.

Oklahoma, Division of Wildlife Services. Annual Fiscal Report, 1976, Region 2. Oklahoma City, Okla.

Olsen, Jack. Slaughter The Animals, Poison The Earth, Simon & Schuster, 1971.

Oppian (of Apamea). Cynegetica. Consult a major library.

Orr, Robert T. Mammals of North America. Doubleday.

Owens, Harry J. The Scandalous Adventures of Reynard the Fox. A modern American version. Knopf, 1945.

Perry, Richard. Desert and Plain. Taplinger, 1977.

Petrie, Constance C. Tom Petrie's Reminiscences. Watson Ferguson 1904.

Pimlott, D. H. Wolf. Canadian Wildlife Service, Hinterland Who's Who, 1973.

Rasmussen, Knud. People of the Polar North. Gale. 1908.

Reed, A. W. Myths and Legends of Australia. Taplinger, 1973.

Ride, W. D. L. A Guide to the Native Mammals of Australia, Oxford University Press, 1970.

Robinson, Roland. Aboriginal Myths & Legends. Paul Hamlyn, 1969.

Roche, Frank. The Coyote That Cried Wolf. The American Way, Oct. 1973.

Rutter, R. J. and Pimlott, D. H. The World of the Wolf. Lippincott, 1968.

Rue, Leonard Lee, III. The World of the Red Fox. Lippincott, 1968. Pictorial Guide to the Mammals of North America, Crowell, 1967.

Ryden, Hope. God's Dog. Coward, McCann & Geoghehan, 1975.

Sadler, R. M. F. X. The Ecology of Reproduction in Wild & Domestic Animals. Methuen, 1969.

Sahagun, Friar Bernardino de Sahagun, General History of Affairs in New Spain., 1560–61.

Sanderson, Ivan T. Living Mammals of the World. Doubleday, 1967.

Senecal, D. Coyote. Canadian Wildlife Series, Hinterland Who's Who, 1977.

Seton, E. T. Lives of Game Animals. Doubleday Page, 1925. Great Historic Animals. Mainly About Wolves, Scribner's, 1937.

Smith, Col. Charles Hamilton. The Naturalist's Library. Sir William Jardine, Vol. IX, 1839.

Spect, Robert. Tisha. St. Martin's Press, 1976.

Speller, S. W. Arctic Fox. Canadian Wildlife Series, Hinterland Who's Who, 1977.

Squires, P. C. Wolf Children of India. American Journal of Psychology, No. 38, 1927.

Stallybras, William. The Epic of the Beast. Broadway Translations. Routledge-Dutton.

Stevens, Joe T. Almost Gone. Texas Parks & Wildlife, May, 1977.

Stigand, C. H. and Mrs. C. H. Black Tales For White Children, Houghton Mifflin, 1904.

Texas Parks and Wildlife Magazine (See Stevens, Joe. T.)

Theberge, John B. Wolf Management In Canada Through A Decade Of Change. Nature Canada 2 (1) 1973. Canadian Nature Federation.

Thomas, Joseph B. Hounds and Hunting Through The Ages, Windward House, 1928.

Tindale, Norman B. Aboriginal Tribes of Australia, Their Terrain, Environmental Controls, Distribution, Limits and Proper Names. University of California Press, 1974.

Turner, Kay. Serengheti Home. Dial-James Wade, 1977.

Van Lawick, Hugo. Solo, The Story of an African Wild Dog. Houghton Mifflin, 1974. Innocent Killers, Houghton Mifflin, 1971.

Van Wormer, Joe. The World of the Coyote. Lippincott, 1964.

Walker, Ernest P. Mammals of the World. Johns Hopkins Press, 1968.

Waters, Joseph H. Red Fox and Gray Fox From New England Archaeological Sites. Journal of Mammology, Vol 45, 1964.

Xenophon. Cynegeticus (Try major city libraries).

Young, Edgerton R. Algonquin Indian Tales. Eaton & Mains, 1903. Winter Adventures of Three Boys in the Great Lone Land, Eaton & Mains, 1903.

Young, Stanley P. The Wolf in North American History, Caxton, 1946. The Wolves of North America, Part I, Their History, Life Habits, Economic Status, and Control. American Wildlife Institute, 1944. Part II, Classification of Wolves by E. A. Goldman.